A HANDBOOK OF VERBAL GROUP EXERCISES

A HANDBOOK OF VERBAL GROUP EXERCISES

By

KENNETH T. MORRIS, PH.D.

Associate Professor and Certified Consulting Psychologist
Counseling Center—Central Michigan University
Mount Pleasant, Michigan

and

KENNETH M. CINNAMON, M.A.

With A Foreword By
Robert L. Shelton, Ph.D.

Assistant Professor
Speech Communications and Human Relations
University of Kansas
Lawrence, Kansas

CHARLES C THOMAS • PUBLISHER
Springfield • Illinois • U. S. A.

Published and Distributed Throughout the World by
CHARLES C THOMAS • PUBLISHER
Bannerstone House
301-327 East Lawrence Avenue, Springfield, Illinois, U.S.A.

© 1974, by CHARLES C THOMAS • PUBLISHER
ISBN 0-398-03010-3 (Cloth)
ISBN 0-398-03011-1 (Paper)
Library of Congress Catalog Card Number: 73-15524

With THOMAS BOOKS careful attention is given to all details of manu-
facturing and design. It is the Publisher's desire to present books that are
satisfactory as to their physical qualities and artistic possibilities and
appropriate for their particular use. THOMAS BOOKS will be true to
those laws of quality that assure a good name and good will.

Printed in the United States of America
EE-11

Library of Congress Cataloging in Publication Data

Morris, Kenneth T
   A handbook of verbal group exercises.
   1. Group relations training—Handbooks, manuals, etc. I. Cinnamon,
Kenneth M., joint author.
   II. Title.
   HM134.M67   361.4   73-15524
   ISBN 0-398-03010-3
   ISBN 0-398-03011-1 (pbk.)

*To our families, whose inspiration
and patience have proved invaluable assets,
this book is affectionately dedicated.*

CONTENTS

FOREWORD

For those who make a serious and responsible effort in helping others toward their human potential, there is certainly no need for a new set of gimmicks. This book could be seen as such a collection. I hope it will not be.

One thing very much needed by those who work with individuals in learning groups is an acquaintance with a variety of structured exercises—tools to be utilized in assisting an exploration, an expansion, or a deepened understanding of interests and needs being demonstrated in a group. This book can be a resource for such tools. I hope that the reader, if he or she uses it, will use it in that way.

Some insist that the word "facilitator" is nothing but a nicer word for "manipulator." There are those with responsibility for giving direction to the learning and growth of others who *do* fall into the ancient art of manipulation. That is true for lecturers, lab instructors, division managers, preachers, TV personalities, political speakers, etc., etc., and thus also for those known as "facilitators" or "trainers" (or whatever group consultants prefer to call themselves). The use of an exercise to *produce* a particular experience desired by one for others may well be considred manipulation. On the other hand, the use of exercises to facilitate learning, growth and expansion of creativity, all of which are there in the persons who have agreed by their presence to be exposed to a widening of opportunities for themselves, is an appropriate and often very helpful enterprise.

Most of my work with groups is in university teaching. I am always astounded by the wealth of resources latent within those with whom I work—resources for their own learning, as well as resources for the growth and development of others around them. It is often the case that such resources are not readily available, for the myriad of reasons known to the student of human behavior. To help these resources become available, a structured exercise may, very productively, be employed. In order to make good use of such structure, the "facilitator" must have an understanding of the persons with whom he/she is working, and sensitivity to the priorities of their concerns, needs, and possibilities. Otherwise the exercise is "something to do" and might better be left undone.

In the following pages, you will find exercises designed to assist in getting acquainted, developing empathy, gaining skill in listening, etc. It is essential to keep in mind that you are helping *persons to get acquainted,* to *develop empathy,* to *become better listeners—not* to go through an exercise with efficiency and good feelings. There *is* a *difference.* It is the difference between real growth and learning in the group setting, and going through the motions of a "good group experience."

I encourage careful selection and use of these exercises. Some of them have been helpful in my own work. Many—including some of mine—were "invented" in the midst of a "real, live" group situation, or significantly modified to be appropriate to a given situation. The key word is "appropriate." The goal is the "freeing up," or "unfreeing," or expansion of growth and communication possibilities within and between individuals. The basic set of "facilitator" tools is one's own imagination, inventiveness and sensitivity.

Lawrence, Kansas   ROBERT L. SHELTON, PH.D.

ACKNOWLEDGMENTS

THIS VOLUME AS is the case for most books, is the result of the aid and contributions of many persons.

We are unable to acknowledge everyone who assisted us, but we do wish to mention a few whose contributions were essential.

First, Robert L. Shelton and Robert Brook who creatively contributed to the development of the Handbook.

Second, Elizabeth Asch, who patiently typed revision after revision.

Third, the colleagues of the Central Michigan University Counseling Center who gave support to us in our endeavors.

Fourth, to Judy Morris, Dorothy and Molly Cinnamon, whose moral support was invaluable.

Last, and most important of the contributors, are all the members of our encounter and t–groups. We learned from them and loved them. Without them and other group members, a volume such as this is unneeded.

K.T.M.
K.M.C.

INTRODUCTION

W E HAVE BEEN APPROACHED, quite frequently, by both professional facilitators and laymen, with questions concerning group exercises. These people wonder where they can find such exercises. They ask about the effectiveness of exercises. They ask what goals can be met. This book is our way of answering their queries.[1]

We decided to write the Handbook because we noticed that many of the exercise books currently available to the facilitator have at least three weaknesses:

1. First of all, they seldom list exercises by specific goals. Therefore, the practitioner desiring an exercise devoted to attainment of a specific goal has to hunt laboriously through such books in an attempt to meet his need. Our handbook does away with this "hunt and find" method.

2. Second, many volumes, if they do list exercises by goal, use global, non–specific listings. Such listings lead to the same "hunt and find" process cited above. Our volume, by being specific, not global, aids the facilitator's finding what he wants with minimal effort.

3. Third, the handbook incorporates, through condensation, simplification, and avoidance of repetition, the same material that would be covered in numerous books, thereby making unnecessary the practitioner's purchase of a multitude of volumes on the subject of group exercises. Both authors own numerous books describing group exercises. We know that the repeated duplication from book to book is enormous. We (and we assume other facilitators) would

---

[1] NOTE: This handbook covers only verbal group exercises. A *verbal* group exercise is defined as one in which 50 per cent or more of the member activity is verbal in nature.

The idea of writing a handbook listing verbal *and* non–verbal exercises was entertained. However, the enormous amount of data available did not make such an effort feasible. Non–verbal group exercises will be covered in a subsequent volume entitled *A Handbook of Non-Verbal Group Exercises.*

definitely prefer owning *one* all–encompassing source such as the one here made available.

Our handbook does not possess the weaknesses listed above, but, instead, makes the needed material readily accessible. In this book the group facilitator will find 175 exercises and 135 exercise variations. No longer will he need to buy five or six volumes which are usually disjointed and unorganized: he can now consult this one source with the flexible type of format that can help him locate or discover some viable group exercises. Those marked with an asterisk (*) will indicate to him that they dynamically and most effectively meet a specified goal.

Thus, the present volume offers the professional an opportunity to find specific exercises rapidly. For example, if he needs an exercise for *feedback,* he simply opens the book to the chapter on feedback and locates the exercise most in accord with his needs. And if, in this same grouping, he wants an exercise that is particularly potent and that will achieve the desired effect, he can choose a feedback exercise marked with an asterisk. In the introductory section of each chapter (for example, VIII. Feedback), both primary and subsidiary goals or objectives are carefully spelled out. Moreover, said chapters are listed alphabetically from I Assessment, to XXI Ungrouped Exercises (*see* Contents).

The advantages for the facilitator in using A HANDBOOK OF VERBAL EXERCISES, therefore, are many. We enumerate some of them as follows:

1. Each chapter has an introductory section which provides basic information on the use and appropriateness of each exercise under the (chapter) heading under consideration.
2. The order of main headings (*i.e.,* chapter titles) under which the various exercises are listed, is alphabetical as well as numerical.
3. The goal for each exercise is clearly and specifically delineated.
4. Subsidiary goals are also listed for each exercise, again assuring the choice of an exercise appropriate to the facilitator's goal and subgoals.
5. A consistent format is used for every exercise, thereby

facilitating application of the exercise and, from it, the development of *new* exercises.

As we noted above, it is this type of format uniformity which is so sorely lacking in most volumes dealing with group exercises.

6. Clear indications are given concerning the group applicability of each exercise. Therefore, the practitioner needing an exercise suitable for an encounter group need only read the Group Application section of the exercise to determine its suitability for his purpose and group.

7. The ratio of verbal to non–verbal behavior is indicated in each case. Thus, the facilitator who is suspicious of non–verbal efforts can easily avoid utilizing exercises requiring non–verbal behavior.

8. Suggestions for processing are given, thereby aiding the facilitator in his procedure, analysis, and discussion efforts.

9. Dynamic, more effective exercises are marked with an asterisk.

10. The handbook acquaints the facilitator with a multitude of verbal group exercises, thereby increasing his expertise.[2]

Exercise Format

Each exercise is described, using a standardized format devised by the authors. We believe the format includes information on all the variables necessary for the facilitator to insure successful use of an exercise.

The reader will notice that usually the exercise goal is not indicated except in the chapter on Ungrouped Exercises. The reason for this is that each exercise listed in any given chapter has that chapter's title as its specific goal. For example, all the exercises described in the chapter on Feedback have, as their specific goal, the elicitation of feedback data.

The information included in the format sections within each Chapter is consistent from one exercise to another. Therefore,

---

[2] Of course, the Handbook does not purport to cover *all* verbal group exercises, as such a task would be economically unfeasible. It does, however, include a representative number of exercises which are usable, effective, and congruent with the human relations area of group activity and endeavor.

the facilitator does not have to read an entire exercise before he decides, for instance, its applicability and suitability for his group and for the group's particular requirements. He need only read the appropriate format sections of the exercise under consideration.

The format sections and an indication of the material included in each one follows:

Subsidiary Goal(s)

Herein are listed those subsidiary goals reached by the group utilizing the exercise.

Group Application

Each of these sections is written in such a manner that the facilitator rapidly develops insight into which groups the exercise may be best suited for. Included, in the order of their appearance, are the following factors:

1. GROUP SIZE. An indication of the size group with which the exercise may be utilized. We use twelve members or less for all encounter, personal growth, marathon and t–groups. The facilitator, if he has more than twelve members, would be wise to modify the exercise in using it with his group.
2. TYPES OF GROUPS WHICH MAY UTILIZE THE EXERCISE. We have included the following groups for consideration with regard to application:
   a. *Encounter.* A group whose purposes are to help foster self-awareness and to help members establish genuine, authentic interpersonal relationships.
   b. *Personal growth.* A group whose purpose is to help the member grow and maturate in his intrapersonal and interpersonal relationships. Particular emphasis is placed on the individual participant's growth as a feeling person.
   c. *Marathon.* A group whose purposes are, over an extended, concentrated period of twenty or more hours, to strip away member defenses so that interaction becomes more real, genuine and authentic.
   d. *T–group.* A group whose purposes are to bring about awareness of self as a group member, to create an intellectual awareness of group dynamics, and to build interpersonal skills which members can utilize in their everyday relationships.
   e. *Problem solving.* A group whose purpose is to solve a problem or satisfactorily complete a task given to it. A subsidiary goal is to create awareness of member group roles.

f. *Classroom*. Herein we refer to *any* high school or college level class-room group of students. Utilization of exercises deemed suitable for the classroom with elementary classes, should be carefully considered by the facilitator or group leader.

3. MEMBER EXPERIENCE AND AGE. Wherever the level of group members' experience or age is important to exercise success, comment is made.

4. SEX RATIO. Where the ratio of males to females is important to exercise success, the facilitator is so informed.

Application Variables

This section of the format includes the following data:

1. TIME REQUIRED. A statement of the time needed to conduct the exercise is indicated in each instance. Note that the time required refers only to *conducting* the exercise. It does not include an estimate of time needed for the facilitator to lead a discussion or to process the exercise, as the time spent on these activities is dependent on the needs of the group and on the facilitator's objectives.

2. VERBAL AND NON–VERBAL RATIO. The ratio between verbal and non-verbal activity for the exercise is indicated accordingly. We do this so that the facilitator desiring an exercise which does *not* include non–verbal activity, will be able to decide easily whether to utilize the exercise in question. In cases where the non–verbal behavior is a written activity, such is indicated.

3. MATERIALS NEEDED. Where materials are needed for an exercise, specific mention is made.

4. ROOM SETTING. Where a certain type of room setting is needed for exercise success, that is also noted.

Administrative Procedure

This section of the format contains step-by-step instructions to the facilitator regarding the proper administration of the exercise.

Suggestions for Facilitator Process

Herein are contained a list of the questions the facilitator should use during the "processing" stage, *i.e.,* to effect the changes that will lead to the desired goal or result. We realize we cannot include all the queries the facilitator will use during processing, but we have supplied a sufficient number of these not only to help make his processing productive, but also to suggest further questions the facilitator may develop.

Variations

For a sizable majority of the exercises, variations on the original exercise are available. We have included such variations for the facilitator, and we urge him to use these whenever he feels they will be more suitable to his group's requirements than will be the original exercise. We also urge the facilitator to develop *his own* variations or to alter any of the exercises in this book so that they may more appropriately meet his needs and those of his group.

Again we wish to emphasize *the asterisked exercises.* The authors and other professionals have discovered that the exercises which have thus been singled out possess above average potential in achieving the stated goal and subsidiary goals. However, because such exercises are more advanced and subtler, we do wish to caution that only the experienced facilitator should make use of them. Anxiety, frustration, feelings of rejection, and so forth, may in many cases be related to such dynamic exercises. Therefore, the facilitator utilizing them must be adept at processing and at helping members to cope with the feelings elicited by the particular activity. As the facilitator grows in expertise, he will wish to make greater use of exercises so designated.

How To Use The Handbook

As we have pointed out, the facilitator will find that the Handbook is developed in such a way that he will have easy access to the exercise he desires. We have attempted to develop a more orderly approach to the exercise domain of human relations training than is presently available. The facilitator using this volume, will also appreciate the fact that he no longer need rely on the "hunt and find" effort required in other books dealing with group exercises.

For the most effective use of A HANDBOOK OF VERBAL GROUP EXERCISES, we suggest that the facilitator approach it in the following fashion:

1. Decide what goal he wishes the needed exercise to meet.
2. Look for the appropriate chapter and/or use the Index at the back of the book to determine *which* exercises meet the goal in question.

3. Then, if certain variables are important to him, such as time required, materials needed, group size, etc., let him pay particular attention to the appropriate format sections of the exercise under consideration.
4. After following the above steps, the facilitator will have one or more exercises at his disposal. He may then choose whichever of these he deems most appropriate for his particular group, *or* he may use an asterisked exercise, knowing *beforehand* that the exercise chosen has definite potential for meeting the goal in question.

Exercise Sources

We have given credit to exercise designers wherever such credit was necessary or appropriate. We could not give credit for each exercise, for the majority have reached us by word of mouth or are fifth– and sixth–hand versions of exercises developed by unknown contributors to the field of group interaction. We have discovered that the majority of our exercises existed in people's heads, on scraps of notebook paper, on unsigned handouts, etc. We have not copied any known copyrighted material without the copyright owner's permission.[3]

Concluding Comments

In this volume we have set out to develop a handbook of verbal group exercises that is easy for the facilitator to use, presents him with a wealth of readily accessible new material, provides all the necessary information as to various aspects of these exercises, offers the facilitator ease of duplication and application, and—hopefully—furthers the professional and public stature of the human

---

[3] The professional facilitator will note that some extremely well–known exercises are not included. For example, we have not included the Johari Window, One–Way Two–Way Communication and the Prisoner's Dilemma, to name just a few. We have eliminated such exercises for two reasons. First, these exercises are so well known that duplicating them one more time seemed unnecessary and we wanted to avoid gross reduplication. Second, we wished to use the space made available by these omissions to present innovative, never before published exercises. By omitting the first type of exercises, we have succeeded in our second desire.

relations training field. We believe we have been successful in these efforts.

Lay Use Versus Professional Use

Many of the exercises in this book can be used by the "layman." However, we caution the non–professional concerning his attempts to use such exercises in his everyday group situations. We do not propose that this book be a guide to Everyman's group efforts. It is designed for use by professional group facilitators and group leaders. Laymen, if they wish to conduct an exercise, should restrict themselves to those exercises listed as "applicable to any group," still using caution. This is not a party book, nor a "game" and "gimmick" book for instant self–growth. It is a professional effort to be used by experienced professionals. Regardless of who uses the book, *any* exercise is to be regarded as a tool rather than as an end in itself.

A HANDBOOK OF VERBAL GROUP EXERCISES

I

ASSESSMENT

THE PRIMARY GOAL for each exercise in this chapter is to allow members the opportunity to assess themselves, other members, and/or the group.

Assessment exercises are appropriate for all types of groups, but are particularly useful when used with problem solving and t–groups. Since assessment usually involves feedback, the use of such exercises can be expanded to any type of group.

Assessment exercises typically use writing as an initial form of communication. The following questionnaires and charts are intended to be reproduced for individual and group use. The facilitator should also feel free to alter them so they will more easily meet his or his group's assessment needs.

Assessment exercises are designed to elicit a multitude of dynamics. It is suggested that the facilitator familiarize himself thoroughly with any exercises being considered for use before making a final decision on which exercise is most appropriate for his and his group's specific needs.

It is the authors' belief that assessment exercises, if properly used, can enhance and further the group's development. The facilitator is encouraged to make any variations of the following exercises that he deems necessary.

* ASSESSING PARTICIPATION

Subsidiary Goal(s)

a. To compare a member's estimate of his participation with the predictions of other group members.
b. To encourage participation.
c. To give and receive feedback.

Group Application

Group size is unlimited, but the most successful experiences will occur with twelve members or less. Applicable, with modification, to any group, but most frequently used early in the life of encounter, personal growth, marathon and t–groups.

Application Variables

Thirty minutes. The exercise is 70% verbal, with 30% non–verbal being written. Participation Forms, pencils and a chalkboard are needed.

Administrative Procedure

a. About thirty to forty minutes before the end of the session, the facilitator stops the group discussion and asks that each member fill out a Participation Form.
b. He makes sure each member understands that he is to rate his own participation and that of *every* other member.
c. He plots the results on the chalkboard and leads a discussion on the data.

Suggestions for Facilitator Process

Concentrate on the following during processing:
a. Were your self–assessments significantly higher or lower than those ratings you received from others? Why? Which ratings are the most accurate, your's or the group's, and why?

---

* Dynamic, more effective exercises are marked with an asterisk.

b. What participation strengths and weaknesses in yourself did you learn about? What can you do to overcome the low rated areas?

c. Are these ratings indicative of your participation level in past group sessions? If not, is your participation level today higher or lower, and why?

d. In question six, why did you ask questions instead of making the statements behind them? For example, "Are you bored?" equals "I see you as being bored," etc.

Variations

Variation I

a. Conduct the exercise as above, but chart the results anonymously, so only the member will know the results he obtained.

b. During processing, encourage self-disclosure about the results.

**Variation II*

a. To encourage verbal participation and confrontation, have each member read his self-assessment, then have the other members read him their assessments.

b. Allow the member to react to, challenge, defend, etc., his and other members' assessments.

PARTICIPATION FORM

Assess your verbal participation level for each question. Also, assess the level for all other members. Use percentages, from 1% to 100%.

OTHER MEMBERS
Me 1 2 3 4 5 6 7 8 9 10 11 12

1. In this session I contributed _____% to the overall verbal participation.

2. _____% of my participation dealt with the feelings of myself and others.

3. _____% of my partici-
   pation dealt with the thoughts
   of myself and others.
4. _____% of my partici-
   pation was self-disclosing.
5. _____% of my partici-
   pation was giving feedback to
   others.
6. _____% of my partici-
   pation consisted of my asking
   questions of others.

DIMENSIONS OF GROUP EFFECTIVENESS [1]

Subsidiary Goal(s)

a. To help in recognizing aspects of the group needing improvement.

Group Application

Twelve members or less. Applicable to any group, but
particularly relevant to problem solving and task oriented
groups.

Application Variables

Thirty minutes, fifteen for completing scale and fifteen
for tabulation. The exercise is 50% verbal, with 50% non–
verbal being a written exercise. Pencils, chalkboard and
copies of the Group Effectiveness Scale are needed.

Administrative Procedure

a. The facilitator has the members complete the Group Effectiveness Scale.
b. He tabulates the ratings on the chalkboard, identifying
those dimensions where there was much disagreement and
those which rated low.
c. The group discusses the results, attempting to diagnose

---

[1] This is a variation of an exercise developed by the Youth Office, Lutheran
Church of America.

why there were low and/or diverse ratings. The facilitator should attempt to get the group to devise plans for improving those dimensions that show a need for improvement.

Suggestions for Facilitator Process

Concentrate on the following during processing:
a. Why did (name the dimension) get a low rating?
b. Where were disagreeing ratings achieved for (name the dimension)?
c. What can we do to remedy the situation?

Variations

None

GROUP EFFECTIVENESS SCALE

DIRECTIONS: *Circle the number indicating the rating you think the group deserves at this time.*

A. Task Dimensions

1. How clear are the goals for our group?

1	2	3	4	5
Very Confused	Vague	Average	Fairly Clear	Very Clear

2. How involved are we in what the group is doing?

1	2	3	4	5
No Involvement	Not Much Involvement	Average	Some Involvement	Very Involved

3. How accurate are we in group problem diagnosis?

1	2	3	4	5
Disregard Diagnosis	Some Diagnosis	Average	Considerable Diagnosis	Very Involved in Diagnosis

4. Are our group norms and procedures appropriate with our group goals?

1	2	3	4	5
Inappropriate	Of Little Appropriate-ness	Average	Appropriate	Very Appropriate

5. How much attention do we give to contributions from other members?

1	2	3	4	5
Disregard Them	Slight Attention Given	Average	Attention Given	Much Attention Given

6. What process do we use in decision making?

1	2	3	4	5
Tsaristic	Minority	Majority	Forced Consensus	True Consensus

7. To what extent do members contribute to reaching our goals?

1	2	3	4	5
No One Contributes	A Few Contribute	Average	Most Contribute	All Contribute

B. Maintenance Dimensions

8. To what extent do we find pleasure in working with each other?

1	2	3	4	5
Hate It	Discontented	Some Pleased, Some Displeased	Most Pleased	All Enjoy It

9. How much do we show our appreciation, support and encouragement to others?

1	2	3	4	5
We Don't	Very Few Supported	Average	Often Show Support	Every Member Given Support

10. To what extent do we express feelings?

1	2	3	4	5
We Don't	Positive Feelings, No Negative	Low-Level Positive and Negative Feelings	Negative Feelings, No Positive	Share All Feelings At All Levels

11. How do we handle conflicts?

1	2	3	4	5
Avoid Them	Seldom Explore Them	Change The Subject	Do Explore Them	Explore Them All And Resolve Them

12. Are we sensitive to unexpressed feelings?

1	2	3	4	5
Insensitive	Seldom Sensitive	Average	Often Sensitive	Fully Sensitive

13. What is the level of our feedback?

1	2	3	4	5
Never Give It	Give Negative Feedback Only	Give Judgmental Feedback	Give Positive Feedback Only	Give Both Types Without Being Judgmental

14. How many members are growing in their understanding of self and others?

1	2	3	4	5
None	A Few	Half	Most	All

* I'VE LEARNED

Subsidiary Goal(s)

a. To give and receive feedback.
b. To facilitate member involvement.

Group Application

Twelve members or less. To be used with any group. Most commonly used at one of the last two meetings.

Application Variables

Forty-five minutes to one hour. The exercise is 90% verbal, with 10% non–verbal being written. An overhead projector is recommended.

Administrative Procedure

a. The facilitator gives each member an I've Learned Form and asks that it be completed.
b. He then has a volunteer read his form. (If an overhead projector is available, the facilitator places the volunteer's form in it so all can see it.)
c. All other members read to the volunteer their I've Learned

Form responses concerning him. The member is urged to react to the group members' discoveries about him.

d. Steps b and c are repeated until all members have participated.

Suggestions for Facilitator Process

Concentrate on the following during processing:

a. Have your perceptions of yourself changed? In what way? How have your perceptions of other members changed?

b. Which member (s) did we, as a group, share uniform learnings with? Why? Which member (s) did the group have diverse learnings about? Why?

c. Did your learnings about yourself and others deal with factual, feeling, thinking, believing, or valuing data? Why were your learnings factual with (name the member) and feeling with (name the member) ? Continue such questioning, investigating the reasons for the types of learnings.

Variations

*Variation I

a. Ask for a volunteer.

b. Then ask each member to write *one* learning they have for the volunteer from the following list. Have the member write one learning he has for himself for *each* statement.

1. I've learned this fact about (volunteer's name) ＿＿＿＿＿
2. I've learned (volunteer's name) values ＿＿＿＿＿
3. I've learned (volunteer's name) believes ＿＿＿＿＿
4. I've learned (volunteer's name) thinks ＿＿＿＿＿
5. I've learned that on a feeling level (volunteer's name) is＿＿

c. Have the statements read to the volunteer. All who wrote on statement 1 should read their learning to the volunteer. He then reads his response to statement 1. Brief interaction is encouraged. Statement 2 is read, then responded to. Statement 3 and so on.

d. Continue the exercise until all who wish to participate have done so.

I'VE LEARNED FORM

Complete the following for every member. Include yourself.

Examples: I've learned Ken is a loving person.
I've learned I am a lover.

1. I've learned I _____ _____
2. I've learned _____ is _____
3. I've learned _____ is _____
4. I've learned _____ is _____
5. I've learned _____ is _____
6. I've learned _____ is _____
7. I've learned _____ is _____
8. I've learned _____ is _____
9. I've learned _____ is _____
10. I've learned _____ is _____
11. I've learned _____ is _____
12. I've learned _____ is _____

SELF ANCHORING SCALE [2]

Subsidiary Goal(s)

a. To gain insight into one's self–concept.
b. To explore the dynamics involved in self–disclosure.
c. To differentiate present from past experiences.

Group Application

Twelve members or less. To be used in any group. Best results are obtained if the exercise is used in the early stage of development so that knowledge gained can be utilized in future sessions.

Application Variables

One hour and thirty minutes. The exercise is 50% verbal, with 50% non–verbal being written. A pencil and copy of the Self Anchoring Scale are needed for each member. The

---

[2] This is a variation of an exercise developed by the Youth Office, Lutheran Church of America.

room should be large enough to allow members to spread out without feeling unduly restrained.

Administrative Procedure

a. The facilitator gives a copy of the Self Anchoring Scale to each member.
b. He then tells the members they have forty-five minutes to complete the form. Members are to spread out around the room.
c. When members are finished filling out the form, the group reforms.
d. The facilitator asks if any members are willing to share what they have written on their form. (Start with question #1, wait for response and proceed to question #2, etc.)
e. After all members have had an opportunity to share what they have written the facilitator initiates discussion.

Suggestions for Facilitator Process

Concentrate on the following during processing:
a. What have you learned about yourself? Would you say you have a constructive or destructive self–concept? What have you learned about other members that surprise you?
b. Do you feel the results of the Self Anchoring Scale are indicative of your behavior in the group? If not, why? Where do you go from here?
c. If you were unwilling to share what you have written, can you let the group know why?

Variations

None.

SELF ANCHORING SCALE

1. (A) Everybody wants certain things out of life. When you think about what really matters in your life, what are your wishes and hopes for the future? In other words, if

you *imagine your future* in the *best* possible light, what would your life be like then?

Take time in answering; such things aren't easy to put into words.

(B) Now, taking the other side of the picture, what are your fears and worries about the future? In other words, if you *imagine your future* in the *worst* possible light, what would your life be like then?

Again, take time in answering.

(C) Where on the ladder do you feel you personally stand at the *present* time?

Step number_____

(D) Where on the ladder would you say you stood five years ago?

Step number_____

(E) And where do you think you will be on the ladder ten years from now?

Step number_____

Diagram I presents the picture of a ladder. Suppose we say that at the top of the ladder is the very best state of affairs you have described; at the bottom is the very worst state of affairs.

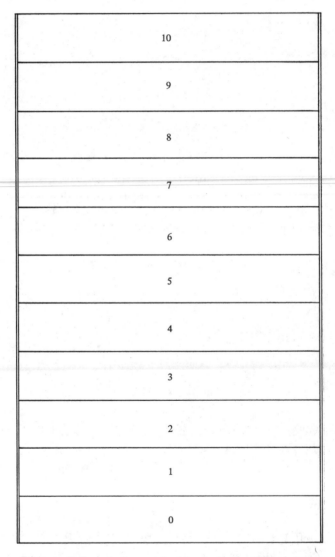

Diagram I. Sample Success Ladder in Group Effectiveness.

2. (A) As you look at things the way they are for you *today*, what do you feel are the *best* aspects of your own personal life?

(B) And what do you feel are the *worst* aspects of your own personal life today as you look at things the way they are for you now?

(C) Some people seem to be quite happy and satisfied with their lives, while others seem quite unhappy and dissatisfied. Now, look at the ladder again. Suppose that a person who is entirely satisfied with his life would be at the top of the ladder, and a person who is extremely dissatisfied with his life would be at the bottom of the ladder.

Where would you put yourself on the ladder at the present time in terms of how satisfied or dissatisfied you are with your own personal life?

Step number_____

Why?

* WHAT'S WRONG WITH US

Subsidiary Goal(s)

a. To give and receive feedback.
b. To facilitate member involvement.
c. To allow the group to work together in resolving group problems and difficulties.

Group Application

Twelve members or less. To be used with any group, but most frequently used with encounter, personal growth, marathon and t–groups whose members have developed rapport, warmth and care for each other. This exercise is ideal for use with groups which are experiencing some communication problems. Since negative feedback is elicited, the facilitator should process diligently to insure that the group members do not leave the session with negative reactions and feelings.

Application Variables

Forty-five minutes to one hour. The exercise is 90% verbal, with 10% non–verbal being written. An overhead projector is recommended. If a projector is unavailable, a chalkboard is needed.

Administrative Procedure

a. The facilitator gives each member a What's Wrong With Us Form and asks that it be completed.
b. He then asks that a volunteer read his form to the group. (If an overhead projector is available, the facilitator places the volunteer's form in it so all can see it.) If a projector is unavailable, the facilitator writes each member's response on the chalkboard. (See Example 1.)

EXAMPLE 1

Members Responding	Problem	Members Creating the Problem
Ken	group too closed	Ed, Bill, Mary
Ed	group too structured	Bill (the facilitator)
Judy	not enough touching	all members
Phil	too problem oriented	Ed, Jack, Mary

c. After all responses have been read, the group decides which problems they want to overcome. A discussion follows, oriented to resolving the problems chosen.
d. The facilitator is urged to wait two or three sessions and then have the group decide whether they overcame the problems discussed during this exercise.

Suggestions for Facilitator Process

Concentrate on the following during processing:
a. Do we agree that everything listed is a problem? If no, which ones are not problems and why?
b. Why did you choose the problems you did for corrections? Why did you ignore others?
c. Which members were frequently listed as contributors? Why? *To those members:* Do you agree or disagree about your role in the problems? Why?

Variations

None.

WHAT'S WRONG WITH US

Complete the following open–ended statement as many times as you wish. If you write more than one statement, rank your responses from 1 most important to (last number) least important.

> *Example:* **One of the groups problems is** being too structured **and** Ken **member (s) help create the problem.**

1. One of the group's problems is _____
_____ and _____ member (s) help create the problem.
2. One of the group's problems is _____
_____ and _____ member (s) help create the problem.
3. One of the group's problems is _____
_____ and _____ member (s) help create the problem.
4. One of the group's problems is _____

_____ and _____ mem-
ber (s) help create the problem.
5. One of the group's problems is _____
_____ and _____ mem-
ber (s) help create the problem.
6. One of the group's problems is _____
_____ and _____ mem-
ber (s) help create the problem.

* WHO ARE YOU

Subsidiary Goal(s)

   a. To give insight into one's concept of others.
   b. To increase one's ability to evaluate other participants
      more accurately.
   c. To give and receive feedback.

Group Application

Twelve members or less. To be used with encounter, personal growth, marathon and t–groups.

Application Variables

One hour. The exercise is 70% verbal, with 30% non–verbal being written. Paper and pencils are needed.

Administrative Procedure

   a. Names of all members are written on slips of paper. The slips are randomly distributed (no member, however, should receive his own name).
   b. The facilitator asks that the name received remain secret.
   c. Each member then writes a personality evaluation of the name received (short paragraph). The evaluation is to include such things as drive, good and bad points, motivation, etc.
   d. Without revealing the name, one member reads his de-

scription. (The first description is assigned A, the second is B, etc.).

e. The facilitator then asks the group to write down who they think the person is that has been described by the member.

f. Steps **d** and **e** are repeated until all members have read their descriptions and voted.

g. The facilitator collects the votes of the members and divulges who A is, B is, etc. The right votes are then counted.

Suggestions for Facilitator Process

Concentrate on the following during processing:

a. How did you feel about evaluating other members? Were you hesitant about putting in bad points? Why?

b. What did you feel about your own evaluation? Was it accurate? Did the other members think so?

c. Why do you think we disagreed with some of the descriptions? What does that tell us about ourselves?

d. Whose description received the least correct guesses? How do you account for this? Whose descriptions received the most correct guesses? How do you account for this?

e. What have we learned about our perceptions of other members?

Variations

None.

II

AWARENESS

THE PRIMARY GOAL for each exercise in this chapter is the elicitation of greater member awareness of himself or other members.

Awareness, for the purposes of this chapter, is defined as a heightened ability to perceive in oneself and/or other members the predominant thoughts, feelings, values, beliefs, etc., which are operating in the relationships between group members.

Awareness is essential for any small group, as well as for the facilitator, and member utilization of such awareness is an essential dynamic to the success of personal growth and interpersonal relationships.

The following exercises are created to perpetuate the process of self–exploration and personal integration of the group experience. The above two factors combined with processing (provided after each exercise) will lead to increased awareness for all members concerned.

The facilitator should feel free to use awareness exercises whenever he feels they will be beneficial to the group. They are particularly useful in situations in which the members are perceived by the facilitator as being "unaware" or not "tuned in" to the dynamics operating in themselves and the group.

Although the following exercises can be relied on as extremely useful and effective tools, the facilitator should keep in mind that the final responsibility for gaining increased awareness lies with the member himself.

RANKING MEMBER INFLUENCE

Subsidiary Goal(s)

a. To develop insight into other member self–concepts concerning their influence quotient.
b. To recognize coping methods used when confronting anxiety, acceptance, rejection, and conflict.

Group Application

Twelve members or less. To be used with any group, but caution should be used when used with problem–solving and task oriented groups so that excess anxiety, if created, is dealt with. Best results obtained from mixed groups having had sufficient group sessions to adequately measure member influence.

Application Variables

Forty-five minutes to one hour. The exercise is 70% verbal and 30% non–verbal. A chalkboard is required. The room must be large enough to allow the members to mill comfortably.

Administrative Procedure

a. The facilitator asks the group to mill around.
b. He then instructs the group to non–verbally rank themselves according to member influence on the group so that the member first in line is seen as most influential, the second in line is second in influence, etc., to the last member who is considered least influential.
c. After the group has completed the ranking, the facilitator writes the ranking on the chalkboard so that all members can easily see and read it.
d. The group discusses the ranking exercise concentrating on feelings aroused, differences of opinion concerning the final ranking, reasons why individuals were ranked where they were, etc.

Suggestions for Facilitator Process

Concentrate on the following during processing:

a. *To all:* How did you feel during the ranking process? How did you handle your feelings?

b. *To high ranked members:* How did you feel about your position? Why did you take it? or Why do you feel other members gave it to you?

c. *To low ranked members:* How did you feel about your position? Why did you take it? or Why do you feel other members gave it to you?

d. Who does not agree with the ranking? Quiz those who respond as to why they disagree and how they would change the rank order.

Variations

Variation I

a. Tell the group to write down their estimate as to how the members should be ranked, from high to low, using influence on the group as the dimension considered.

b. Continue as in the original exercise.

c. Process, but have members deal with the differences between their written rank orders and that order achieved in the milling stage.

RESOURCE IDENTIFICATION [1]

Subsidiary Goal(s)

a. To identify the resources, or special skills and abilities helpful to others in the group.

b. To assist individual members in understanding and enhancing the resources he/she has to offer.

c. To provide feedback assessment of self and group.

Group Application

Twenty members or less. To be used with any group having

---

[1] Adapted from Robert Shelton and Robert Brook, University of Kansas.

considerable previous experience as a group. Best results are obtained if the exercise is introduced during the middle of the group's life.

Application Variables

Forty-five minutes. The exercise is 100% verbal. Sufficient space is required for the entire group to be comfortably seated.

Administrative Procedure

a. It is suggested that the facilitator give a brief talk regarding the way in which persons are "resources" for one another. The group should be told that this is not a typical "feedback" exercise but identification of specific ways in which persons help others to do their tasks, be more disclosing, etc. The facilitator should distinguish between resources, in this sense, and support. Examples of this distinction should be given as well as elicited from the group.
b. The facilitator asks the group to stand in a large circle, leaving space between members. Individuals are to look around the circle, being aware of particular individuals who have provided a helpful "resource."
c. Members are to go to that person and tell him/her briefly about it. After a brief discussion, the member is to return to the original position in the circle.
d. After each member has had ample time to go to other members, as well as having other members come to him, reassemble for discussion.

Suggestions for Facilitator Process

Concentrate on the following during processing:
a. Any surprises? Were there ways in which you were helpful that you didn't realize before? Has this confirmed your own self–perceptions?
b. Do you feel you have increased your self–awareness or awareness of others? Do you have any new ideas about what

is resourceful to you or to others? Have your feelings changed toward any members? If so, why?

Variations

Variation I

a. If the group is very large, the follow–up discussion might best be done in groups of eight or so, rather than in the total group.

SEMANTICS

Subsidiary Goal(s)

a. To learn to dissociate objects from their labels.
b. To note the inadequacy of words.

Group Application

Twelve members or less. To be used with any encounter, personal growth, marathon and t–groups whose members have had sufficient experience in self–awareness.

Application Variables

Thirty minutes. The exercise is 60% verbal and 40% non–verbal. A number of objects are needed, preferably small objects (*i.e.*, pencils, rocks, leaves, books, etc.). Each member should have access to at least three objects.

Administrative Procedure

a. The facilitator gives each member an object.
b. He then asks that each participant try to notice as many qualities of the object as possible (*i.e.*, texture, color, size, weight, smell, etc.).
c. As the members are getting acquainted with their object, they are to say the word for it aloud (every twenty seconds).
d. After a member feels he is acquainted with his object he may proceed to the next object.

e. After thirty minutes, the facilitator asks the group to form a circle and introduce their objects.

Suggestions for Facilitator Process

Concentrate on the following during processing:

a. Which objects did you find the most appealing and why? Which objects did you find the most unappealing and why?
b. Did you stay with one object a significantly longer period of time? If so, why?
c. How did saying the word associated with the object affect you? Did it gain or lose meaning? Did the word still represent the object?
d. Did you present your object verbally or non–verbally? Why? Did your object take on qualities you hadn't seen before?

Variations

Variation I

a. Have members choose their objects from a composite pile.
b. Have the members explain why they chose the object.
c. Let members share their object while making initial investigations.
d. Ask members to create new words for their objects.

SIMILARITIES AND DIFFERENCES [2]

Subsidiary Goal(s)

a. To understand similarities and differences in goals and styles of group participation.
b. To explore stereotypes and first impressions.
c. To identify the values of similarities and differences in group experience.

Group Application

Twelve members or less. To be used with encounter, per-

_____
[2] Adapted from Robert Shelton and Robert Brook, University of Kansas.

sonal growth, marathon and t–groups who have had considerable interaction experience within the group.

Application Variables

One hour and thirty minutes. The exercise is 90% verbal, with 10% non–verbal being written. Pencils and paper are needed for each member. The room must be large enough to allow for clustering of a small group within a large circle for "fishbowling."

Administrative Procedure

a. The facilitator passes out a pencil and paper to each member.

b. The facilitator asks members to think about the other members in the group whose goals for and style of group participation are most similar to and different from his own. Each member should make two lists on his sheet of paper (similarities and differences) with the names of the appropriate members.

c. Members are now to cluster (stand together) in groups with those on their most similar list. (Groups will shift as members decide to join another group when more of their list appear to be in another group.)

d. Once clusters are formed, each group, in turn, sits in the middle of the larger circle formed by the other group members. The group in the center is to discuss their feelings about their similarities, those in the group not on their list, members outside the cluster, etc.

e. When the group in the center has finished the discussion, those on the outside may comment.

f. Rotate another cluster into the center, repeat.

g. Repeat steps c to f with members they feel different from.

h. Group reforms for discussion.

Suggestions for Facilitator Process

Concentrate on the following during processing:

    a. What have you learned about the other members in your group? Were there any members in your cluster that you felt dissimilar to? Have your feelings changed toward any members? If so, in what way?

    b. Did verbalizing your differences change your perceptions of any members in your subgroup? Do you feel that you are able to accept differences in other members? What have you learned about yourself?

Variations

Variation I

    a. If there are strong feelings that differences have dominated the group's interaction, a "splitting" of the group may result. It is suggested that a follow–up design which permits the experience of differences as a contribution to personal and group growth be used. Example, an exercise in which each person comes prepared to share his creativity, talent, or individual interest with the entire group.

* TELL ME WHAT YOU SEE

Subsidiary Goal(s)

    a. To achieve greater insight into how other members are perceiving and being perceived.

    b. To establish a deeper sense of openness and honesty.

    c. To give and receive feedback.

    d. To encourage self–disclosure.

Group Application

Twelve members or less. To be used with encounter, personal growth, marathon and t–groups whose members have had an ample number of sessions to develop member identity.

Application Variables

One hour and thirty minutes. The exercise is 100% verbal.

---

* Dynamic, more effective exercises are marked with an asterisk.

Administrative Procedure

a. The facilitator is to make up in advance four negatively oriented questions which a member might ask of himself (*i.e.,* Am I hostile? Do I represent myself as being dishonest? Am I materialistic? Etc.).

b. He then asks for a volunteer to stand in the middle of the circle.

c. The volunteer in the center then asks the questions given to him by the facilitator to the members in the group.

d. The group member addressed is to reply to the question asked of him.

e. Each member is to have an opportunity to answer the questions about the person in the center but *no other* discussion is to take place.

f. The person in the center then answers the questions he has been asking others.

g. After he is finished he rejoins the group and another volunteer is asked for.

h. Steps c through f are repeated.

i. After all members have had an opportunity to participate, the group discusses the experience.

Suggestions for Facilitator Process

Concentrate on the following during processing:

a. Were you surprised at the answers you received to your questions? If so, in what way? How did you feel about the feedback you received? Do you perceive it as being accurate?

b. How did you feel about being in the center of the circle? Did your feelings change as you asked more questions? If so, in what way?

c. What did you learn about yourself? About other members in the group? Have your feelings changed towards anyone in the group? If so, in what way?

d. Were you hesitant about asking or answering any questions? If so, which questions and why?

Variations

Variation I

a. Have the members write the negative questions.

b. The volunteer then answers any four questions other members wish to ask him. He chooses the four questioners *before* he is told their questions.

c. During processing, concentrate on the volunteer's reasons for choosing questions, the place projection played in the member questions, etc.

VERBAL SOCIALIZATION

Subsidiary Goal(s)

a. To recognize differences between social get–togethers and growth awareness get–togethers.

b. To give the member insight into his own social behavior.

Group Application

Twelve members or less. To be used with any group although most effective with encounter, personal growth, marathon and t–groups. The exercise is most appropriate with a group in the early stages of development.

Application Variables

One hour. The exercise is 60% verbal and 40% non–verbal.

Administrative Procedure

a. The facilitator asks the group members to socialize with each other.

b. During the socialization he makes rounds and asks members to change partners from time to time.

c. After half an hour the facilitator stops the socializing and asks the group to form a circle.

d. The facilitator asks each member to greet every other participant by giving him a hug.

e. He then has the group divide into pairs non–verbally.
f. The facilitator asks the group members to communicate non–verbally with their partner using eye contact, physical gestures, etc.
g. After five minutes with each partner the group is asked to change dyads until each member has communicated with at least three other members.
h. Each member is given a few minutes to meditate about the experience.
i. The facilitator then asks the members to discuss the experience.

Suggestions *for* Facilitator *Process*

Concentrate on the following during processing:
a. What did you learn about your ability to socialize and communicate verbally as opposed to non–verbally? How did you interpret the word "socialize?"
b. How did you go about choosing partners? What were your feelings as to physical contact (*i.e.,* being touched or touching)? Ask those who say they felt fearful, uneasy, etc., why this was so.
c. How did we react to having to leave our partners and meet other members?
d. Did you find the experience rewarding? If so, why? If not, why not?

Variations

Variation I
a. Have members introduce their partners non–verbally to the group after the initial exercise is finished.
b. After the non–verbal introduction, the members are to verbally introduce their partners.
c. Check out differences between verbal and non–verbal introductions.

Variation II
a. Instead of dyads, form triads.
b. During processing, determine whether the addition of a

third person facilitated or hindered communication and socialization.

ZEROING IN

Subsidiary Goal(s)

a. To develop new perspectives in dealing with one's environment.
b. To recognize differences in perception of the group environment.

Group Application

Twelve members or less. To be used with encounter, personal growth, marathon and t–groups whose members have had group experience in awareness.

Application Variables

Thirty minutes. The exercise is 90% verbal and 10% non–verbal.

Administrative Procedure

a. The facilitator states "many of us go through our daily routines without being aware of our environment and our body. Almost every object has its own 'uniqueness' which we fail to discover. To approximate this sense of 'uniqueness' we are going to explore the 'familiar'."
b. He then asks that each member explore the room, concentrating on objects. He says "Verbally state your observation of the object starting with the word 'this' (i.e., this brick, this hole, this floor, this chair, this crack). Be sure at least one other member hears your statement. Do not, however, explore the room in pairs."
c. Each member is told to explore as many objects as he can, including his own body.
d. After thirty minutes the facilitator asks the group to form a circle and share their insights.

Suggestions for Facilitator Process

Concentrate on the following during processing:

a. How specific did you get in explaining "this"? In example, did you stop with the object as a whole or go further?

b. Did you explore your own body? Why not? If you did, what parts did you explore and why? Which did you ignore and why?

c. How did you feel "discovering" a familiar object? Did you find your awareness for it expanding?

d. Did you explore another person? Why or why not?

Variations

Variation I

a. Have the members explore the environment in pairs and compare and contrast their perceptions.

Variation II

a. Conduct the exercise as above, but ten minutes before the end say: "Now, explore your body and the bodies of other members. Instead of the word 'this' substitute 'my' or 'your'. For example, my hair, my teeth, your eyes, your mouth."

III

COMMUNICATION

THE PRIMARY GOAL for each exercise in this chapter is to expose the group members to the dynamics of communication.

Communication is the foundation for any group, regardless of type or purpose. Without accurate, efficient, give–and–take communication, the group experience will be frustrating, exhausting, and, possibly, detrimental for the group members.

The exercises in this chapter do not *create* communication and its accompanying skills. Instead, they help members experience the art of communication. They are designed to help members who are communicating with each other *improve* that communication.

Since communication exercises expose the members to many of the dynamics involved in efficient communication, the facilitator is urged to use the processing stage to foster and enhance the learning which should be taking place.

CHAIN COMMUNICATION

Subsidiary Goal(s)

    a. To examine the dynamics of distortion.
    b. To gain an awareness of member perception.
    c. To stimulate more critical examination of gossip.

Group Application

Twelve members or less. To be used with any group. Best results are obtained if the exercise is used early in the group's development so that the information learned may be utilized in future sessions.

Application Variables

Thirty minutes. The exercise is 90% verbal, with 10% non–verbal being written. Pencils, paper, and a photograph chosen by the facilitator for its ambiguity are needed.

Administrative Procedure

    a. The facilitator asks for a volunteer to initiate the exercise.
    b. The volunteer is taken to the side and is shown the ambiguous photograph and is asked to write down ten attributes of the picture. (The other group members are not to view the photograph or hear the instructions concerning the attributes.)
    c. After a few minutes the facilitator takes the photograph and the written attributes from the volunteer. He and the volunteer now rejoin the group.
    d. The facilitator instructs the group that the volunteer is going to pass information on concerning a photograph. He will start by whispering the information to the member on the right of him. The member listening may ask questions but only two minutes are allowed in passing on the information. (The members transmitting the information should make sure they are not being overheard.)
    e. The member who has received the information now passes

Suggestions for Fa...

Concentrate on

a. *To the volu...*
   behavior? W
   handle them

b. *To other p...*
   drama? Did
   If so, why?

c. *To non–pla...*
   for remedyir

Variations

None.

W

Subsidiary Goal(s)

a. To gain insig
   in communic

b. To gain insi

c. To gain insig

Group Application

Twelve mem
are used. Ea
classroom. Be
when used w
port and expe

Application Variabl

Forty-five mir
non–verbal b
ber are requi
commodate c

h

i.

Sugg...

(

a

h

(

Var

Sub

Gr

it on to the member on his right and so on until all members have participated.

f. The last member receiving the information is to report to the group what he has heard.

g. The facilitator reads the initial description made by the volunteer and now presents the photograph to the group.

h. The facilitator initiates discussion.

Suggestions for Facilitator Process

Concentrate on the following during processing:

a. Did the final description differ substantially from the initial one? If so, why do you feel this happened? Can you pinpoint any areas of breakdown in communication?

b. When viewing the photograph did you agree with the descriptions given to you? What does this tell us about our photograph?

c. How can we tie this exercise into dynamics that may be occurring in the group? How can we become more accurate in our perceptions?

Variations

Variation I
a. Use a very distinctive photograph.
b. Repeat basic exercise.

Variation II
a. Have members non–verbally describe the characteristics of the photograph (still having volunteer write down ten attributes).
b. Repeat basic exercise.

* LET'S EAT

Subsidiary Goal(s)

a. To gain awareness of familiar objects.
b. To emphasize the dynamics involved in dependency.

---

* Dynamic, more effective exercises are marked with an asterisk.

Applicatio

Tim
the
run.
ticip
mate
a ne

Administra

a. The
    persc
b. He t
    in an
    select
    act s
c. The
    1. C
        go
    2. Se
        in
    3. A
        se
    4. B
d. Wher
    have
    dram
e. He le
    Did it
    roles
    were
f. The f
    replay
    has th
    copes
g. After
    and le

Administrative Procedure

a. The facilitator has the group separate into dyads.
b. One member is assigned the leader role, the other assumes his own identity.
c. The facilitator tells the dyads to engage in written conversation on a sheet of paper to be passed back and forth between them.
d. The member with the leader role communicates first by writing any angry statement he wishes and handing it to his partner. The statement must be directed at his dyadic partner.
e. The partner responds by writing his reply and handing it back to the leader–member.
f. This process is continued for twenty minutes, then stopped.
g. The facilitator leads a discussion by having dyads share their conversation with the rest of the group.

Suggestions for *Facilitator Process*

Concentrate on the following during processing:
a. Did you feel angry at your partner? If so, how did you cope with this feeling?
b. What did you learn about yourself? What did you learn about your partner?
c. What did you learn about your method of communication?
d. *To the members playing a leader:* Did you feel authoritative? How did you communicate your authority?
e. *To the members not assigned a role:* Did you feel as if you were being confronted by an authority figure? If so, how did you cope with his authority?

Variations

*Variation I
a. Develop dyads in which there is some anger or hostility between the dyadic partners.
b. Use the same instructions, but have the dyads deal with the real anger or hostility they feel for each other.
c. It is feasible that the dyads, after writing, will want to continue verbally until they resolve their difficulty. This opportunity should be made available to them.

IV

CONSENSUS SEEKING

THE PRIMARY GOAL for each exercise in this chapter is to facilitate the examination and exploration of consensus seeking behavior.

Consensus seeking occurs in a group when the members must reach a decision which is agreeable to all, without using majority rule or voting procedures. It is readily apparent that such exercises investigate the dynamics involved in "true consensus" situations as opposed to "false consensus" situations.

The following exercises are designed to create an environment which allows for examination of member behavior in task oriented groups. Although consensus seeking exercises are most frequently used with t–groups and problem solving groups, their use can be expanded to other groups.

The structures and situations devised for each exercise are intended to provide feedback which will generalize to member behavior exhibited outside the group in what are usually "false consensus" situations. The facilitator is encouraged to pay close attention to the processing stage and to getting members to discuss their consensus seeking behavior.

* CONTRACTING

Subsidiary Goal(s)

a. To investigate the dynamics present in decision making.
b. To encourage participation.
c. To allow members the opportunity to decide how the group will be conducted.

Group Application

Twelve members or less. To be used *only* with advanced encounter, personal growth, marathon and t–groups, preferably at the second session. The facilitator should announce the exercise at the *end* of the previous session.

Application Variables

Time is unlimited. The exercise will frequently take up an entire session's time. If the facilitator wishes to add the dynamic of working under pressure, he will follow the time limits enclosed in parentheses in the Administrative Procedure section. The exercise is 90% verbal, with 10% non–verbal being written. The exercise will be more effective if the written material is prepared *before* the session starts. The room must be large enough to accommodate the sub–groups available and allow for fish–bowl observation.

Administrative Procedure

a. Prior to the end of the *first* session, the facilitator gives a (brief) lecturette about the Gerard Egan theory of the use of contracts in groups (we recommend having sample contracts available for distribution).
b. The facilitator says: "Between now and next week, write a contract for the group and bring it with you to the next meeting. Do not collaborate and do not tell others what is in your contract. Type it up and have copies available for each member."
c. At the start of the next session, the facilitator distributes

the copies of the members' contracts. Each member then reads his contract to the group.

d. If the group size is eight members or less, the facilitator can ask that they come up with a consensus as to what the group contract will be, using their eight copies as guides. (We do not recommend this procedure, for two reasons: 1. many members will sit back and allow the "few" to draw up the contract; and 2. consensus might be too difficult to reach with more than six people in the group.)

e. For best results, the facilitator is advised to break the group into triads or quartets and inform the subgroups: "Using your contracts as guides, reach a consensus as to what should be in a final draft of the group contract." *(Thirty minutes)*

f. After the subgroups have finished (or after time is up) he says: "Pick a member to represent your subgroup in consensus negotiations. He will represent your subgroup's consensus contract, devising a final form of the group contract." *(Three minutes)*

g. The representatives are seated in the middle, with the rest of the group seated in a circle around them. One chair in the middle is left open.

h. The facilitator says to the representatives: "You represent your subgroup and are to enter into negotiations with each other. You are to reach consensus as to what should go into a final draft of our group contract. The following rules must be followed." *(Thirty minutes)*

Rules:
1. You cannot communicate with your subgroup.
2. You are not to reach consensus by voting, trading one inclusion for another, polling, etc.
3. You must all agree with and accept the final draft.

i. He tells the observers: "If you feel your agent is misrepresenting your group, take the open chair and give him your input, then leave the chair. You *may not* enter into a conversation with your representative, nor may he ask you questions, so make your feedback and input clear."

j. After consensus has been reached (or after time is up)

the facilitator stops the exercise *whether consensus has been reached or not.*

k. If consensus has been reached and material for inclusion in a final draft of the group contract has been delineated, the facilitator tells the group they will make a final decision about following the contract at the next meeting. If consensus has *not* been reached, he may end the exercise or poll the members as to whether they wish to reach consensus at the next session.

Suggestions for Facilitator Process

Concentrate on the following during processing:

a. *To subgroups:* What criteria did you use in deciding what would be in your final contract? How did you feel when one of your ideas was rejected for inclusion? (If you used time limits, ask how the time limit affected the consensus seeking.)

b. *To representatives:* How did it feel to be your subgroup's representative? How did you feel when you got feedback that you were misrepresenting your subgroup? What did you do with the input you received? For example, did you ignore it, did you change your tactics because of it, etc.?

c. *To observers:* Did you feel your subgroup was represented well? If not, why not? If yes, why do you feel this way?

d. *To all:* Can we accept the concept of a group contract? If not, why? If yes, why? (If a final draft has been agreed upon by the representatives, ask if the group will accept it. Find out why they will or will not accept the contract reached through their representatives' consensus.)

Variations

None.

SAMPLE GROUP CONTRACT [1]

Purpose

The contract provides a general structure and framework

---

[1] AUTHORS' NOTE: This sample does not exhaust the possible procedural rules. It is, however, far too comprehensive to be given to members as an example of a contract. The facilitator would be wise to alter this contract, possibly by including only four or five of the procedural rules, before giving it to his group.

from which the group may operate. It also helps to clear up some of the misconceptions many of us have about encounter groups. In addition the contract enables the members to avoid coercion by leaving the option of non–participation open to each individual before the group begins.

General Goals

The general goal of the group is to provide an atmosphere in which interpersonal growth may be facilitated and explored. This is achieved by establishing relationships which are open, honest, caring and genuine.

Procedural Rules

1. Members are to deal with the here–and–now as much as possible, and not the then–and–there. It is impossible for the other group members to deal with your past or future, so it should be avoided.
2. It is essential for each member to express feelings. Without disclosing how we feel we begin to intellectualize and not interpersonalize.
3. Openness and honesty are the prerequisites upon which the relationships in the group should develop.
4. Self–disclosure is essential for interpersonal growth. Members must be willing to risk revealing themselves to others.
5. Group business is to be taken care of in the group. If you have something to say, say it in the group.
6. Members are responsible only for themselves. No group member should ever take the responsibility *for* another person. This does not mean that we are not responsible to each other.
7. Each member is to speak for himself and no one else. When speaking be aware of whether you're using the pronouns "I" or "We".
8. Members express willingness to engage in any exercises the group feels appropriate in facilitating communication between members.
9. The members should feel free to experiment with physical contact if such will be conducive to better communication.

10. Finally, each group member must be willing to take the initiative to reach out and contact others.

Commitment

A commitment to the group and its members is necessary. It is assumed that acceptance of the contract constitutes a pledge of commitment to yourself and the group.

CRISIS CONSENSUS

Subsidiary Goal(s)

a. To investigate the dynamics involved in decision–making.
b. To encourage participation.
c. To recognize the role our values play in the decision we make.
d. To give and receive feedback.

Group Application

Size is unlimited, for more than one group can utilize the exercise at one time. Applicable to any group, but most frequently used with encounter, personal growth, marathon and t–groups.

Application Variables

One to one and one half hours. The exercise is 100% verbal. Crisis Consensus forms and pencils are needed. The room must be large enough to accommodate the subgroups on hand and protect against undue distractions between them.

Administrative Procedure

a. The facilitator divides the group in subgroups. (We recommend the forming of quartets or quintets. If you have less than ten members, use *Variation I*.)
b. We recommend that the facilitator conduct a brief fantasy exercise with the group to allow them to get a feeling for the elimination situation.
c. He gives each member a copy of the Crisis Consensus form

and says: "Elect a recorder. The recorder is to make sure the rules are followed and record on his form the sub-group's consensus. You have thirty minutes to reach a consensus."

d. After thirty minutes he says: "Elect a member to represent your subgroup in consensus negotiations. He and the other subgroup representatives will each represent his subgroup's consensus in an attempt to reach one consensus. You have five minutes."

e. The representatives are seated in the middle, with the rest of the group seated in a circle around them. One chair in the middle circle is left open.

f. The facilitator tells the representatives: "You represent your subgroups and are to enter into negotiations with each other. You are to reach consensus as to which individuals are to be eliminated from the bomb shelter. The rules are the same as before. You have thirty minutes."

g. He tells the observers: "If you feel your agent is mis-representing your group, take the open chair and give him your input, then leave the chair. You *may not* enter into a conversation with your representative, nor may he ask you questions, so make your feedback and input clear."

h. After thirty minutes the facilitator stops the exercise and discusses it with the group.

Suggestions for Facilitator Process

Concentrate on the following during processing:

a. *To subgroups:* What was your approach to solving the task? Did you establish some criteria? If so, what were they and why? How did you feel about performing such a task?

b. *To representatives:* How did it feel to be your subgroup's representative? How did you feel when you got feedback that you were misrepresenting your subgroup? What did you do with the input you received? For example, did you ignore it, did you change your tactics because of it, etc.?

c. *To all:* Can we accept the negotiators' final choices? If not, why? Were you pleased with your behavior throughout the exercise? If so, why? If not, why not?

Variations

Variation I

a. If you have less than ten members, you may:
   (1) Have the entire group reach a consensus, thereby by–passing the use of subgroups; or
   (2) Have four or five of the members sit in the middle and decide who is to be eliminated. The rest of the members observe the inner group and give them feedback after the elimination has been completed.

Variation II

a. If you do not have time to conduct the exercise in its original form, have four to six members sit in the middle and complete the elimination exercise. The rest of the members observe and give them feedback after the exercise has been completed.

Variation III

a. Have ten members role play the people in the bomb shelter, with instructions that four must be eliminated.
b. Extend the time to one hour.
c. Have other members observe and give feedback after the exercise has been completed.

CRISIS CONSENSUS DATA

SITUATION: *You are a civil defense committee appointed by the President to make decisions on fall–out shelter occupancy. War has been declared. It appears that only the occupants of a fall–out shelter in Death Valley have a good chance for survival. The Death Valley civil defense director has wired Washington that at present ten people are occupying the shelter. The computers have calculated that the shelter can guarantee survival for only six people. Your committee is to decide which four are to be excluded from the group. Four must go so that six may live to rebuild a society.*

The recorder is to make sure the following rules are followed:

1. Everyone must agree with the choice.
2. No voting.

3. The final decision must be acceptable to everyone.

Your committee has thirty minutes to inform the President as to which four people will be excluded. A decision *must* be reached.

1. Thirty–six year old female physician—known to be a confirmed racist.
2. Marine drill instructor.
3. Black militant—biological researcher.
4. Bio–chemist.
5. Olympic athlete—all sports.
6. Hollywood starlet.
7. Third year medical student—homosexual.
8. Sixteen year old girl of questionable IQ, high school dropout, pregnant.
9. Thirty–year old Catholic priest.
10. Thirty–eight year old male carpenter and "Mr. Fix–It" man, served seven years for pushing narcotics, has been out of jail for seven months.

MOON EXPLORER PROBLEM [1]

Subsidiary Goal(s)

a. To explore the dynamics involved in member roles.
b. To compare individual effort with group effort.

Group Application

Group size is unlimited, for more than one group can be directed at one time. Most effectively utilized with groups of twenty members or less. To be used with any group.

Application Variables

One hour. The exercise is 80% verbal, with 20% non–verbal being written. A copy of the Moon Explorer Sheet is needed for each member and one for each subgroup.

---

[1] We wish to thank the Youth Office, Lutheran Church of America for giving us permission to reproduce this exercise.

Pencils are also needed. The room should be large enough to allow subgroups to spread out in the room comfortably.

Administrative Procedure

a. The facilitator asks members to divide into subgroups of four to six depending on the size of the group.

b. He then passes out pencils and hands a copy of the Moon Explorer Problem Form to each member.

c. The facilitator tells the members they have fifteen minutes to complete the Moon Explorer form individually.

d. After fifteen minutes the facilitator passes out one Moon Explorer Problem Form to each subgroup and tells them: "Fill out the form as a group. Arguing is to be avoided as well as members changing their mind, only in order to reach an agreement and avoid conflict. The group *must* reach a consensus, majority rule vote is not valid. Decisions must be agreed upon *by all members*."

e. After thirty minutes the facilitator stops the exercise.

f. The key is now read by the facilitator. Differences are tallied and scored for both individuals and the subgroups. Results are posted for individual and subgroup scores.

g. The group discusses the experience.

Suggestions for Facilitator Process

Concentrate on the following during processing:

a. Which scores were lower, individuals in the subgroup or the subgroup's score? Why do you think this occurred?

b. What types of roles developed among members in your subgroup? How did your group compare to other groups in scoring? Was it difficult for your group to reach a consensus? If so, why?

c. If you felt you knew your answer was correct, did you have a difficult time convincing the rest of the group? What are the advantages or disadvantages of working in a group compared to working as an individual?

Variations

None.

MOON EXPLORER PROBLEM

INSTRUCTIONS: *You are a space crew originally scheduled to rendezvous with a mother ship on the lighted surface of the moon. Due to mechanical difficulties, however, your ship was forced to land at a spot some 200 miles from the rendezvous point. During re–entry and landing, much of the equipment aboard was damaged and, since survival depends on reaching the mother ship, the most critical items available must be chosen for the 200 mile trip. Below are listed the fifteen items left intact and undamaged after landing. Your task is to rank order them in terms of their importance in allowing your crew to reach the rendezvous point. Place the number 1 by the most important item, the number 2 by the second most important, and so on through number 15, the least important.*

		INDIVIDUAL RANKING	GROUP CONSENSUS
_____	a. Box of matches	_____	_____
	b. Food concentrate	_____	_____
_____	c. 50 feet of nylon rope	_____	_____
_____	d. Parachute silk	_____	_____
_____	e. Portable heating unit	_____	_____
_____	f. Two .45 calibre pistols	_____	_____
_____	g. One case dehydrated Pet Milk	_____	_____
_____	h. Two 100 lb. tanks of oxygen	_____	_____
_____	i. Stellar map (as seen from moon)	_____	_____
_____	j. Life raft	_____	_____
_____	k. Magnetic compass	_____	_____
_____	l. 5 gallons of water	_____	_____
_____	m. Signal flares	_____	_____
_____	n. First aid kit containing injection needles	_____	_____
_____	o. Solar–powered FM receiver–transmitter	_____	_____

MOON EXPLORER SCORING KEY

KEY	ITEM	REASON
15	a. Box of matches	The matches won't work because there is no oxygen.
4	b. Food concentrate	Man can live well over a week without food.
6	c. 50 feet of nylon rope	Will prove useful for carrying and climbing over rocky, rough terrain.
8	d. Parachute silk	Will prove useful for wrapping and carrying items.
13	e. Portable heating unit	No need for heat since the light side of the moon is extremely hot.
11	f. Two .45 calibre pistols	The propelling effect of the pistol blast may be needed.
12	g. One case dehydrated Pet Milk	Water is needed and there's not enough to spare.
1	h. Two 100 lb. tanks of oxygen	With no air on the moon, oxygen becomes absolutely essential.
3	i. Stellar map (as seen from moon)	The map is needed for navigational purposes.
9	j. Life raft	Could be used for carrying and/ or for shelter from the sun.
14	k. Magnetic compass	The magnet won't work properly due to the difference of the moon's magnetic pull.
2	l. 5 gallons of water	Man needs water to live.
10	m. Signal flares	Won't work properly because there is no oxygen.
7	n. First aid kit containing injection needles	The first aid kit could be needed, but the needles are useless.
5	o. Solar–powered FM receiver–transmitter	Can be used to communicate with the mother ship.

Score the individual and group consensus results by using the following procedures:

a. Subtract the individual and group score from the score found in the key. Make all differences positive.

	Individual Ranking	Group Consensus
e.g. Box of Matches	10	12
Key score	15	15
Difference	5	3

b. Repeat step a for all fifteen scores.

c. Total the differences.

V

COPING

THE PRIMARY GOAL for each exercise in this chapter is to expose each member to his coping behavior and to exercise his own ability to cope. The question we ask here is this: How does the individual member cope with a variety of feelings and experiences? Within the coping chapter, the reader will find a number of primary goals—*i.e.*, coping with anger, coping with authority, coping with the here–and–now. The facilitator should select the coping exercise which is most appropriate for the group in its particular stage of development. For example, if the group appears to be having difficulty coping with anger, the facilitator would use an exercise designed to elicit anger and expose the members to their "coping with anger" behaviors.

Coping exercises are appropriate for most encounter, personal growth, marathon and t–groups. This chapter is differentiated from other chapters by the fact that recognition of various coping mechanisms relates to the feelings elicited in the primary goal. In other words, the facilitator is not so interested in exposing the group to the feelings of "anger" as he is interested in getting them to investigate how they *cope* with anger.

The dynamics which are elicited by coping exercises can be of great benefit to both the group and individual members. It is suggested that the facilitator pay special attention to the processing stage for each coping exercise.

ANGER

Subsidiary Goal(s)

a. To recognize the difference between feeling anger and intellectualizing about it.
b. To tune into one's angry feelings.
c. To disclose to others one's anger areas.

Group Application

Twelve members or less. Applicable to any group. Potency is increased with member experience and level of self-disclosure.

Application Variables

Approximately five minutes per open–ended statement and ten minutes for graphing, equalling thirty-five to forty-five minutes. The exercise is 95% verbal, with 5% non–verbal being written. Paper, pencils and a chalkboard are needed.

Administrative Procedure

a. The facilitator asks the group members to respond verbally to open–ended statements dealing with the experience of being angry. Some examples are:
  1. I become angry when. . .
  2. When I become angry, I. . .
  3. When someone becomes angry with me, I. . .
  4. I reduce my angry feelings by. . .
  5. I find it easiest to become angry at. . .
  6. Etc. The facilitator should feel free to develop other open–ended statements dealing with anger.
b. The facilitator leads a discussion based on the members' statement completions.
c. Each member writes down an estimation of the number of

times he becomes angry, annoyed or irritated each week
(or each day).
d. These estimates are placed on a chalkboard and a discussion follows concerning differences between amount of
anger reactions per member.

Suggestions for Facilitator Process

Concentrate on the following during processing:
a. How did you feel during the exercise? Did you become
angry at yourself or others?
b. Did we find out anything about how we handle anger?
c. Can we see the difference between *intellectualizing* versus
feeling in our reactions to and coping with anger?
d. What was the level of your self-disclosure in completing
the statements?

Variations

Variation I
a. Have members write completions to the statements.
b. Read all completions to the first statement and lead a discussion concentrating on the differences and similarities
between the member responses.
c. Read completions to the second statement and continue
as above.

*Variation II
a. Have members complete only the following: I have become
angry in this group. . . .
b. Lead a discussion between participants who have experienced angry feelings.

GET ANGRY

Subsidiary Goal(s)

a. To experience the feeling of anger.
b. To experience the feelings aroused by having someone
angry at you.

Group Application

Twelve members or less. To be used with encounter, personal growth, marathon and t–groups with adult members after rapport has been developed.

Application Variables

Ten minutes. The exercise is 90% verbal and 10% non–verbal. A room large enough to allow milling is needed.

Administrative Procedure

a. The facilitator tells the group members to mill around.
b. As they mill he tells them, "Look at your fellow members. Let their being sink into you. Now, develop angry feelings toward one or more of them. Let the anger seethe inside you. Go to a person and be angry at him. Do whatever you wish to express your anger except physically hurting the person."
c. He joins in the milling and the exercise if he so desires, or he stays outside the milling and observes member behavior.
d. After ten minutes, he tells the group, "Begin to lose your anger. Find a person or persons whom you care for and go to him. Express your care for each other and then find your seat."

Suggestions for Facilitator Process

Concentrate on the following during processing:
a. How did you feel during the exercise stages?
b. Was it hard to become angry? How did you accomplish the task of becoming angry? How did you stop being angry?
c. Did you go in the last stage to anyone you had been angry with? If any respond positively, ask them why?

Variations

None.

* SCOLDING

Subsidiary Goal(s)

a. To explore member reactions to anger from an authority figure.

Group Application

Twelve members or less. To be used with encounter, personal growth, marathon and t–groups with adult members after rapport has been developed.

Application Variables

Five to ten minutes. The exercise is 100% verbal.

Administrative Procedure

a. The facilitator, without forewarning any member, interrupts the ongoing process and angrily exclaims, "You have all been wasting my and your time with this garbage discussion! I think it stinks and you'd better stop it and get on to meaningful things!" (Pay close attention to verbal and non–verbal reactions.)
b. He then states he was role–playing and leads a discussion of member reactions to his anger.

Suggestions for Facilitator Process

Concentrate on the following during processing:
a. How did you feel when I became angry at the group?
b. What did you do with these feelings?
c. Illustrate non–verbal reactions you noticed and inquire as to the feelings and thoughts the member had while he was reacting.

Variations

*Variation I

---

* Dynamic, more effective exercises are marked with an asterisk.

a. Make the angry statement to one or more specific individuals.
b. Process by concentrating on the attacked member (s) reaction and the reactions of non–attacked members to the verbal onslaught.

*Variation II

a. Inform a member ahead of time of your plan and have him join with you in the attack.
b. Explore differences in attacked members' reactions to you as opposed to their reactions to attack by a peer.

Coping with Anxiety

* NO QUESTIONS

Subsidiary Goal(s)

a. To learn new ways of communicating.
b. To encourage responsibility in communication.

Group Application

Twelve members or less. Applicable to any group except the classroom. Best results are obtained when used with encounter, personal growth, marathon and t–groups, especially during the early stages of group development.

Application Variables

Time unlimited. The exercise is 100% verbal. A bell is needed.

Administrative Procedure

a. The facilitator gives a (brief) lecturette covering the use and misuse of questions in a group. He explains that most questions are defensive maneuvers used to avoid responsibility for making the statement that lies behind them.
b. He adds that the group will not use *any* questions during that day's session. If a question is asked, he will ring the bell, and the questioner will stop his question and make

the statement it covers. For example, "Are you angry?" becomes "You are angry."
c. The facilitator stops the session prior to its ending time and leads a discussion of the experience.

Suggestions for Facilitator Process

Concentrate on the following during processing:
a. How did you feel about having one of your prime means of communication taken from you? How did you cope with these feelings?
b. Did you find it easier as the time progressed to make statements instead of questions. If yes, why? If no, why?

Variations

Variation I
a. After informing the group of the "no question" rule, establish a three–member appeal panel.
b. Any member who feels he has a legitimate question may make a plea to the panel to allow him to ask his question. They are to listen to his question, hear his reasons, and make a decision.
c. During discussion, concentrate on the fact that most appeals were denied because there were concealed statements behind the question or because the question would elicit meaningless data. Ask appealers how they felt about being turned down.

Coping with Authority

*ARGUING WITH THE FACILITATOR

Subsidiary Goal(s)

a. To confront in oneself the feelings created by being harassed.

Group Application

Twelve members or less, although the exercise can be utilized with larger groups. To be used with encounter, personal growth, marathon and t–groups.

Application Variables

Ten to fifteen minutes. The exercise is 100% verbal. The room should be large enough to allow the leader–member dyad to be seated in the middle of an observer circle without the dyad feeling unduly cramped.

Administrative Procedure

a. The facilitator asks two or three volunteers to leave the room. It is best to pick the volunteers from active, energetic, leader–type members.

b. He tells the group he will debate a topic relevant to the group with them. He asks the group to observe what happens. Note: *Do not* tell the group that you will not debate fairly! *Do not* tell them what you will debate!

c. One volunteer is returned. The unused volunteers join the observer group. The facilitator and the member sit in the middle and the observers form a circle around them.

d. The facilitator debates with the volunteer on any topic relevant to the group (*e.g.*, the member's lack of participation, his reliance on intellectualizing, his failure to self–disclose, etc.). Try to pick a topic area diametrically opposed to the volunteer's real group behavior.

e. During the debate, the facilitator is to be as unfair as he can be. (Use an air of authority, interrupt the volunteer, contradict yourself, point out volunteer behavior which doesn't exist, etc.)

f. After five or ten minutes the facilitator stops the debate and leads a discussion dealing with volunteer and observer feelings and behavior.

Suggestions for Facilitator Process

Concentrate on the following during processing:
a. How did the volunteer feel?

b. How did he react? What behaviors did the observers notice?

c. What feelings did the observers have? Were they angry, sympathetic, amazed, etc.

d. What was learned about coping with authority?

Variations

Variation I

a. Engage a volunteer to side with you in the debate.

b. Continue as above, but in processing, explore the differences in the coping behavior used with you as opposed to that used with a peer.

CORRECTING A CORRECT SENTENCE [1]

Subsidiary Goal(s)

a. To illustrate members' uncritical attitudes toward authority.

b. To illustrate the anxiety which countering authority creates.

Group Application

Group size is unlimited. Applicable to any group.

Application Variables

Ten minutes. A chalkboard is needed. The exercise is 95% verbal, with 5% non–verbal being written. The room must be so shaped that all members can read the chalkboard.

Administrative Procedure

a. The facilitator asks the members to write down the following instructions so that they may refer to them:
"Look over each of the words in the sentence on the chalkboard carefully. Can you find just one word in the sen-

---

[1] This is a variation of an exercise developed by Daniel Malamud and Solomon Machover.

tence which, if you crossed it out, might correct the sentence?"

b. Then write the following sentence on the chalkboard: "The words in this sentence do not add up to ten."

c. Caution the group not to talk to each other during the written phase.

d. After the members have written their responses, inform them that the sentence is correct as it stands. (Most members will have crossed out the word *not*.)

e. Lead a discussion investigating the dynamics of blindly following the authority figure, feelings aroused, etc.

Suggestions for Facilitator Process

Concentrate on the following during processing:

a. Why did those who corrected the sentence do so?

b. If a member objects to your trick, inquire what was going on in him to make him vulnerable to it.

c. Some members will say they knew it was right, but still changed it. Again, ask why? What was going on to make them deny their rational, logical, valid conclusions?

d. Some members will have left the sentence intact. Ask them what factors governed their behavior? Were they suspicious, mistrustful, etc?

Variations

None.

INTERVIEW THE FACILITATOR

Subsidiary Goal(s)

a. To gain insight into the member–facilitator relationship.

Group Application

Twelve members or less, but any size group can utilize the exercise. Applicable to any group. The exercise is more dynamic and revelatory if group rapport has been established.

Application Variables

Fifteen to twenty minutes. The exercise is 100% verbal.

Administrative Procedure

a. The facilitator informs the group that he is willing to be interviewed by three volunteers with "no holds barred," one at a time. He does not guarantee an answer to all questions.

b. He answers the interviewer's questions as frankly and openly as he comfortably can. He does, however, exercise his right to refuse to respond to questions he feels are too personal.

c. The facilitator continues this procedure for each volunteer.

d. He has the group discuss reactions, insights gained about him, observations made, etc.

Suggestions for Facilitator Process

Concentrate on the following during processing:

a. *To interviewers:* How did you decide what questions to ask? How did you feel while interviewing me? Did my authority hinder you?

b. *To observers:* What behavior did you observe on the part of myself and the volunteers? How did you feel about not getting a chance to interview me?

Variations

*Variation I

a. Add the following reciprocal statement to your introduction: "The interviewer must be willing to answer any question he asks me, whether I answer it or not."

b. During processing, point out the effect this statement had on the interviewer. Most interviews conducted on this basis will deal with safe, non–embarrassing, non–revealing data as opposed to those conducted without the reciprocal statement.

Variation II

a. Allow each member three questions.
b. Respond as above, then discuss the extent to which one learns about others through the questions they ask. Questioner's values, priorities, etc. will be revealed through question level and content.

Variation III
a. Repeat step a of Variation II, but use the reciprocal statement.
b. Process, using the dynamics discused in Variation Ib and Variation IIb.

Coping with Confrontation

* GETTING IT OUT

Subsidiary Goal(s)

a. To increase honesty among members.
b. To air out underlying feelings, both complimentary and critical.
c. To enrich relationships.
d. To give and receive feedback.

Group Application

Twelve members or less. To be used with encounter, personal growth, marathon and t–groups with adult members who have developed warm, caring relationships. Caution should be used if the exercise is utilized early in the group's formation.

Application Variables

One hour and thirty minutes. The exercise is 100% verbal.

Administrative Procedure

a. The facilitator states that the exercise is intended to produce honest feedback. Compliments and criticism are to be used. Idle conversation, small talk and debate are *not* permitted.

b. Chairs are formed into a semi–circle with one in the middle.

c. The facilitator asks for a volunteer to take the inside chair.

d. Any group member may now address the volunteer by giving him feedback in statement form.

e. After each comment the person in the inside chair is given a chance to agree or disagree.

f. After approximately five minutes the facilitator asks for another volunteer and steps **d** and **e** are repeated until all members have been given the opportunity to be confronted.

g. The facilitator then asks the members to form dyads with the person they think has been most critical of them. They are given ten minutes for discussion.

h. Step **g** is repeated with the person they feel has been the most supportive.

i. The group discusses the experience.

Suggestions for Facilitator Process

Concentrate on the following during processing:

a. How did you feel about going into the inside chair? Why? Did your feelings change once you were in the chair?

b. How did you react to the feedback? In most instances, did you tend to agree or disagree? Why? Did the feedback surprise you? Did you feel it was honest?

c. Were you hesitant about giving feedback? Why? Was your feedback primarily negative or positive? Why?

d. What did you learn from the people you felt were most complimentary and critical? Have your feelings changed about these people? Has your self–concept changed? In what way?

Variations

Variation I

a. Have members write feedback for each member instead of verbalizing it.
b. The facilitator reads the feedback to the member inside the circle.
c. Discussion takes place after *all* members have received feedback.

Variation II

a. Conduct the exercise in its original form, but during step **e** have members shout "yes" or "no" depending on whether or not they agree with the feedback given the member.
b. During processing, concentrate on the amount of agreement during voting. Attempt to discover why members agreed or disagreed and how the member being voted on felt.

FACING FEAR

Subsidiary Goal(s)

a. To develop sensory awareness.
b. To recognize the differences between "thinking" about "fearful" situations versus "feeling" them.

Group Application

Twelve members or less. To be used with encounter, personal growth, marathon and t–groups. The group should have reached the stage where supportive behavior can occur unrestrained.

Application Variables

Thirty minutes. The exercise is 90% verbal and 10% non–verbal.

Administrative Procedure

a. The facilitator asks the group to form dyads.
b. The facilitator then tells the members to think of a fearful situation and try to experience it.

c. He then gives the following instructions: "Choose one of you to go first. After this is done, the person going first is to lie on the floor face up, open his eyes wide, and breathe deeply. Your partner is to press both sides of your nose, just below the bones under your eyes. While doing this, the person on the floor is to voice 'Oh-h-h-h-h-h.' This is to continue until the sound of 'oh' is occurring spontaneously."

d. The facilitator allows this to continue for fifteen minutes. Then the positions in the dyads are reversed and step c is repeated.

e. Return to group circle and process.

Suggestions for Facilitator Process

Concentrate on the following during processing:

a. Did you feel your body change (*i.e.*, tension, breathing, heart beat) ?

b. Were you able to experience a fearful situation? If not, why not? Did the fear turn into any other emotion? If so, what?

c. Were you conscious of your surroundings? Of your feelings? Of your thoughts?

d. Has your concept of fear changed? If so, how?

Variations

Variation I

a. Have each member open his eyes wide and murmur "I'm scared."

b. Then tell the members to exaggerate their fear (*i.e.*, shaking legs, breathing rapidly, etc.) .

c. Members are to continue as long as they choose.

Coping with the Here–and–Now

* AT THE MOMENT

Subsidiary Goal(s)

a. To increase awareness in terms of time and space, past, present and future.

    b. To facilitate understanding of member perceptions of the present and to stimulate specific attention towards self–evaluation.

Group Application

Twelve members or less. To be used with encounter, personal growth, marathon and t–groups. Best results are obtained during the early stage of a group's development or in groups where members are having difficulty relating to the here and now.

Application Variables

Thirty minutes. The exercise is 100% verbal. The room must be large enough to allow members to move about unrestrained.

Administrative Procedure

    a. The facilitator asks the members to mill around and choose a partner.

    b. He then instructs the dyads to find a private spot in the room.

    c. The facilitator makes a brief statement concerning the difficulty and importance of staying in the "here and now."

    d. He then asks one of the partners in each group to begin verbalizing everything he sees, beginning with the words, "At this time I am aware of . . ." Every sentence must begin with these words. The other member in the dyad is to listen and correct any statements making reference to the past or future.

    e. After five minutes the same member is told to concentrate on his body, again beginning each sentence with the words, "At this time I am aware of . . ." The other member is to keep acting as a monitor for any statements not dealing with the present.

    f. After five minutes the member is told to concentrate on what he perceives himself to be as a person. The same instructions apply as in steps **d** and **e**.

g. After five minutes the members alternate roles and steps
d through f are repeated.

Suggestions for Facilitator Process

Concentrate on the following during processing:

a. How did it feel relating only in the "here and now?" Did
you find it difficult? If so, why? How many errors did you
make? Did they decrease or increase during the fifteen
minutes? Why do you think they increased or decreased?

b. Which phase did you find most difficult (room, body, or
self)? What does that tell us about ourselves?

c. What did you learn by observing? Are you now conscious
of the difference between the "here and now" and the
future or past? When speaking about yourself, did you feel
uncomfortable? Did silence occur? If so, how did you deal
with it? What does this exercise tell us about our self–
images?

Variations

Variation I

a. Conduct the exercise in its original form. However, do *not*
use dyads. Instead, have the *entire* group engage in the
three phases, communicating with the group as a whole.
For example, in phase one, every member is to use "At
this time I am aware of . . ." as his sole means of communicating with the group.

* I'M THINKING AND FEELING

Subsidiary Goal(s)

a. To practice self–disclosure.
b. To learn the differences between thinking and feeling.
c. To recognize non–verbal communication.
d. To encourage participation.

Group Application

Twelve members or less. To be used with beginning encounter, personal growth, marathon and t–groups. The exercise is very effective if used when the group members are experiencing difficulty staying in the here and now and expressing feelings.

Application Variables

Time unlimited. The exercise is 100% verbal.

Administrative Procedure

a. The facilitator presents a brief lecturette conveying the differences between thinking and feeling, the need to express here and now instead of there and then feelings, and the necessity of watching for non–verbal clues that another member is "sitting on" his thoughts and feelings.

b. He then says: "During this session we are to pay particular attention to sharing our here–and–now thoughts and feelings. Stay away from the there and then. Try to tell us how you feel. Let's pay close attention to each other's non–verbal behavior. If you feel another member has something to say, ask him what he's thinking and feeling. If you are asked to share your thoughts and feelings, you *must* respond by saying "I'm thinking . . . and that makes me feel. . . ."

c. Early in the session, the facilitator will have to model the desired behavior and take the initiative for inviting members to share their thoughts and feelings. As the session progresses, the members will become more comfortable with this communication method and shoulder most of the load.

d. About fifteen minutes before the session ends, the facilitator leads a discussion of the experience.

Suggestions for Facilitator Process

Concentrate on the following during processing:

a. What were your feelings when you were first asked to share your thoughts and feelings? Did you find it easier to respond later in the session? If so, why?

b. What non–verbal clues did you use in your decision to ask a member to respond?
c. Did you find it easier near the end to respond at a feeling, rather than thinking, level? If so, why? If not, why not?
d. Who was asked to share his thoughts and feelings the least? Why? Were we afraid to address this person, did we ignore him, etc.?

Variations

*Variation I

a. Conduct the exercise as above, but allow *only* feeling responses. Let members ask each other what they are feeling and share these feelings.

* MAKE CONTACT

Subsidiary Goal(s)

a. To provide feedback.
b. To tune into feelings elicited by engaging in physical contact.
c. To experiment with new behavior.

Group Application

Twelve members or less. To be used with encounter, personal growth, marathon and t–groups. It is preferable that the group size be balanced by sex so that one can experience contact with members of both sexes.

Application Variables

Thirty-five to forty minutes. The exercise is about 90% verbal, with physical contact being used to elicit "here and now" feelings.

Administrative Procedure

a. The facilitator tells the group they will engage in a six–phase exercise designed to help generate "here and now" feelings. We encourage the facilitator to design physical contact experiences appropriate to his particular group.

b. Phase one *(five minutes)*. Seated as usual, the group members share feelings about the exercise, the group, etc. (During each phase the facilitator should be sure that feelings and *not* thoughts are being shared.)

c. Phase two *(five minutes)*. The group stands in a circle, with arms around one another's waists and heads bent into the middle of the circle. They share "here and now" feelings of this experience and feelings they have for each other as a result of it.

d. Phase three *(five minutes)*. The group stands in a circle, holding hands, with their *backs* facing *inward*. Speaking toward the walls, they share "here and now" feelings of this experience and feelings they have for each other as a result of it.

e. Phase four *(five minutes)*. The group kneels in a circle, holding hands and facing each other. They share "here and now" feelings of this experience and feelings they have for each other as a result of it.

f. Phase five *(ten minutes)*. The group forms dyads. One member places his head in another member's lap. The other "cares" for his head, touching it, massaging it, etc. They do this for five minutes, then switch. During both stages, the members share "here and now" feelings of this experience and feelings they have for each other as a result of it.

g. Phase six *(five minutes)*. New dyads form. The partners sit back–to–back with arms intertwined. They again share feelings of the experience and feelings they have for each other as a result of it.

h. The group reconvenes and shares reactions to the total exercise.

Suggestions for Facilitator Process

Concentrate on the following during processing:

a. Did the feelings created by physical contact change from Phase one to Phase six? If so, how and why?

b. How did your feelings for each other change? Why?
c. Which phase was hardest for you to perform? Why? Which was easiest? Why? Which was most beneficial?
d. Did some of you enjoy the dyad contact more than the entire group contact? If yes, ask why.

Variations

None.

Coping with Risk

* WHO'S WILLING TO TAKE A CHANCE?

Subsidiary Goal(s)

a. To experience anxiety.
b. To recognize the internal dialogue that occurs in us during decision making.
c. To recognize the difficulty in being willing to enter into a "taboo" task.

Group Application

Twelve members or less. Applicable to any group, but most frequently used early in the life of beginning encounter, personal growth, marathon and t–groups.

Application Variables

Five minutes. The exercise is 100% verbal.

Administrative Procedure

a. The facilitator tells the group he needs some volunteers, members who are willing to enter into a stressful, but dynamic, non–verbal exercise involving excessive physical contact.
b. He says: "Who is willing to take a chance?" (If members question him, he responds vaguely and ambiguously, being sure not to say anything which will alleviate their anxiety.)
c. After a few minutes, he says, "The exercise is over. We

have just encountered our willingness to take a risk. Let's talk about it."

Suggestions for Facilitator Process

Concentrate on the following during processing:

a. *To non–volunteers:* What thoughts and feelings were present in you? Describe the positive–negative dialogue you were conducting inside yourself. For example, "I want to," "No, you don't, you're scared," "I am not, it's just that . . . ," "It's just nothing, you're scared," etc.

b. Why wouldn't you take a chance? If responses avoid the "taboo" area of physical contact, confront the members with the fact that this might really be the reason for their unwillingness.

c. *To risk–takers:* Why did you decide to raise your hand? What thoughts and feelings did you have before and after you volunteered? If they respond that they were scared, nervous, anxious, etc., ask them: "Isn't it incongruous that a scared person would volunteer? Why did you do it?"

Variations

None.

Coping with Tension

ASSERT YOURSELF

Subsidiary Goal(s)

a. To release inhibitions.
b. To explore the dynamics involved in releasing hidden agendas.

Group Application

Twelve members or less. To be used with encounter, personal growth, marathon and t–groups. Caution should be used if the exercise is used before a supportive group atmosphere has been adequately developed.

Application Variables

Fifteen minutes. The exercise is 50% verbal, 50% non-verbal. The room must be large enough to allow individual members to spread out comfortably within the room.

Administrative Procedure

a. The facilitator makes the following introduction: "This exercise is intended to give you an opportunity to totally exert yourself and express feelings of hostility, resentment and anger."
b. He then asks members to spread out over the room so that each participant has ample freedom of movement.
c. The facilitator asks members to concentrate on feelings of resentment and anger which may have been lying unattended to.
d. Members are to lie down on the floor and throw a tantrum, rhythmically kicking and pounding the floor while yelling anything that comes to mind. Members should be encouraged to shout, scream and totally let their feelings run free.
e. After ten to fifteen minutes, the facilitator stops the exercise.

Suggestions for Facilitator Process

Concentrate on the following during processing:
a. How did you feel at the start of the exercise? If you felt awkward, why do you think this occurred? How did you feel at the end of the exercise?
b. Which had the most meaning for you, your body movements or your verbalization? Can you share with the group the mental dynamic you went through in trying to remove restraints from inhibiting anger? Do you feel you were successful in achieving this? If not, why?

Variations

Variation I
a. Have members form dyads.

   b. Taking turns have one member throw a tantrum while the other member encourages and reinforces his behavior (restraining his arms so that the member must fight to free them, etc.) .

VI

EMPATHY

THE PRIMARY GOAL for each exercise in this chapter is to allow members the opportunity to increase their empathic understanding.

The ability to empathize is a vital dynamic in the small group interaction process, especially in encounter, personal growth, marathon and t–groups. The appropriateness of empathy exercises lies entirely with the facilitator's decision. However, it is suggested that the following exercises be used only after enough sessions have been given to allow for the spontaneous development of empathic behavior to occur, for we believe that, ideally, empathic behavior and understanding should be naturally expressed rather than elicited through a structured means. We hope the facilitator will use empathy exercises to *enhance* empathic understanding, not *create* it.

The use of empathy exercises is usually found in encounter, personal growth, marathon and t–groups. However, the facilitator is encouraged to broaden the use of these exercises with other groups whenever he feels it is appropriate.

Since empathy exercises often lead to intense emotional states, we suggest that the facilitator pay close attention to the processing stage of the specific exercise in use.

*ALTER EGO

Subsidiary Goal(s)

a. To help a member bring out feelings he does not recognize or hopes to conceal.

b. To learn a new method for increasing one's understanding of hidden factors in individuals.

Group Application

Twelve members or less. To be used with encounter, personal growth, marathon, and t–groups with adult members. This exercise is especially valuable when used in t–groups in which the increase of empathic ability is a goal.

Application Variables

Time is unlimited, although most alter ego exercises will run thirty to forty–five minutes. The exercise is 100% verbal. The room must be large enough to allow the alter egos to stand behind their subject without feeling cramped and without disturbing the ongoing discussion.

Administrative Procedure

a. The facilitator gives a (brief) lecturette about empathy, non–verbal clues we give off indicating we are hiding or covering our feelings, and the alter ego concept.

b. He then asks that a member volunteer to be an alter ego.

c. The volunteer stands behind the member he is observing. He is told: "When you feel that the member you are observing is not saying what he really feels, place your hands on his shoulders and tell the group what is being left unspoken. Use the word "I", just as if you are the other person."

d. The facilitator tells the other group members that they should also serve as alter egos if they feel (1) that the alter ego is misinterpreting or missing hidden feelings, or (2) that another member is also covering up significant feelings. (Note: two alter egos operating at once should be the limit.)

---

* Dynamic, more effective exercises are marked with an asterisk.

e. The group begins a discussion with the volunteer commenting as an alter ego *whenever* he feels his member is covering up and with other members performing alter ego functions when they feel someone is not revealing his true feelings.

f. After five or ten minutes the facilitator stops the discussion and reviews with the group what took place.

g. Select a new alter ego and continue until all who want the experience of having, or being, an alter ego have had their chance.

Suggestions for Facilitator Process

Concentrate on the following during processing:

a. Were the alter egos accurate in their interpretation of your hidden feelings?

b. *To alter egos:* What clues did you use in determining that something was unsaid? Did you believe you were accurate?

c. Why did some of you spontaneously get up and serve as another member's alter ego? Why did others not do this?

Variations

Variation I

a. Instead of getting a specific volunteer, simply use the lecturette and request that members spontaneously serve as alter egos *whenever* they feel another is hiding significant feelings.

b. During processing concentrate on the dynamics of empathy and the reasons for serving, or refusing to serve, as another member's alter ego. (It is the authors' observation that few members alter ego the facilitator. We find it beneficial to point this out to the group and to attempt to find out why they did not alter ego us.)

COUNSELING A MEMBER

Subsidiary Goal(s)

a. To learn the variables involved in giving and receiving help.

b. To learn the values of sharing problems.

    c. To learn the value of self–disclosure.

    d. To learn about giving and receiving feedback.

Group Application

Twelve members or less. Triads are used, so the group should be divisible by three. If not, drop the observer role. To be used with encounter, personal growth, marathon and t–groups. Especially valuable in t–groups where development of empathy is a goal. Group composition should be equal by sex so that the members gain insight as to whether their method of helping differs according to the sex of the counselee.

Application Variables

One to one and one–half hours. The exercise is 100% verbal. The room must be large enough to accommodate the available triads and guarantee that one triad's conversation does not unduly interfere with that of any other triad.

Administrative Procedure

    a. The facilitator gives a (brief) lecturette on giving and receiving help and the dynamics of feedback.

    b. He then has the group form triads. One member is to be the counselor, one the counselee, and the third an observer.

    c. The member playing the counselee is told to present a real life problem to the member–counselor.

    d. The facilitator tells the member–counselor to try to help the counselee resolve the problem.

    e. The member–observer is told to observe the interaction and to be prepared to give feedback to both members at the end of the exercise.

    f. The facilitator should move from triad to triad to insure that no member is getting in too deeply.

    g. After fifteen to twenty minutes the exercise is stopped. Observers are to give feedback to the members. The two members are asked to share their feelings about the counseling experience.

h. Roles are changed and the procedure is repeated until each member has been an observer, a counselor and a counselee.

Suggestions for Facilitator Process

Concentrate on the following during processing:
a. What feelings did you have as you played each role?
b. What did you learn about your counselee?
c. What did you learn about your counselor?
d. Did you find it difficult to tune into the other member's feelings? If so, why?
e. What difficulties did you encounter in giving and receiving feedback?

Variations

Variation I
a. Have the counselee present a problem he is having (a) in the group; or (b) with the member who is playing the counselor.

Variation II
a. Place three chairs in the middle of the room and have the group form an observing circle around them.
b. Have two members who do have a problem *between* them occupy two of the chairs.
c. The two present their difficulty to each other. Other members are to enter the middle of the circle and occupy the empty chair *whenever* they have some important feedback or insight to share with the two. They are then to leave *immediately* and rejoin the large circle.
d. The two members in the middle are to listen to the feedback or insight but are *not* to communicate in *any way* with any other members.

* EMPATHY PRACTICE

Subsidiary Goal(s)

a. To compare individual empathic insights with those of the group and those of a specific member.
b. To recognize the differences between thinking and feeling.

c. To develop feedback skills.

Group Application

Twelve members or less. To be used with encounter, personal growth, marathon and t–groups with adult members who have had sufficient group sessions to have developed rapport and some measure of insight into other members.

Application Variables

Half an hour. Empathy Observation Forms, pencils and a chalkboard are needed. The exercise is 70% verbal, with 30% non–verbal being written.

Administrative Procedure

a. The facilitator stops the group about a half hour before the ending time.

b. He picks a member who has interacted frequently during that session (or he may ask for a volunteer to be rated empathically).

c. The facilitator then gives each member an Empathy Observation Form and asks him to complete it for the member in question. The member picked rates himself, using the form.

d. The facilitator tallies the Empathy Observation responses on the chalkboard.

e. A discussion is held covering differences in ratings, accuracy and fallacy of ratings, reasons for ratings, etc.

Suggestions for Facilitator Process

Concentrate on the following during processing:

a. Why did we rate the member as we did?

b. Why do you think you were accurate or inaccurate?

c. Did you have difficulty separating the member's thoughts from his feelings? If so, why do you think this happened? What can you do in the future to ignore thinking and concentrate on feelings?

Variations

None.

EMPATHY OBSERVATION FORM

Describe the feelings the member exhibited. Indicate when he was revealing these feelings.

FEELING	INSTANCE
Example: Anger	When he was talking of his wife.

1.
2.
3.
4.
5.
6.
7.
8.
9.
10.

WHERE ARE YOU AT?

Subsidiary Goal(s)

   a. To help members key in on each other's non–verbal communication.

   b. To encourage participation.

Group Application

Twelve members or less. To be used with encounter, personal growth, marathon and t–groups.

Application Variables

Time unlimited. The exercise is 100% verbal.

Administrative Procedure

   a. The facilitator tells the group at the beginning of the

session that they are to concentrate on one another's participation and/or lack of participation during the session.

b. He adds: "Whenever any of you feel that another member is sitting on his feelings or is not disclosing where he is at, you are to point at him and say 'Where are you at?' The member addressed *must* reply."

c. Prior to the end of the session, the facilitator stops the group and discusses the experience.

Suggestions for Facilitator Process

Concentrate on the following during processing:

a. What were the verbal and non–verbal clues you used in deciding that another member was sitting on feelings or not disclosing? Were you right? If you were wrong, why?

b. How did you feel when someone asked you where you were at? Was your response at a feeling or thinking level? Why did you respond the way you did?

c. If any member was not asked where he was at, ask the group why? Did they not notice him? Was he evidently at a feeling and revealing level all through the session? Etc.

Variations

Variation I

a. Members who have difficulties expressing feelings and self–disclosing are assigned a watchdog.

b. The member serving as watchdog asks the "Where are you at" question whenever he feels his partner is not revealing feelings or is not self–disclosing.

VII

FANTASY

THE PRIMARY GOAL for each exercise in this chapter is to
expose the members to fantasy material. It is hoped that
exploration of fantasy data will help increase the member's
awareness and facilitate his ability to utilize fantasy in his
group interaction.

Fantasy exercises are most appropriate with encounter,
personal growth, marathon and t–groups. However, they may
be implemented in other small groups.

It is suggested that the following exercises be used when
the group has developed an environment which is relatively
non–threatening, caring and creatively directed. Since fantasies may have great personal meaning to the members sharing them, the facilitator should never force any member to
reveal his or her fantasy.

The use of fantasy may lead to a number of dynamics (see
Subsidiary Goals) . Therefore, the facilitator is encouraged to
pay special attention to the processing stage.

The fantasy exercises are designed to provide exploration
of one's self. Also, relationships with others are explored
using a different type of communication level. The interpretation of fantasy should be dealt with as such. By this, we
mean that literal interpretations should be avoided.

ANIMAL, FOOD, OBJECT

Subsidiary Goal(s)

a. To give one insight into how he is perceived by others.

Group Application

Size is unlimited, but is most effective with groups of twelve or less. To be used with any group. Is very effective in groups having difficulty communicating.

Application Variables

Thirty to forty–five minutes. The exercise is 80% verbal, with 20% non–verbal being written. Paper and pencils are needed.

Administrative Procedure

a. The facilitator tells the group to write down each member's name on a sheet of paper.
b. He then tells the group: "After each name, write down an animal, food object, and inanimate object which you fantasize as being representative of the member in question." (He might wish to illustrate by sharing his fantasies about one of the members. For example, "I see Dave as a fish, a hamburger and a statue.")
c. The group members read their responses to each other and attempt to explain the reasoning behind their fantasies.

Suggestions for Facilitator Process

Concentrate on the following during processing:
a. Did you experience difficulties fantasizing? If so, why?
b. What do you think made it easy to fantasize about some members and difficult to fantasize about others?
c. What did we learn about ourselves from the fantasies others had about us?

Variations

None.

GROUP FANTASY

Subsidiary Goal(s)

   a. To share feedback with the group as to one's perceptions of it.
   b. To facilitate involvement in the group.

Group Application

   Twelve members or less. To be used with encounter, personal growth, marathon and t–groups. Particularly effective with advanced groups.

Application Variables

   Time is unlimited, but the exercise will usually last fifteen to thirty minutes. The exercise is 100% verbal.

Administrative Procedure

   a. The facilitator asks the group to create a fantasy about the group. Each member should add to the fantasy whenever he feels the need to do so.
   b. If the group has difficulty, the facilitator might start the fantasy. After he has started it, he *should not* speak again until the group has started to spontaneously develop the fantasy.

Suggestions for Facilitator Process

   Concentrate on the following during processing:
   a. What difficulties did you encounter in creating a group fantasy? Why do you think you had problems fantasizing?
   b. What have we learned about our group from this fantasy experience?

Variations

   Variation I
   a. Structure the fantasy by telling the group to develop a group fantasy dealing with an emotion or feeling the group has experienced. For example, have the fantasy center around fear or anger or frustration, etc.

Variation II

a. Have the group develop a fantasy about one member.

SHAPING DREAMS

Subsidiary Goal(s)

a. To gain insight into one's inner feelings and thoughts.
b. To recognize coping methods used when confronting ambiguity.

Group Application

Twelve members or less. To be used with encounter, personal growth, marathon and t–groups.

Application Variables

One hour and fifteen minutes. The exercise is 60% verbal and 40% non–verbal. The room must be large enough for the members to move around comfortably.

Administrative Procedure

a. The facilitator informs the group that they will attempt to realize and act out their fantasies about the group.
b. He asks for a volunteer to select a scene (home, zoo, football game, school, etc.) and assign roles to the group members as his fantasies see fit.
c. Since the purpose of the exercise is to allow for a spontaneous "stream of consciousness approach," no other directions are given.
d. Step **b** is repeated until all members have had a chance to participate.

Suggestions for Facilitator Process

Concentrate on the following during processing:
a. How did you cope with the ambiguity of the exercise? Did you look for direction? If so, why?
b. Were you actually able to act out a fantasy about the group? Did this change your perceptions of the group?
c. Were you surprised at the role you were assigned in other

people's fantasies? If so, why? Were you left out of most of the member's fantasies? How did this make you feel?

d. When selected for a fantasy did you fit into the role you were assigned? If not, why not? Why did you assign members the roles?

Variations

Variation I

a. The facilitator, during stage **b** (see under Administrative Procedure), tells the volunteer to limit his fantasy to the group. Outside scenes are not allowed.

SPECTRUM OF COLORS

Subsidiary Goal(s)

a. To learn to express fantasies in terms of symbols.
b. To allow members to experience a sense of creation by utilizing an artistic approach.
c. To give insight into self.
d. To give and receive feedback.

Group Application

Twelve members or less. To be used with encounter, personal growth, marathon and t–groups.

Application Variables

One hour. The exercise is 60% verbal and 40% non–verbal. Ten percent of the non–verbal activity is written. Approximately one hundred magazine clippings are required (clippings are to be of various colors rather than pictures or words). Paper and pencils are also needed.

Administrative Procedure

a. The facilitator places the magazine clippings in a pile at one side of the room.
b. He then asks for four volunteers to go over to the clippings and create a "montage" (each individual is to make his own).

c. After this is completed, the group goes over and views the four creations.

d. Step **b** is repeated until each member has had an opportunity to make his own "montage."

e. The clippings are returned to the original pile.

f. The facilitator asks each member to select a single clipping which represents his life.

g. He then asks each member to write a short paragraph on why he chose the clipping.

h. The facilitator collects the papers with the clippings attached and randomly distributes them, making sure no member receives his own material.

i. The member receiving the clipping reads the description and shows the clipping.

j. The members are to share insights and feelings about the statement and clipping until all have been discussed. They are to guess who wrote the statement, giving reasons for their guesses.

Suggestions for Facilitator Process

Concentrate on the following during processing:

a. How did you select your clippings in making your "montage?" How did you feel when someone else took a clipping you wanted?

b. What significance did your "montage" have for you? In terms of color, size, shape, etc.? What significance did you intend it to have for the group?

c. How did you feel when your creation was destroyed? How did you feel when you discovered we liked or disliked your "montage?"

d. What did you consider when selecting the single clipping? How disclosing were you in writing your descriptive statement? Did we easily guess you had written the statement? If so, why? If not, why not?

e. Did you mind sharing your symbolic creation? If so, why? If not, why not?

Variations

Variation I
a. Have the group as a whole create a "montage."

Variation II
a. Have dyads form "montages."
b. Then have the group decide which dyad's "montage" is the "best" and which is the "worst." Do *not* define "best" and "worst."

Variation III
a. Tell the members to make their "montage" out of one color with various shadings.

STEP ONTO THE STAGE

Subsidiary Goal(s)
a. To allow expression of alternative roles.
b. To develop an environment conducive to imaginative self–expression.

Group Application
Twelve members or less. To be used with encounter, personal growth, marathon and t–groups. Best results obtained from groups who have had experience in role playing and fantasizing.

Application Variables
Forty-five minutes. The exercise is 100% verbal. The room must be large enough to allow members unrestricted movement.

Administrative Procedure
a. The facilitator states that he is going to direct a play.
b. He then informs the members to follow his instructions about the role assigned them and the scene of the play.

c. He tells the members, "Do not be limited by your roles. Try to create from them."

d. The facilitator then proceeds to describe the scene of the play (a boat, a park, a stage, an airbase, etc.). It can take place in the past, present or future. He urges the members to dissolve the walls and the ceiling in the room and create the scene described.

e. The facilitator should assign roles according to his perceptions of the viable alternatives it allows individual members and the appropriateness of the role for the member receiving it.

f. After the scene is described and the roles are assigned, the play begins. There is to be no other direction by the facilitator.

g. After forty-five minutes, the group reforms for discussion.

Suggestions for Facilitator Process

Concentrate on the following during processing:

a. Were you happy with the roles assigned to you? Did you change that role during the play? In what way? What role would you like to have had? Why?

b. How did you deal with the ambiguity of the play? Did you act spontaneously? If not, why?

c. Did you take this opportunity to try an alternative role? If not, why? If so, how did it feel?

d. Did you try to give the play more direction? If so, why? Most plays have directors. Who among you was the director?

Variations

None.

* STORY CREATION

Subsidiary Goal(s)

a. To give feedback to another member.

---

* Dynamic, more effective exercises are marked with an asterisk.

b. To gain insight into how other members perceive us.
c. To gain insight into the place projection plays in fantasy experiences.
d. To experience rejection.

Group Application

Twelve members or less. To be used only with encounter, personal growth, marathon and t–groups whose members have developed rapport and some insight into each other.

Application Variables

Thirty to forty-five minutes. The exercise is 80% verbal, with 20% non–verbal being written. Paper and pencils are needed.

Administrative Procedure

a. The facilitator asks the group to *silently* choose another member they would like to write a fantasy story about.
b. He then tells the members to create a fantasy story about how the member they chose would handle an attack of anger in the group. (The facilitator can create any situation he desires, as long as it can occur in the group. For example, how would the member cope with confrontation, a silent member, frustration, etc.?)
c. The story should be no longer than one page.
d. After the stories are finished, the members read their story to the group, specifying the member in question.

Suggestions for Facilitator Process

Concentrate on the following during processing:
a. Why did we pick the individuals we did? Why did we ignore others?
b. *To members who were* not *picked as fantasy subjects:* How do you feel about being ignored?
c. What did we learn about how others perceive us? Do their perceptions match ours? Were the stories accurate in pre-

dicting your coping behavior? If not, what predictions were wrong?

d. What feelings do we have for each other now that the fantasy stories have been completed? If our feelings for others have changed, in what direction and why?

Variations

*Variation I
a. Get a volunteer to serve as the subject in a fantasy story.
b. Have every member write the fantasy story with the volunteer as the central character.
c. Have the stories read and then process.
d. Continue until all who wish to volunteer for the experience have had the opportunity to do so.

VIII

FEEDBACK

THE PRIMARY GOAL for each exercise in this chapter is the elicitation of feedback material.

Feedback is essential for most encounter, personal growth, marathon and t–groups, for feedback and self–disclosure are essential dynamics to the success of such groups.

We recognize three types of feedback exercises. First, those eliciting only positive feedback. These should be used when members need to learn how to give and receive positive feedback, when a particular member is exhibiting an inability to positively perceive himself, and whenever it becomes apparent to the facilitator that the group needs to be exposed to a positive feedback exercise.

Second, some exercises elicit only negative feedback. These are to be used when members need to learn to give and receive negative feedback, when a particular member is exhibiting an inability to negatively perceive himself, and whenever the facilitator believes the group needs to be exposed to a negative feedback exercise.

Third, the majority of exercises elicit general feedback. That is, feedback which can be negative and/or positive. Unless the facilitator specifically desires a preponderance of negative or positive feedback, he should consider utilizing an exercise falling in the general feedback classification.

The Index lists each feedback exercise and whether it deals with negative, positive, or general feedback.

*ASSIGNING MONEY VALUES

Subsidiary Goal(s)

  a. To assess the relative value each member has in the group.
  b. To determine how a member deals with differences between his own self–perception and others' perceptions of him.

Group Application

Twelve members or less. Should *only* be used with encounter, personal growth, marathon and t–groups with adult members after rapport has been developed.

Application Variables

Thirty to forty-five minutes. The exercise is 70% verbal, with 30% non–verbal being written. Money Value Forms, pencils and a chalkboard are needed.

Administrative Procedure

  a. The facilitator explains that each member is to assign a money value to himself and to every other member. Money value is to be determined by the estimated worth (or value) of the member to the life of the group.
  b. He explains that money values are to be no lower than one dollar nor higher than one hundred dollars.
  c. He urges the members to be as honest in assigning value as they can be.
  d. After the group completes the written section, the facilitator collects the Money Value Forms and charts the assigned values on the chalkboard.
  e. He returns the forms to the members and leads a discussion dealing with feelings aroused, differences between self–value assignment and others' value assignments, reactions to the feedback, etc.

Suggestions for Facilitator Process

Concentrate on the following during processing:

---

* Dynamic, more effective exercises are marked with an asterisk.

a. What feelings do you have about the money values you received?
b. Why do you think there is disparity between the value you gave yourself and that others gave you?
c. Why did you rate others and yourself as you did?
d. Whose values would you change now and why?

Variations

Variation I

a. Assign letters to each member so that only he knows his letter after collecting the Money Value Forms.
b. Chart the results on the chalkboard using the assigned letters instead of names.
c. Process as above. Members should be encouraged to share ratings, but not forced to do so.

MONEY VALUE FORM

DIRECTIONS: *Assign a money value from $1 to $100 to each member, including yourself.*

MEMBER'S NAME	MONEY VALUE	REASON
1.		
2.		
3.		
4.		
5.		
6.		
7.		
8.		
9.		
10.		
11.		
12.		

* BIRTHDAY PRESENTS

Subsidiary Goal(s)

a. To perpetuate and strengthen deeper and more caring relationships.
b. To explore the dynamics involved in giving and receiving.

Group Application

Twelve members or less. To be used with encounter, personal growth, marathon and t–groups. Best results are obtained if the exercise is used in the latter stages of group development.

Application Variables

One hour. The exercise is 70% verbal and 30% non–verbal. Members must have access to materials, so that they may create presents for other members in between sessions.

Administrative Procedure

a. The facilitator informs the members that they are going to have a birthday party for the group at the next meeting.
b. He then asks the members to bring birthday presents for any individual or the group as a whole, contingent on their feelings. The only restriction is that the member must actually make the present (s), not buy them. There are no other restrictions.
c. At the next meeting, the presents are placed in the middle of the circle.
d. Each member opens his present (s), and the member (s) giving it to him explain the meaning behind it.
e. The presents to the group are then opened, and again the member giving the present explains the meaning behind it.
f. The group discuss the experience.

Suggestions for Facilitator Process

Concentrate on the following during processing:
a. What types of feelings did you have when you gave your presents? When you received them? How did you decide on what type of present to give? Were you disappointed with what you received? If so, why?
b. Have your feelings changed towards any members in the group? If so, in what way? What have you learned about

yourself? Why did we wait for a birthday party to give part of ourselves?

c. Who received the most presents? Why? Who received the least? Why?

Variations

None.

CLASSIFYING MEMBERS

Subsidiary Goal(s)

a. To recognize the part projection plays in feedback.
b. To note differences in perception of others between members.

Group Application

Twelve members or less. To be used with any group, but is most effective with encounter, personal growth, marathon and t–groups whose members have developed some insight into one another.

Application Variables

Time unlimited, depending on the amount of triads rated. Paper and pencils are needed.

Administrative Procedure

a. The facilitator asks for three volunteers who wish to learn what impression the group has of them.
b. He then asks the other members to judge which two of the three volunteers are most alike. The members are to write down as many reasons for their choice as they can think of.
c. The members read their impressions to the three volunteers.
d. The facilitator leads a discussion focusing on the similarities and differences between impressions, the diversity of reasons, the feelings of the volunteers, etc.

e. A new triad is formed until all who wish to be judged have had the opportunity.

Suggestions for Facilitator Process

Concentrate on the following during processing:

a. To what extent were your pairings illustrative of projection? (He may illustrate a case where he perceived projection.)
b. *To volunteers:* Did you agree with the pairing? Why? If you disagreed, why?
c. Why were the pairings for (name the triad in question) so similar? Why did we get diverse pairings for (name of triad in question)?
d. What did we learn about how other members perceive us? Why did we get so many diverse perceptions?

Variations

None.

CONSENSUAL COMMANDMENTS REVISITED

Subsidiary Goal(s)

a. To compare self–estimates of behavior with the estimates of other members.

Group Application

Twelve members or less. To be used only with encounter, personal growth, marathon and t–groups whose members have previously experienced the CONSENSUAL COMMANDMENTS exercise found in the CONSENSUS chapter of this book. This exercise is to be conducted two to four sessions after the Consensual Commandments session.

Application Variables

One hour. The exercise is 70% verbal, with 30% non–verbal being written. Consensual Commandments Forms, pencils and a chalkboard are needed.

Administrative Procedure

a. The facilitator gives each member a copy of the Consensual Commandments form. (The facilitator should note that the forms list the "consensual" or "self–chosen" command-ment for each member. He therefore needs the list of those commandments he obtained when the Consensual Commandments exercise was conducted.)

b. He reads the "consensual" or "self–chosen" commandment for each member. The members write this information on the form and then complete it.

c. The facilitator charts the results on the chalkboard and leads a discussion of the exercise.

Suggestions for Facilitator Process

Concentrate on the following during processing:

a. What accounts for the difference between self–estimates and the group's estimate? What accounts for the discrep-ancies between the members' estimates concerning various individuals?

b. Who seemed to have the lowest estimates? Why? *To those people:* Did you follow your "consensual commandment"? If not, why not? If you did, why did we rate you so low?

c. Who had the highest estimates? Why?

Variations

None.

CONSENSUAL COMMANDMENTS FORM

Using percentages, estimate the effort made by yourself and each member in following the consensual commandment listed. Example: Joe: Start expressing your feelings.

60% effort to follow the commandment

NAME	CONSENSUAL COMMANDMENT	SELF–CHOSEN COMMANDMENT	EFFORT MADE TO FOLLOW COMMANDMENT
1.			
2.			

3.
4.
5.
6.
7.
8.
9.
10.
11.
12.

*CREATE A FAMILY

Subsidiary Goal(s)

a. To recognize how one copes with acceptance or rejection.
b. To self–disclose the warmth or coldness of one's relationship with other members.
c. To check one's perception of his relationship in the group
   with those of other group members.

Group Application

Twelve members or less. To be used only with encounter,
personal growth, marathon and t–groups whose members
have had sufficient sessions to have developed warm, intimate, caring relationships with one another.

Application Variables

One hour. The exercise is 90% verbal, with 10% non–
verbal being written. Family Forms and pencils are needed.

Administrative Procedure

a. The facilitator gives the members a Family Form and tells
   them to create a family comprised of other group members.
b. After the members have finished, they read their family
   choices, explaining each choice.

Suggestions for Facilitator Process

Concentrate on the following during processing:

a. Who was most frequently chosen for each role? Why? How did it make you (the members in question) feel?
b. Who was least frequently chosen for each role? Why? How did it make you (the members in question) feel?
c. What did we learn about our relationships with other members? Did our perception of relationships differ from those reported? Why?
d. Whose family were you pleased to be in? Why? Were you satisfied or dissatisfied with the family roles others gave you? Why?

Variations

Variation I
a. Omit the forms and have a volunteer choose his family verbally.
b. Have him gather the created family together. He then reveals a problem to them and they react to it, trying to act as they believe their role dictates.
c. After five minutes the facilitator stops the drama and checks out how the created family's reaction to the problem compares with that of the volunteer's real family.
d. Continue until all who wish to choose a family have had the opportunity.

*Variation II
a. Inform the members of the task, then have each member predict in writing: (a) which other members will choose him for their family; (b) what role they will assign him; and (c) why they will assign him the particular family role.
b. Proceed as before. In processing, pay particular attention to the accuracy or inaccuracy between predicted family groups and family groups assigned, roles predicted *versus* roles assigned, and reasons predicted *versus* reasons given.

FAMILY FORM

Choose another member to fill each of the following family roles. Indicate your reasoning.

ROLE	REASONS
1. Your mother	

2. Your father
3. Your younger sibling
4. Your older sibling
5. Your spouse
6. Your son
7. Your daughter

DESERT ISLAND [1]

Subsidiary Goal(s)

   a. To gain awareness of perceptions.
   b. To identify roles and stereotypes.
   c. To explore the dynamics involved in decision making.

Group Application

   Fifteen members or less. To be used with any group. Best results are obtained if the group members have had ample sessions to have developed feedback information with one another.

Application Variables

   One hour and thirty minutes to two hours and thirty minutes. The exercise is 100% verbal. The room must be large enough to allow up to five members to sit in the center of the room while the other members are seated around the inner group.

Administrative Procedure

   a. The facilitator initiates a discussion about the value of feedback concerning feelings and perceptions.
   b. The facilitator then gives the following instructions: "Each member is, in turn, to be marooned on a desert island. Each member may take as many as five other members from the group with him on this island."

---

[1] Adapted from an exercise developed by Robert Shelton and Robert Brook, University of Kansas.

c. He then asks for a volunteer.

d. The member being marooned enters the center of the circle. He is now told to choose up to five members to join him (the suggested number may be smaller if the total group is small enough to warrant it).

e. The facilitator informs all members that, if selected for the marooned group, they have the option to decline.

f. Those agreeing to be chosen join the "chosen" in the middle.

g. The chooser then tells each member (and the total group) why he chose that person, how he or she will be of help, etc., on the island.

h. Members chosen are asked to describe their feelings about being chosen.

i. When the chooser has explained each of his choices and each member has responded, the facilitator should encourage the island group to discuss survival needs, work responsibilities on the island, sexual problems.

j. The facilitator then asks the larger, outside group to comment on their feelings about the make–up of the island group, its possibilities and problems, etc.

k. When the whole procedure is completed, another volunteer is asked for.

l. Repeat steps **d** through **j** until all who wish to be a "chooser" have had the opportunity.

Suggestions for Facilitator Process

Concentrate on the following during processing:

a. *To the "choosers":* Was it difficult to decide which member to be stranded with? If so, why? Have you changed your mind about any of the members you selected? Did you pick fewer members than the suggested number? If so, why? What did you learn about your previous perceptions? If you were rejected by a member, what types of feelings did you have?

b. *To the "chosen":* How did it make you feel to have been chosen? Did you ever reject being chosen, if not why? Did you see any commonality between yourself and other members that were chosen? If so, what? Were you surprised at being selected? If so, why?

c. *To the outside members:* What were your feelings about not being chosen? What type of communication did you perceive going on in the center? What have you learned about other members? Were you surprised at any of the selections? If so, why?

d. *To the facilitator:* Maintain a sense of timing. The process can become exhausting. It is suggested that breaks be taken between "islands." Be prepared to help move the group along, for it is sometimes very time–consuming for each member to create the "island."

Variations

None.

*EGO TRIPPING

Subsidiary Goal(s)

a. To check the validity of a member's self–perceived positive characteristics with those perceived in him by other members.

b. To learn how to give and receive positive feedback.

Group Application

Twelve members or less. Applicable with any group, but particularly effective with encounter, personal growth, marathon and t–groups.

Application Variables

Thirty to forty-five minutes. The exercise is 100% verbal. A bell is needed.

Administrative Procedure

a. The facilitator sets one chair, the "ego chair", in the

middle of the room. All other members sit in a circle around the ego chair.

b. A volunteer is sought, one who is willing to receive *only* positive feedback. If any member makes a negative statement, the volunteer rings the bell as an indication that the comment is out of order.

c. The volunteer occupies the "ego chair." He is bombarded, verbally, by positive feedback from the other members.

d. When the group has exhausted itself of positive feedback for the volunteer, another member takes his place and the process is repeated.

e. The exercise ends after all members who wish to occupy the "ego chair" have had their opportunity.

Suggestions for Facilitator Process

Concentrate on the following during processing:

a. How did you feel about receiving only positive feedback? (Most will express difficulty in handling positive feedback.) Ask them why this is so and how they handled their difficulties?

b. How did you feel giving only positive feedback?

c. Did you disagree with any of the feedback you received? Why?

Variations

*Variation I

a. If two members are experiencing difficulty in establishing a relationship, are angry at each other, are not communicating well, etc., have them sit in the middle of the group and verbally bombard each other with positive feedback.

*Variation II

a. If you see that a member is continually "down" on himself, unable to recognize his positive qualities, expressing a negative self–concept, etc., have him assume the "ego chair" position and be bombarded positively by the group.

FIRST IMPRESSIONS

Subsidiary Goal(s)

a. To determine immediately one's impact on the group.
b. To check one's predicted impact with one's true impact.
c. To facilitate the getting–acquainted process.
d. To learn the part projection plays in our first impressions.

Group Application

Twelve members or less. Applicable with any group, but more often used in the first session of encounter, personal growth, marathon and t–groups.

Application Variables

Forty-five minutes to one hour. The exercise is 80% verbal, with 20% non–verbal being written. First Impression Forms and pencils are needed.

Administrative Procedure

a. The facilitator asks that each person take the opportunity to introduce himself to the group. The member should spend about three minutes telling the group about himself.
b. After all members have introduced themselves, each member writes all other members' names on the First Impression Form. If they have difficulty remembering a name, they may ask the member in question for additional data.
c. When each member has every other member's name on his form, the facilitator tells the group to complete the form.
d. After completion, each member reads his prediction, then all other members read their first impressions for him.
e. The group discusses the experience. The facilitator should save the First Impression Forms, for he may wish, later in the life of the group, to conduct an Updating First Impressions exercise (found in this chapter).

Suggestions for Facilitator Process

Concentrate on the following during processing:

a. Was your prediction of the impression you would make wrong? Why was this so?

b. Why did we get so many different impressions? Did projection play a part in our impressions of other members?

c. Did you have any difficulty determining your first impression of another member? Why? Similarly, why was it easy for you to establish first impressions of certain members?

Variations

Variation I

a. Before the group starts to talk, have each member write brief statements describing the first impressions he has of the other members. They should rely only on what they see. If a member knows another member, he should omit that person in his impression sketches.

b. During processing concentrate on the accuracy and inaccuracy of first impression sketches and the part projection and stereotyping play in such activities.

FIRST IMPRESSION FORMS

Write a prediction of the impressions you made on the group. Then write your first impresions of all other members.

My Prediction: _____

Other Members	My First Impression
1.	
2.	
3.	
4.	
5.	
6.	
7.	
8.	
9.	
10.	

11.

12.

* FISHBOWLING

Subsidiary Goal(s)

a. To learn to empathize with others.
b. To learn to observe more carefully than might be possible if one were actively participating.
c. To deal with anxiety, frustration, and intrusion.

Group Application

Size unlimited. To be used with any group, but especially effective with encounter, personal growth, marathon and t–groups.

Application Variables

Thirty minutes. The room must be large enough to handle two sets of circles, with six chairs in the middle and all other members seated around the inner circle.

Administrative Procedure

a. The facilitator and four other members sit in the inner circle. One chair is left open.
b. The facilitator tells the observing members: "We in the fishbowl will conduct a thirty minute session. You are to observe. *Whenever* you feel you have feedback for one or all of us, occupy the empty chair, give us your input, and *immediately* depart and rejoin the observing circle. You are *not* to carry on a conversation with us in any way!"
c. He tells the fishbowl members: "We are to listen to *all* feedback. What we do with it is up to us. We are not allowed to question the empty chair occupant or respond to him in any way. In other words, he can talk to us, but we *cannot* respond."
d. The fishbowl begins its session. After thirty minutes the

facilitator stops the session. He then leads a discussion about the experience.

Suggestions for Facilitator Process

Concentrate on the following during processing:

a. *To fishbowlers:* How did it feel to receive feedback but not be allowed to respond? How did you cope with these feelings? Whose feedback was helpful? Why? Whose was not helpful? Why?
b. *To observers who used the empty chair:* What made you decide to give us feedback? Why do you think we needed it? If we ignored it, how did that behavior on our part make you feel?
c. *To observers who did not use the empty chair:* Why didn't you give us feedback?

Variations

Variation I
a. Have the facilitator and five members occupy six chairs in the middle. There is *no* empty chair.
b. Tell observers: "If you wish to join our session, come into the middle, tap someone on the shoulder, and occupy his chair. You then *stay* in the fishbowl until some other member "taps you out.""

*FISHBOWLING FOR FEEDBACK

Subsidiary Goal(s)

a. To develop empathic ability.
b. To learn to focus on one individual.
c. To recognize how one copes with anxiety.

Group Application

Twenty members or less. To be used with encounter, personal growth, marathon and t–groups who are attempting to learn how to give and receive feedback and how to empathize with others.

Application Variables

One hour. The exercise is 100% verbal. The room must be large enough to allow the observers' circle to sit around the fishbowl circle without unduly interfering with it.

Administrative Procedure

a. The facilitator asks for volunteers (half the group) to "fishbowl" a discussion. They will be observed by the remaining members and receive feedback about their participation in the fishbowl.

b. He asks that each of the members from the inner group pick an alter ego (observer) from the outer group. Each alter ego then positions himself in the outside circle so that he has an unobstructed view of his member.

c. The facilitator tells the alter egos that: (1) they will position themselves in the fishbowl eventually; (2) they will have new partners as alter egos; (3) they are each to give feedback to their member after the fishbowl session; and (4) they should concentrate on what the member did and how he affected the fishbowling group.

d. The inner circle participates in a group session. You may structure it by suggesting areas for discussion or leave it unstructured and let the fishbowl group go where it wishes (we recommend the latter as it provides data as to how the fishbowl members cope with ambiguity).

e. After twenty minutes the facilitator stops the discussion and has the alter egos and observed members form dyads. The alter egos then each have ten minutes to give their member feedback.

f. Process this data, concentrating on what feedback was given, its accuracy or inaccuracy, and how it affected the member receiving it.

g. Have the alter egos go into the fishbowl and pick new alter egos so that all dyads are different.

h. Repeat steps **d**, **e**, and **f**.

Suggestions for Facilitator Process

Concentrate on the following during processing:

a. Did you receive negative feedback? How did you deal with it? Did you have difficulty giving negative feedback? Why?
b. Did you feel anxiety about the alter egos? How did you cope with it?
c. If you left the fishbowl session unstructured, ask the members how they dealt with the ambiguity it created. Ask alter egos what maneuvers they noticed fishbowling members used to deal with the ambiguity.

Variations

Variation I
a. Have prepared observation forms available for alter egos to use. Examples may be found in most books on group dynamics.

* FIVE QUESTIONS

Subsidiary Goal(s)

a. To gain insight into how other members perceive us in our relationships with them.
b. To learn of the strengths others see in us.

Group Application

Twelve members or less. To be used with encounter, personal growth, marathon and t–groups after the members have had sufficient meetings to gain some insight into each other. Easily adaptable to any group.

Application Variables

Thirty minutes. The exercise is 90% verbal, with 10% non–verbal being written. Five Questions Forms, pencils and a chalkboard are needed.

Administrative Procedure

(We urge the facilitator to make up his own questions depending on the feedback he wishes to elicit.)
a. The facilitator has the members complete the Five Questions Form.

b. He collects the forms and tallies the results on the chalk-board.

c. The group discusses the experience.

Suggestions for Facilitator Process

Concentrate on the following during processing:

a. What reasons do we have for our choice? How do you feel about the choices you were given by others?

b. Why do some members appear more on one list than others? Why are some not chosen at all?

c. If you weren't chosen, how do you feel about this?

Variations

Variation I

a. Have each member predict on his form who in the group will pick him for each question.

b. During processing, concentrate on the accuracy and/or inaccuracy between predictions and actual results.

*Variation II

a. Change the form to read, "Who would be the last person in this group you would choose?"

b. Proceed as before, but concentrate on the reactions to negative feedback, the reasons for choices, discrepancies in choice, etc.

FIVE QUESTIONS FORM

Whom would you choose in this group:

QUESTION	NAME	REASON
1. To spend two weeks with on a desert island?		
2. To have on your side during an argument?		
3. To ask for help in resolving a personal problem?		
4. To reveal yourself to?		
5. To give you honest feedback?		

* FOCUSING

Subsidiary Goal(s)

a. To learn to fantasize.
b. To learn the differences between thinking and feeling.
c. To learn how one deals with rejection.

Group Application

Twelve members or less. To be used only with encounter, personal growth, marathon and t–groups whose members have developed rapport and have established some insight into each other.

Application Variables

Thirty to forty-five minutes. The exercise is 70% verbal and 30% non–verbal.

Administrative Procedure

a. The facilitator tells the group they will learn to differentiate between thought and feeling and to give feedback to another member concerning his impact on them.
b. He tells the members: "Non–verbally, without indicating who you are picking, decide which member you wish to focus on. You will be giving him feedback concerning his impact on you."
c. After a minute he proceeds: "During the three phases of the experience, try to retain all the thoughts and feelings the focusing arouses so they can be shared with the member you are focusing on. Close your eyes. Concentrate on your member. Now, focusing on him and him only, fill in, in your mind, the following statement: 'I think you. . .' Repeat this statement until you have exhausted possible completions."
d. After five minutes he says: "Now, still focusing, complete the following until you exhaust possible completions: "I think you . . . and that makes me feel. . .' "
e. After five minutes he says: "Still focusing, complete the

following as exhaustively as you can 'Toward you I feel. . .' "

f. After five minutes, he tells the group to stop focusing and to go to the member focused on and give him feedback concerning his statement completions. (Note: Some members will have been focused on by more than one person. Others will not have been focused on at all. Still others will be receiving feedback before they get the chance to give it to their focused member. *Do not* help the group deal with these factors. Let them cope with them.)

g. After all have given and received feedback, discuss the experience with the group.

Suggestions for Facilitator Process

Concentrate on the following during processing:

a. What did you learn about the differences between thinking and feeling?

b. How did you feel during the feedback phase? How did you cope with the frustration and other feelings you encountered?

c. *To members not focused on:* How did you feel when you found out no one focused on you? Why do you think you were ignored? Check with other members as to why they did not choose the member (s) in question.

d. What did we learn about our impact on others as a result of the feedback we received?

e. Why did you choose the person you did to focus on?

Variations

Variation I

a. To eliminate non–picked members and the frustration of the feedback stage, have dyads form and conduct the exercise as above.

*Variation II

a. Ask for a volunteer who wishes to receive feedback from the group concerning his impact on the members.

b. Have the entire group focus on the volunteer.

c. Process, then repeat the focusing exercise until all who wish to be focused on have had the opportunity.

* GROUP INVENTORY [2]

Subsidiary Goal(s)

a. To gain insights into member roles.
b. To explore hidden resources in members.
c. To gain awareness of members' self–concepts.

Group Application

Twelve members or less. To be used with any group. Ample sessions must have occurred to enable the group to develop member identity.

Application Variables

One hour and thirty minutes. The exercise is 50% verbal, with 50% non–verbal being written. Pencils are needed. A copy of the Group Role Inventory is needed for each member.

Administrative Procedure

a. The facilitator passes out a copy of the Group Role Inventory to each member in the group.
b. He then asks members to read the directions at the top of the form and complete it.
c. After all members have finished filling out the inventory, the facilitator asks each member to read, in turn, his response to question no. 1.
d. This procedure is repeated until all twenty-six questions have been shared.
e. The facilitator should encourage members to note the number of times their names are mentioned according to specific responses.
f. The facilitator then initiates discussion.

---

[2] Permission to reproduce this exercise was granted by the Youth Office, Lutheran Church of America.

Suggestions for Facilitator Process

Concentrate on the following during processing:
a. Were you surprised at the number of times your name was mentioned? Did you see yourself in the roles the group most commonly associated you with? If not, why not?
b. If your name was infrequently mentioned, what do you feel this means? Are you satisfied with the way the group perceives you? If not, how do you feel you can change it?

Variations

Variation I
a. Repeat steps **a** through **d**.
b. Have members act out the roles most commonly assigned them.

Variation II
a. Repeat steps **a** through **d**.
b. Have members break up into small groups comprised of those members the group has perceived as being the most similar, and discuss why.

GROUP ROLE INVENTORY

Your Group _____ Your Name _____
_____ Date _____

DIRECTIONS: *Who, in your group, is most likely to take the role described (or one rather like it)? Write his or her name in the blank.*

Any members may be identified with several different roles. More than one person can be named for a given role, if you can't choose one who fits better than the other(s). You may nominate yourself whenever you think you fit best into the role.

If no one seems to come close to the description, you may leave the question blank.

Who in your group, as you now see it, is most likely to:
1. Take initiative, propose ideas, get things started?

_____

2. Sit back and wait passively for others to lead?

3. Express his own feelings most freely, frankly, openly?

4. Keep his feelings hidden, reserved, unexpressed?

5. Show that he truly understands the feelings of other members?

6. Be wrapped up in his own concerns and not very responsive to others?

7. Interrupt others when they are speaking?

8. Daydream; get lost in his own thoughts during group sessions; be "far away"?

9. Give you a feeling of encouragement, warmth, friendly interest, support?

10. Understand you, even if you do not speak?

11. Make you feel you might be criticized; put you on your guard?

12. Express group feelings in excellent symbols, images or fantasies?

13. Feel superior to other members; look down on them?

14. Feel inferior to other members?

15. Contradict, disagree, argue, raise objections?

16. Agree, conform, go along with whatever is said?

17. Understand not only *what* members say but *why*, and what lies beneath their words?

___

18. Be aware of group processes; point out what the group is doing; diagnose and suggest better procedures?

___

19. Accept you and affirm you as you really are?

___

20. Try to improve you, change you, make you over?

___

21. Be the one you fully accept and affirm as he now is?

___

22. Be the one you would most like to improve, to change, to make over?

___

23. Lead the group toward deeper experiences and more profound feelings?

___

24. Avoid and fear conflict; be eager to harmonize and smooth things over?

___

25. Accept and explore conflict to get at the real differences?

___

26. Test proposals to see how many really agree; be sure any disagreement is expressed.

___

GROUP SOCIOGRAM

Subsidiary Goal(s)

a. To learn how other members perceive us in relation to them and the group.
b. To recognize differences of perception concerning member strengths and weaknesses.

Group Application

Twelve members or less. To be used with encounter, personal growth, marathon and t–groups.

Application Variables

Forty-five minutes to one hour. The exercise is 80% verbal, with 20% non–verbal being written. Paper and pencils, tape and a chalkboard are needed.

Administrative Procedure

a. The facilitator asks each member to draw a sociogram for all members, including himself, on the following categories *(here the facilitator should feel free to make up categories relevant to his group):*
 1. Trust level
 2. Closeness of relationship
 3. Willingness to self–disclose
b. He may wish to illustrate the sociogram procedure by doing his sociogram on the chalkboard. Draw a sociogram of the ease with which you relate to the group members.
c. The facilitator collects the sociograms and tapes them on the wall or chalkboard. Members go around and check the various sociograms.
d. The members discuss the exercise, concentrating on where they were on one another's sociograms and why; how they felt about being listed high or low on various sociograms; differences in member sociograms; etc.

Suggestions for Facilitator Process

Concentrate on the following during processing:
a. Why were some members listed high in one sociogram and low in others? What can we do to guarantee our moving from a low spot on a member's sociogram to a high spot on his list?
b. Were you surprised at the ranking you received on certain members' lists? Whose lists and why?
c. Why did *you* rank members where you did?
d. What did you learn about how other members perceive your trust level, degree of closeness in relation to the group, and willingness to accept self–disclosure? What can you do to improve these perceptions?

Variations

None.

* GUESSING REAL LIFE REACTIONS

Subsidiary Goal(s)

a. To recognize the part projection plays in giving feedback.
b. To gain insight into others copying behaviors.
c. To gain insight into the way other members perceive us.
d. To learn how to fantasize about another member.

Group Application

Twelve members or less. Applicable with any group. Is particularly effective when used with encounter, personal growth, marathon and t–groups whose members have developed some insight into one another.

Application Variables

Thirty to forty-five minutes. The exercise is 100% verbal.

Administrative Procedure

a. The facilitator asks for a volunteer who wishes to receive feedback as to how his coping behavior is seen by other members.
b. The members are told to predict to the volunteer how he would react in real life to the following: (1) hostility from a loved one; (2) anger from a peer; (3) a violation of confidence.
c. After the predictions, the volunteer reacts, indicating the extent of accuracy and inaccuracy.
d. The exercise is continued until all members who wish such feedback have had an opportunity.

Suggestions for Facilitator Process

Concentrate on the following during processing:
a. What predictions were inaccurate? Why? Were these inaccuracies the result of projection?

b. Your predictions were deemed inaccurate. Do you agree? If you disagree, why do you believe you were right?
c. Did you experience difficulty in making predictions for someone? Why?

Variations

Variation I

a. The facilitator asks the members to predict *his* behavior in real life in (name a situation).
b. During processing, concentrate on the effect your authority and assumed expertise might have played in member predictions.

Variation II

a. The facilitator asks the members to predict *his* behavior in a group situation. Make up a situation you have not yet encountered in the group.
b. Process as in *Variation I*.

Variation III

a. Have the members predict a volunteer's reaction to a group situation. Make up a situation the member has not yet encountered.

IMPROMPTU FEEDBACK

Subsidiary Goal(s)

a. To provide feedback to the group.
b. To recognize the feelings aroused by being the center of attention.

Group Application

Twelve members or less. Applicable to any group but most frequently used in beginning encounter, personal growth, marathon and t–groups. Can be especially effective when adopted to a classroom setting.

Application Variables

Five to seven minutes per participant. The exercise loses its value if more than two members are given "impromptu" assignments. The exercise is 100% verbal.

Administrative Procedure

a. The facilitator, about half–way through the session, says, "I want someone to give a five minute presentation about our session today. Any volunteers?"

b. He ignores the volunteers and chooses another member, saying "Give us some feedback. Tell us what's been happening today and why." (We recommend that the facilitator make up a presentation topic relevant to this group.)

c. The facilitator stops the exercise after five minutes. He may wish to repeat it with as many members making presentations as desire to do so, but he should note that participants three and on will have little excess anxiety, for they will have had adequate time to overcome it.

Suggestions for Facilitator Process

Concentrate on the following during processing:

a. *To presenters:* What feelings and thoughts did you have when I picked you? How did you cope with them? What feelings did you have *during* your presentation?

b. *To others:* What feelings did you have when you found out I wasn't going to pick you? What would *your* presentation have covered?

Variations

Variation I

a. If you wish all members to experience the anxiety created by making an impromptu address, make up new presentation topics for each round.

*Variation II

a. To create excessive anxiety, announce the talk, and *immediately* pick a member whose participation has been minimal.

* NEGATIVE FEEDBACK

Subsidiary Goal(s)

a. To check the validity of one's self–perceived negative characteristics with those perceived in us by other members.

b. To learn how to give and receive negative feedback.

Group Application

Twelve members or less. To be used only with encounter, personal growth, marathon and t–groups with adult members. The members should have developed warm, caring, intimate relationships with one another before they encounter this experience.

Application Variables

One hour. The exercise is 90% verbal, with 10% non–verbal being written. Negative Feedback Forms and pencils are needed.

Administrative Procedure

a. The facilitator presents a (brief) lecturette on the principles of effective feedback.
b. He then asks the members to write down negative feedback items for *every* other member as well as for themselves on the Negative Feedback Forms.
c. After they are finished, he collects the forms and reads the feedback data to the group, reading all feedback for member A, then all feedback for member B, etc., *without* revealing who gave the feedback.
d. He leads a discussion about the experience.

Suggestions for Facilitator Process

Concentrate on the following during processing:
a. How did you feel about giving and receiving negative feedback? How did you cope with these feelings?
b. What were the similarities and dissimilarities between your feedback to yourself and that feedback you received from others? How do you explain this?
c. Do you disagree with some of the feedback? Why?

Variations

*Variation I

a. Have members complete the Negative Feedback Form.
b. Now have each member read his own form. Members re-

ceiving feedback are allowed to react to feedback at the moment they receive it.

Variation II

a. After members complete the form, tally the feedback data on a chalkboard. Tally feedback for one member, process, then tally for another member and process, continuing until all member feedback has been charted.

Variation III

a. If two members appear to have *too* positive a relationship, never confront or disagree with one another, share only positive feelings, etc., have them sit in the middle of the circle and verbally bombard each other with negative feedback.

NEGATIVE FEEDBACK FORM

Write at least one item of negative feedback for each member. Include yourself.

MEMBER   FEEDBACK

1.
2.
3.
4.
5.
6.
7.
8.
9.
10.
11.
12.

PAINTING FEEDBACK [3]

Subsidiary Goal(s)

a. To increase interpersonal communication and understanding.

---

[3] Adapted from an exercise developed by Robert Shelton and Robert Brook, University of Kansas.

b. To explore individual perceptions.
c. To experience creativity.

Group Application

Twelve members or less. To be used with any group. Several hours of previous group experience are essential. Best results are obtained in subgroups of five to six members.

Application Variables

One and one–half to three hours. The exercise is 60% verbal and 40% non–verbal. Large sheets of paper, one per member, or a long sheet of newsprint for each subgroup (large enough to contain five to six paintings) is required. An adequate supply of paint (finger paint or brush on paint) is also needed. There must be sufficient room space for members or subgroups to work independently.

Administrative Procedures

a. The facilitator is to have materials and floor or table spacing prepared beforehand.
b. He then asks the group to divide up evenly into two subgroups. Selection of subgroup members may be determined by current group needs.
c. The facilitator informs the groups that each member will be sent away, one at a time. The member leaving should go outside the room.
d. The group is then asked to discuss impressions and perceptions of the absent member.
e. The group will then jointly paint a picture which represents their impressions and perceptions. It may either be a composite drawing or a collection of individual representations.
f. The absent member then returns and responds to the painting.

g. The group should describe to the member how the painting developed.

h. This process is repeated for each member.

i. The facilitator may desire to make the following statement before the exercise begins: "As in any feedback mechanism, the impressions expressed in the paintings are to be received by the returning members as perceptions which need not be defended or argued. They are simply impressions at the time, to be utilized however the recipient desires. Further inquiry, however, may be desirable. Members are encouraged to use the paint with the assurance that artistic ability is not important."

Suggestions for Facilitator Process

Concentrate on the following during processing:

a. *To members receiving feedback:* How did you feel when you left the room? Were you surprised at the feedback you received? If so, why? Did you feel the perceptions or impressions were accurate? If not, why?

b. *To members giving feedback:* What type of feedback did you give? What type of communication went on within your subgroups? How closely do you feel your drawing represented your feelings? Have your impressions or perceptions changed toward any of the members? If so, in what way? Do you feel your subgroup varied in the style of feedback given as compared to the other subgroups?

Variations

None.

* PARTICIPATION FEEDBACK

Subsidiary Goal(s)

a. To compare one's self–perceived participation level with that level perceived by other members.

b. To give and receive information about the type and level of one's communication in the group.

c. To learn the differences between thinking and feeling.

Group Application

Twelve members or less. Applicable with any group, but most effective with encounter, personal growth, marathon and t–groups.

Application Variables

Thirty to forty-five minutes. The exercise is 80% verbal, with 20% non–verbal being written. Participation Forms, pencils, and a chalkboard are needed.

Administrative Procedure

a. The facilitator stops the group forty-five minutes before the session ends and tells the group to fill out Participation Forms for each member. (If he has never discussed the difference between intellectualizing and revealing feelings, he does so now.)

b. He collects the forms and tallies the results on the chalkboard.

c. The group discusses the exercise, attempting to determine if participation results are unique to this session or representative of previous sessions.

Suggestions for Facilitator Process

Concentrate on the following during processing:

a. What did you learn about your participation level as perceived by other members? Why did your personal estimate differ from the group's estimate? Who is right, you or the group?

b. *To intellectualizers:* Why do you have difficulty sharing your feelings with us? What can you do to change this? How can we help you change?

c. *To low level participants:* Why don't you participate? What can we do to help you? What can you do?

Variations

Variation I

a. Conduct the exercise as before, but chart the results using letters instead of names. Tell each member his letter so he will know which feedback results are his.

    b. Discuss as before. Encourage self–disclosure by members as to which results are theirs. During processing examine the phenomenon of self–disclosure. Who disclosed and why? Who didn't and why?

PARTICIPATION FORM

Using percentages, from 1 to 100, assess the amount of participation for each member in today's session. Rate yourself also.

	TOTAL PERCENT	INTELLECTUALIZING LEVEL PERCENT	FEELING LEVEL PERCENT
My participation:			
Other members:			
1.			
2.			
3.			
4.			
5.			
6.			
7.			
8.			
9.			
10.			
11.			
12.			

STOPPING GUNNYSACKING

Subsidiary Goal(s)

    a. To facilitate verbal communication.

    b. To increase involvement.

Group Application

Twelve members or less. To be used only with encounter, personal growth, marathon and t–groups. Especially effective when used with such groups experiencing difficulty in self–disclosing and giving spontaneous feedback.

Application Variables

Thirty to forty-five minutes. The exercise is 80% verbal, with 20% non–verbal being written. Paper and pencils are needed.

Administrative Procedure

a. The facilitator, when he perceives that members are gunnysacking (*i.e.,* carrying undisclosed thoughts, feelings and values about one another), asks the member to write down what they won't say verbally to each other.
b. He collects the gunnysacked statements and reads them to the group. He does not indicate which member wrote which statements.
c. He leads a discussion, encouraging members now verbally to empty their gunnysack.

Suggestions for Facilitator Process

Concentrate on the following during processing:
a. Why have you been gunnysacking? How do you feel now that your gunnysacks are empty and their contents known?
b. Do you now feel you can stop gunnysacking and tell members what is bothering you *when* it is bothering you? If you receive some "no" responses, ask these members why.
c. What have we learned about the effects gunnsyacking has on the group and on member relationships and communication?

Variations

*Variation I
a. Have the members write their gunnysacked statements.
b. Then have *them* read their statements to the group and to the members they are directed at. This promotes responsibility and creates anxiety which must be dealt with.

Variation II

a. Have the members write a prediction as to who in the group is gunnysacking them and what information is in the gunnysack.
b. Proceed as before. During processing concentrate on the accuracy and inaccuracy of predictions. Inaccurate predictions may indicate unrecognized conflict areas between members, which can now be attended to.

UPDATING FIRST IMPRESSIONS [1]

Subsidiary Goal(s)

a. To gain insight into other members' self–concepts.
b. To recognize differences in perception between members.

Group Application

Twelve members or less. Applicable with any group except the classroom. The exercise is particularly effective if a First Impression exercise was previously conducted.

Application Variables

Thirty minutes. The exercise is 100% verbal. There is a written part to the exercise, but it should be done before the session.

Administrative Procedure

a. The facilitator tells the members at the end of the session to go home and write short impression statements for each member, including themselves. He says: "Write your impression of each member as he is *now* in our group. Write your impression of yourself also. We will discuss these statements at the next session."
b. The next session opens with each member reading his descriptions to the group.
c. The group discusses the impression statements, paying particular attention to the differences between the first

---

[1] This exercise should accompany the First Impressions exercise on P. 114.

impression they had during the first session and those impressions shared today.

Suggestions for Facilitator Process

Concentrate on the following during processing:

a. What discrepancies existed between your impression of yourself and those of other members? Why is this?
b. What discrepancies between our impressions of each other? Why?
c. How have our first impressions changed? Why is this so?

Variations

Variation I

a. To avoid the written aspect and to conserve time, have the members share verbally their current impressions of each other.
b. During processing concentrate on differences between first and current impressions and discrepancies in impressions between members. For example, "We all see Jack as caring, I see him as cold. Why is this so?"

Variations

None.

IX

FEELINGS

THE PRIMARY GOAL for each exercise in this chapter is to elicit behavior dealing with the feelings of oneself and other members in the hopes that members will be able to recognize the presence of such feelings and report, during processing, how they coped with the feelings in question.

Recognizing, dealing with, and getting in touch with feelings is essential for all encounter, personal growth, marathon and t–groups. The following exercises are designed to facilitate exploration of the dynamics involved in feeling rather than thinking. By this, we mean that members will learn to recognize the differences between thinking and feeling. Such differentiation is definitely essential for human relations training groups.

Since feelings are the foundation upon which communication is developed, the facilitator should be aware of dynamic events which may ensue during or after the use of these exercises. These exercises are not designed to substitute or speed up member feelings, but rather to provide an environment through which already established feelings can be better explored, examined, defined, experienced and reported.

Because of the immense spectrum of feelings available for elicitation, the facilitator is encouraged to make variations according to the group's and individual members' specific needs.

141

ECHOING

Subsidiary Goal(s)

a. To provide feedback to members about their impact on the group.
b. To improve empathic understanding.
c. To facilitate self–disclosure.

Group Application

Twelve members or less. To be used with encounter, personal growth, marathon and t–groups.

Application Variables

Fifteen to thirty minutes. The exercise is 100% verbal.

Administrative Procedure

a. The facilitator stops the group about thirty minutes before ending time and asks the members to recall their strongest feelings during that session.
b. All members who wish to share their strongest feelings do so.
c. The facilitator then asks the group to focus on one of the feeling experiences which was revealed. The members are to recall moments in the group when they too shared the feeling under discussion. (In other words, members try to "echo" the feeling experience.)
d. If time allows, choose another member's experience and "echo" it.

Suggestions for Facilitator Process

Concentrate on the following during processing:
a. Could you empathize with the individual? Was echoing a difficult task? Why?
b. Discuss the nature of the feelings experienced. Were they positive or negative? What feelings were easiest to echo and empathize? Why?

Variations

None.

KEY ON FEELINGS AND DEFENSES

Subsidiary Goal(s)

a. To obtain feedback on our perceived defenses.
b. To empathize with others.
c. To check self–perceptions with those of other members.
d. To see the place projection plays in assessing others' strengths and defenses.

Group Application

Twelve members or less. To be used only with encounter, personal growth, marathon and t–groups with adult members who have had sufficient sessions to have developed rapport and some insight into each other.

Application Variables

Forty-five minutes to one hour. The exercise is 80% verbal, with 20% non–verbal being written. Paper and pencils are needed.

Administrative Procedure

a. The facilitator asks the group to write a description of the feeling they most easily reveal and the feeling they most strongly struggle against revealing.
b. He then informs the group to write the same description for each member (*e.g.,* "I see Tom most easily revealing anger, most strongly defending against revealing love," etc.)
c. He has each member read his prediction for himself. All other members then read their statements for the member in question.
d. Discuss the exercise after all have had their turn.

Suggestions for Facilitator Process

Concentrate on the following during processing:

   a. Did your self–predictions differ from those you heard other members read? Why is this so?

   b. What place did projection play in our statements about other members?

   c. If you disagree with other members as to their statements about you, where and why are they wrong?

Variations

Variation I

   a. Have one member volunteer to make a prediction.

   b. Then have the other members write their statements about the individual in question.

   c. Process, then continue until each member who wishes to experience the procedure has had the opportunity.

   d. If some members refuse to participate, examine the dynamics behind their refusal.

MAGNETS [1]

Subsidiary Goal(s)

   a. To elicit self–disclosure.

   b. To deepen member awareness.

   c. To explore the dynamics involved in first impressions.

Group Application

Twelve members or less. To be used with any group. Best results are obtained if the exercise is used after the group has had ample sessions to allow members to form definite perceptions of other members.

Application Variables

Two hours and thirty minutes. The exercise is 60% verbal and 40% non–verbal. An outdoor setting is preferable. Sufficient space is needed to walk and explore surroundings. One blindfold for every two members is required.

---

[1] Adapted from Robert Shelton and Robert Brook, University of Kansas.

Administrative Procedure

a. The facilitator may wish to give a (brief) lecturette concerning the difficulty of disclosing feelings toward other members. Participants are told that they will have an opportunity to explore some of these undisclosed feelings toward other members.

b. The facilitator then asks each participant to select a person in the group toward whom they feel attracted (*i.e.,* like, admire, feel comfortable with), and have not previously discussed this with that person. (The selection will require persons taking responsibility for choosing not to go with one member if they prefer to be with another.)

c. The dyads are to find a place to talk and share their feelings about one another.

d. After thirty minutes all dyads return to the larger group. Members are encouraged to share with the large group their reactions to the experience.

e. After ample time has been allowed for discussion, the facilitator now asks members to select a person to whom he/she is not attracted (uncomfortable with, have no experience with, don't like, etc.). Again, responsibility must be taken by members to say "no" to one person if he/she would prefer to be with someone else.

f. Dyads are to find a place to talk apart from others and to discuss their feelings about one another.

g. After thirty minutes the facilitator asks dyads to form with one or two other dyads. The subgroups are to discuss their experiences.

h. After thirty minutes the subgroups are to break into the original dyads. Each pair is given a blindfold. They are to take turns being blindfolded, each leading the other on a non–verbal exploration walk. (*Note to facilitator:* Although it certainly involves trust, the exploration walk is not primarily a "trust walk," and it is helpful to refer to it as an "exploration" rather than a "trust" walk. For members in the group who have previously been on "trust walks," this difference in language emphasis may be important.) Allow ten to fifteen minutes per member (twenty-five to thirty minutes total). The facilitator should signal the time to change.

i. Members return to large group for discussion.

Suggestions for Facilitator Process

Concentrate on the following during processing:

a. What issues were involved in your discussions? What was the effect of this communication on stereotypes, first impressions, projection of feelings, etc.? Were you able to communicate your feelings accurately?

b. What did you experience during the walk? What were some of your pleasant discoveries? What were your feelings about the person leading you? What connections did you find between your discussion and the walk which followed? What did you feel when you led your partner?

c. What do you feel about the relationship of disclosure and dependence, interdependence and cooperation? Which part of the exercise did you feel was the most valuable for you? What have you learned about yourself?

Variations

Variation I

a. If less time is available, and if there is more need to concentrate on feelings of non–attraction, steps **a–d** may be omitted.

* PLEASURE-PAIN

Subsidiary Goal(s)

a. To receive feedback about members' group relationships.

b. To receive feedback about one's effect on other members.

Group Application

Twelve members or less. To be used with beginning encounter, personal growth, marathon and t–groups.

---

* Dynamic, more effective exercises are marked with an asterisk.

Application Variables

Thirty minutes. The exercise is 90% verbal, with 10% non–verbal being written. Paper and pencils are needed.

Administrative Procedure

a. The facilitator stops the group thirty to forty-five minutes before the end of the session.
b. He tells them to write responses to the following:
   1. Today (insert member's name) hurt me when. . .
   2. Today (insert member's name) pleased me when. . .
c. When they have finished, the members read their responses to each other. They then discuss the experience.

Suggestions for Facilitator Process

Concentrate on the following during processing:
a. Were you surprised by the pleasure–pain your actions stirred up? Were you aware of this before feedback?
b. What have we learned about our relationships with other members? If we seem to stir up pain with certain people, what can we do about it?

Variations

Variation I
a. Have members reply to the original open–ended statements *and* the following:
   1. In the past (insert member's name) hurt me when. . .
   2. In the past (insert member's name) pleased me when. . .
Variation II
a. Have members complete any of the statements verbally to the member in question.

* PURSE AND WALLET

Subsidiary Goal(s)

a. To recognize acceptance and rejection as they operate in the group.

b. To learn a member's worth to the group as perceived by other members.

c. To disclose one's personal estimation of his worth to the group.

d. To investigate the phenomenon of trust in the group.

e. To learn how to confront other members.

Group Application

Twelve members or less. To be used with encounter, personal growth, marathon and t–groups with adult members who have developed rapport with and insight into each other.

Application Variables

Forty-five minutes to one hour. The exercise is 70% verbal, with 30% non–verbal being written. Note pads and pencils are needed.

Administrative Procedure

a. The facilitator asks that each member take all the money in his or her purse or wallet and place it in a pile in front of himself (the member).

b. Each is to count the money piled in front of him and tell the group how much he has. Each member writes down the amount every other member has.

c. The members are then told: (1) "Decide, then write down, how much of your money you are willing to pool with the other members;" and (2) "Make a written prediction as to how much each member besides yourself will contribute."

d. Each member reads his decision for sharing and places that amount on the floor in the middle of the circle. The other members read to him their prediction as to how much he would pool.

e. After all have completed step **d**, conduct a brief discussion on the differences in amounts pooled and the discrepancies in the member predictions for each other revealed. Ask how the members decided how much to pool.

f. The facilitator then tells the group members they will take turns taking money from the pool. (Do not determine the order for taking money. Let the members wrestle with this problem.) Members may take and keep as much as they wish until the pool is emptied. The member taking money approaches the pool and says: "I am taking (state amount) because. . ."

g. Any member who feels the taker is doing himself or the group an injustice now says: "You should not take (state amount) . You should take (state amount) because. . ."

h. The taker then makes his decision, taking the amount *he* determines and rejoins the group. Steps f and g are continued until each member has taken money or the pool is empty.

i. The group discusses the experience.

Suggestions for Facilitator Process

Concentrate on the following during processing:

a. *To takers who were confronted:* How did you feel when you were told you had taken too much (or too little) ? What factors determined the amount you finally took?

b. *To confronters:* What prompted you to confront certain members about the amount they took? Were you pleased or displeased with the taker's final choice? Why pleased? Why displeased?

c. Did any of you fail to confront? If any affirmatives, ask why.

d. Do you now have a more accurate insight into the worth you and others have in this group?

e. Who feels they were cheated? Why? How are you coping with your feelings?

f. If we started again, who would change their actions and how?

Variations

None.

* SENSUALITY

Subsidiary Goal(s)

a. To provide feedback about a member's impact on others.
b. To discover the agreement or disagreement between one's self–perception of his impact and those perceptions held by others.

Group Application

Twelve members or less. The group should have as close a break down by sex as is possible, *i.e.*, even number of men and women. To be used only with encounter, personal growth, marathon and t–groups with adult members who have developed considerable rapport and feelings of warmth and care for each other.

Application Variables

Thirty minutes to forty-five minutes. The exercise is 95% verbal, with 5% non–verbal being written. Paper and pencils are needed.

Administrative Procedure

a. The facilitator gives a (brief) lecturette on the sensual feelings many of the members have for other members. He stresses the lack of willingness most of us have to reveal and discuss such feelings. He points out that hiding such feelings is really a barrier to real, honest communication. He then explains that the purpose of the Sensuality exercise is to help break down the barriers and to allow the group to disclose their feelings and learn to cope with them.
b. He tells the members to write down who in the group they feel has sensual feelings for them.
c. He then asks the member to go to those members who arouse sensual feelings in them and to express their feelings to the person. The dyads formed are to deal with the feelings and discuss their relationship.

d. Dyads are reformed until each member has had all the opportunities he requires to communicate with members his sensual feelings for them.

Suggestions for Facilitator Process

Concentrate on the following during processing:
a. What were your feelings when you learned what we would be doing? How did you cope with them?
b. What difficulties did you encounter in telling other members you were sensually attracted to them?
c. How did you feel when other members told you they were attracted to you?
d. Did any of your written predictions prove false? Why?
e. What has this sharing experience done for our relationships with each other?
f. How did you handle those situations where your feelings were not sensual and the other person's were?

Variations

None.

SHOUTING AND WHISPERING

Subsidiary Goal(s)

a. To build group unity.
b. To encourage participation.

Group Application

Size is unlimited, but best results occur with groups of ten to fifteen. Applicable to any group, but most effective with encounter, personal growth, marathon and t–groups.

Application Variables

Time depends upon the group size. The shouting and whispering experience will take about one minute per member. The exercise is 100% verbal.

Administrative Procedure

a. The facilitator asks for a volunteer who is willing to have his name shouted and whispered.
b. The entire group circles the volunteer and shouts his name at him five times, each time increasing the shouting level.
c. The group members then whisper the volunteer's name five times, each time decreasing the whispering level.
d. The exercise is repeated until all who wish the experience have had an opportunity.

Suggestions for Facilitator Process

Concentrate on the following during processing:
a. What feelings were present in you while you were being shouted at? What effect did the whispering stage have on you?
b. Which stage pleased you the most? Why?
c. What feelings were present in the shouters and whispers? If you found it easier to shout or whisper at some members than at others, how do you explain this?

Variations

*Variation I

a. Have the members shout and whisper using the following phrase: " (Insert member's name) is (fill in with a personal attribute of the member) ."
b. During processing concentrate on what was said during the shouting and whispering. What the volunteer heard, what attributes were picked and why, etc.

* TABOO BEHAVIOR

Subsidiary Goal(s)

a. To recognize the anxiety created by engaging in taboo behavior.
b. To compare one's feeling reaction to those reactions of other members.
c. To encourage participation and build closeness.
d. To recognize the difference between thinking and feeling.

Group Application

Twelve members or less, although size can be unlimited. If there are more than fifteen members, have dyads or triads formed for showing feeling actions. Applicable to any group. Most frequently used during the early stages of group development for encounter, personal growth, marathon and t–groups.

Application Variables

Fifteen to thirty minutes. The exercise is 100% verbal. Small pocket mirrors are needed for each participant.

Administrative Procedure

a. The facilitator tells the group they will engage in some socially taboo behavior and then share their reactions.
b. He then tells the group: "Yawn. Keep yawning until I tell you to stop."
c. He stops the group after one minute. (We recommend eliciting feeling reactions after each stage, but the facilitator can wait until all four stages have been completed. If he elicits feeling reactions after each stage, he should concentrate on eliciting feelings, not thoughts, on the difference in feelings between members, and on the reasons for the feelings being elicited.)
d. The facilitator then tells the group: "Scratch. Keep scratching until I tell you to stop." After one minute he stops them.
e. He then says: "Cough and clear your throat. Keep doing this until I tell you to stop." After one minute he stops the group.
f. He tells the group: "Take your pocket mirror. Look into it. Comb your hair, touch up your make–up. Carry on a bragging, self–admiring conversation with your mirror image. Continue until I tell you to stop." After two minutes he stops the group.
g. If he has not elicited feeling reactions after each phase, he does so now.

Suggestions for Facilitator Process

Concentrate on the following during processing:

a. What feelings arose from engaging in these taboo behaviors? Why? How did your feelings differ from behavior
to behavior?
b. Which behavior elicited the most anxiety, embarrassment,
etc.? Why?
c. Most of us had different feeling reactions to each task. Why
is this so? How did we cope with these feelings?

Variations

None.

* TELL ME YOUR FEELINGS

Subsidiary Goal(s)

a. To learn the differences between thinking and feeling.
b. To help members become more at ease in disclosing feelings.

Group Application

Twelve members or less. To be used with encounter, personal growth, marathon and t–groups. Most effective when
used early in the life of the group, while members are still
coping with communicating at a feeling level.

Application Variables

Fifteen minutes to one half hour. The exercise is 100%
verbal.

Administrative Procedure

a. The facilitator tells the members to close their eyes and
fantasize that they are in a session where they are the center of a massive confrontation. (We recommend that the
facilitator create a fantasy relevant to his particular group.)
b. Describe the experience, naming people, telling of the

confrontation, etc. Continue for three or four minutes, then stop the group and ask: "Tell me your feelings right now."

c. Members respond to the facilitator's statement. He will note that most members respond by revealing their thoughts, *not* their feelings. When a member does this, the facilitator should stop him and urge that he share his feelings, not his thoughts.

d. The experience can be repeated, using a new fantasy. If it is repeated, note that the group will find it easier to separate thought and feeling and report the latter. After a third repetition, you will seldom find members reporting thoughts.

Suggestions for Facilitator Process

Concentrate on the following during processing:

a. Why did you have difficulty revealing your feelings? Do you find it easier now to differentiate between thinking and feeling? Why?

b. Did you have difficulty fantasizing? If so, why?

c. Why were the particular feelings that were elicited present? For example, why did some feel fear and others anger and others aggression, etc., during the confrontation fantasy?

Variations

Variation I

a. Conduct the first fantasy yourself.

b. Then have a member conduct the second fantasy.

c. Continue until all who wish to conduct a fantasy have had the opportunity.

d. During processing concentrate on the significance of and reasons for the member fantasies.

*WHAT TURNS ME OFF

Subsidiary Goal(s)

a. To develop insight into one's negative reactions.

b. To identify the feelings associated with being "turned off."

c. To self–disclose negative reactions and learn how one copes with them.

Group Application

Twelve members or less. The group should be even, as dyads are used. To be used with encounter, personal growth, marathon and t–groups with adult members who have established strong relationships with one another.

Application Variables

Thirty minutes. The exercise is 100% verbal.

Administrative Procedure

a. The facilitator asks each member to determine what behavior, action, attitude, etc. in other people turns them off the most.

b. He then forms dyads and instructs the members: "Decide which partner will role play your turned off behavior. Tell him what that behavior is. The partners then conduct a ten–minute discussion. During this time, the role player is to make every effort to behave in a manner calculated to turn his partner off. If you hate questions, he will question you to death. If you hate inattention, he will not pay attention to you, etc."

c. After ten minutes, stop the discussion and have the dyads spend five minutes relating their feelings during the experience.

d. Switch so that the other partner role plays and repeat step **b.**

e. After ten minutes stop and repeat step **c.**

Suggestions for Facilitator Process

Concentrate on the following during processing:

a. *To role players:* How did you feel about your actions? Did you find it difficult to engage in behavior you knew would turn your partner off? Why?

  b. *To others:* How did it feel to confront the behavior that turns you off? How did you cope with these feelings?

  c. *To the dyads:* Did you feel a strain in your relationship? If so, why and is it resolved?

Variations

*Variation I

  a. Have a volunteer state what turns him off the most.

  b. The *entire* group then exhibits that behavior toward the volunteer during a five to ten minute discussion.

  c. Process concentrating on the volunteer's reactions, feelings, and coping mechanisms.

  d. Repeat until all who wish the experience have had the opportunity to experience it.

* YOU TURN ME ON – OFF

Subsidiary Goal(s)

  a. To bring to light underlying feelings which may be getting in the way.

  b. To increase awareness of one's feelings of physical stimulation.

  c. To enhance relationships.

Group Application

Twelve members or less. The balance between males and females should be fairly even. To be used with encounter, personal growth, marathon and t–groups with adult members who have had sufficient sessions to have developed sexual feelings among members which may be blocking communication.

Application Variables

One hour. The exercise is 70% verbal and 30% non–verbal. The room must be large enough to allow the members unrestrained movement and privacy.

Administrative Procedure

a. The facilitator asks the group to mill around non–verbally and pair off with the member they are most sexually attracted to.

b. He then asks the dyads to go to a private corner or spot in the room where they feel comfortable.

c. The members are to then share their sexual feeling, fantasies, etc. with their partner in any way they deem appropriate.

d. After half an hour the group is asked to mill around and non–verbally pair off with the person who sexually appeals to them the least.

e. Steps b and c repeated and the group rejoins for discussion.

Suggestions for Facilitator Process

Concentrate on the following during processing:

a. How did you choose your partner? Was it mutual or forced? How did you feel about having to choose one partner?

b. How did you express your sexual feelings? Did you use any physical contact? Why or why not? Did you resolve any problems if there were any to begin with? If so, how?

c. How did your choosing of sexually attractive partners differ from choosing sexually unattractive partners? What did you learn about yourself? What did you learn about your partners?

Variations

*Variation I

a. Repeat initial exercise except have males select other males as their partners.

b. Have females select other females as their partners.

*Variation II

a. Repeat basic exercise except the milling becomes verbal.

b. The members are then limited to non–verbal means in expressing their feelings.

X

GETTING ACQUAINTED

T HE PRIMARY GOAL for each exercise in this chapter is the
facilitation of the getting acquainted process.

Getting acquainted is a necessary phase which all groups
must go through, regardless of whether members have had
past exposure to one another or to the group experience. The
exercises in this chapter are designed to provide a structure
which is conducive to initiating interaction between members in the hopes that they will get to know each other more
rapidly.

Since these exercises will be used, for the most part, in the
first session of the group's development, it is suggested that
the facilitator emphasize the processing stage. This will hopefully give members greater awareness of and insight into
their interactions with one another and into the getting acquainted process.

In many instances the impressions formulated during the
getting acquainted stage last much longer than one might
wish. It is our advice that the facilitator pay special attention to dealing with impressions which may be "getting in
the way" during future interaction among members.

A NAME ISN'T JUST A NAME

Subsidiary Goal(s)

a. To exemplify the dynamics of first impressions.
b. To lay the groundwork for deeper and more meaningful relationships to flourish.

Group Application

Twelve members or less. To be used with encounter, personal growth, marathon and t–groups. Best results are obtained when the exercise is used in the early stage of development.

Application Variables

One hour. The exercise is 80% verbal, with 20% non–verbal being written. Paper and pencils are needed.

Administrative Procedure

a. The facilitator distributes a pencil and twelve slips of paper to each member of the group.
b. He then asks the members to write the name of each member on the top of a slip of paper, one name per slip.
c. Beneath the name, each member is to give every other member including himself a new name, one which he feels is appropriate to his perceptions of that member (*i.e.,* Zeus, Mickey Mouse, Superman, Egg Head, etc.).
d. The slips of paper are collected and given to the appropriate members.
e. One at a time each member reads the name assigned to him and then the name he assigned himself.

Suggestions for Facilitator Process

Concentrate on the following during processing:
a. What meanings did the names assigned to you have? Were you surprised at the names assigned to you? If so, in what way?
b. Did the name you assigned yourself correspond with the

names given to you? What does this say about our perceptions? Were you surprised at the names assigned to other members? If so, why?

Variations

Variation I

a. Repeat steps **a** through **e.**
b. Have members reach a majority decision as to which name from those given, the member is to be called for the rest of the session.
c. Each member then wears a name tag with his "new" name written on it.
d. Members, for the duration of the session, are to address each by their "new" names.

CHERISH

Subsidiary Goal(s)

a. To establish a starting point for meaningful interaction among group members.
b. To gain insight into other members' values.

Group Application

Twelve members or less. To be used with any group in the early stages of development.

Application Variables

Thirty minutes. The exercise is 100% verbal. The room should be large enough to allow members to move unrestrained.

Administrative Procedure

a. The facilitator reads the following three statements:
   (1) I cherish my family.
   (2) I cherish myself.
   (3) I cherish my environment.

b. He then asks each member to decide which of the above statements is the most important to him.

c. The group then divides into three small groups according to which statement they valued the most (all members choosing statement no. 1 group together, statement no. 2 together, etc.)

d. The groups are told to discuss their choices for twenty minutes.

e. After twenty minutes the sub–groups reform and discuss the experience.

Suggestions for Facilitator Process

Concentrate on the following during processing:

a. Was it difficult to decide which of the three statements was the most important to you? If so, why? What did you learn about the other members in your group? What, if anything, did you discover about yourself?

b. Have your impressions changed toward any members in the group because of their choices? If your group was smaller than the others, why do you think this occurred? If larger, why do you think this occurred?

Variations

Variation I

a. After step **d** have each group present their rationale for their decisions to the other two groups.

DYADS AND QUARTETS

Subsidiary Goal(s)

a. To facilitate the getting acquainted process in a large group.

b. To develop relationships between members.

c. To develop listening and feedback skills.

d. To initiate feeling reactions.

e. To note the differences between thinking and feeling.

Group Application

Size is unlimited. The exercise is designed to be used with

large groups of twenty or more members, although it is suitable for smaller groups. It can be used with any group. It is especially effective in groups with adolescent members, for they have some degree of difficulty functioning in a large group setting. The exercise helps relieve some of their anxiety.

Application Variables

Thirty to forty-five minutes. The exercise is 100% verbal. The room must be large enough to accommodate the amount of dyads and quartets on hand.

Administrative Procedure

a. The facilitator breaks the group into dyads. Usually he will allow them to select partners, stressing that they *not* choose someone they already know.

b. He tells the dyads to decide which member will speak first. He tells the speaker to spend five minutes telling his partner about himself. The partner is *only* to listen. He may not reply or ask questions.

c. At the fourth minute, the facilitator says: "You have now spent four minutes telling your partner about yourself. For the last minute, concentrate on sharing your feelings with your partner."

d. After the fifth minute he stops the dyads and tells the listener: "You may now ask questions and communicate with your partner. You will have three minutes for this task."

e. After three minutes, the facilitator stops the dyads, has them change partners, and then repeats steps **b, c,** and **d.**

f. After time is up, the facilitator asks the dyads to choose other dyads they want to get to know, thereby forming quartets.

g. He tells the quartets they have fifteen minutes to get to know each other, giving no other directions.

Suggestions for Facilitator Process

Concentrate on the following during processing:

    a. Was it hard to listen and not be able to respond? Why? Did you remember what your partner told you? If not, why?

    b. Did you share feelings during the fifth minute? What kind of feelings? Point out those responses that indicate thoughts were shared and not feelings.

    c. Was it difficult to talk about yourself for five minutes? Why? How did you cope with these difficulties?

    d. Did the communication differ when you got into quartets? If yes, ask why. Did you share thoughts and facts, or feelings and beliefs?

Variations

None.

GOODIES AND BADDIES

Subsidiary Goal(s)

    a. To learn the positive and negative aspects members perceive in themselves.

    b. To practice self–disclosure.

    c. To develop initial relationships.

Group Application

Twelve members or less. Since dyads are used, the group size should be even. Applicable to any group but most frequently used with encounter, personal growth, marathon and t–groups.

Application Variables

Thirty minutes. The exercise is 90% verbal, with 10% non–verbal being written. Paper and pencils are needed. The room must be large enough to accommodate the amount of dyads on hand.

Administrative Procedure

    a. The facilitator tells the members to write three "good" things and three "bad" things about themselves.

b. When members have finished, the facilitator asks them to turn the page over and write one thing about themselves they seldom reveal to others.

c. Each member then reads to the group his list of "goodies" and "baddies."

d. After each member has read his list, the facilitator says: "Now choose a person you want to get to know better."

e. The dyads are told to spend fifteen minutes getting to know each other better. About the thirteenth minute, the facilitator says: "You have now gotten to know each other a little better. If you feel some trust for your partner, take a chance and reveal the information you wrote on the back of your paper. Do this *only* if you want to."

f. The facilitator stops the exercise after the allotted time and discusses the experience with the group.

Suggestions for Facilitator Process

Concentrate on the following during processing:

a. What did you learn about your partner? What are your feelings toward him? What do you think of him? Why did you choose your partner?

b. Who revealed their back of sheet information? Why? Could you share it with *all* of us? If not, ask why?

c. Did you have difficulty picking "goodies" or "baddies?" Which ones and why?

Variations

None.

* HAPPY AND SAD EXPERIENCES

Subsidiary Goal(s)

a. To encourage self disclosure.
b. To introduce the dynamics of empathy.
c. To begin to build relationships and group cohesion.
d. To start a group off at a deeper level than usual.

---

* Dynamic, more effective exercises are marked with an asterisk.

Group Application

Twelve members or less. The group number should be even, for dyads are used. To be used with encounter, personal growth, marathon and t–groups.

Application Variables

Thirty minutes. The exercise is 100% verbal. The room should be large enough to accommodate the dyads on hand.

Administrative Procedure

a. The facilitator asks each member to introduce himself and reveal his happiest experience to the group.
b. The facilitator tells the members: "Form dyads. Choose a partner whose happiest experience was either very easy to identify with or very difficult to identify with."
c. The dyads are given ten minutes to get to know each other better. They are told to be sure to explore why they selected each other.
d. After ten minutes, the group reconvenes. The facilitator asks each member to again introduce himself and to reveal his saddest experience to the group.
e. The facilitator now tells the group: "Form dyads. Choose a partner whose saddest experience was either very easy to identify with or very difficult to identify with."
f. The dyads have ten minutes to get to know each other better. They are told to be sure to explore why they selected each other.

Suggestions for Facilitator Process

Concentrate on the following during processing:
a. Which of the two dyadic encounters was easiest to enter into, the first or second? Why?
b. What were your reasons for selecting the partners you did? Did anybody pick a person whose experience was very difficult to identify with? Most, if not all, will respond negatively. Ask them why they took the safe, easy way out

and picked a person whose experience they could identify with.

c. Ask the members to share with the group what they learned about their partners.

Variations

Variation I

a. Conduct the exercise as above, but have the members establish the dyads based on whose experience they could most easily identify with.

Variation II

a. Conduct the exercise as above, but have the members establish the dyads based on whose experience they had most difficulty identifying with.

I VALUE

Subsidiary Goal(s)

a. To examine members' beliefs and values.
b. To establish more meaningful relationships.
c. To encourage self–disclosure.

Group Application

Twelve members or less. To be used with any group during the initial stage of development.

Application Variables

Forty-five minutes. The exercise is 100% verbal.

Administrative Procedure

a. The facilitator asks each member, one at a time, to take two or three minutes and describe the things he values the most.

b. During the member's disclosure, there is to be no questioning or comments.

c. If a member needs more time to think about his values, he is to be skipped over until the other members have expressed themselves.

   d. After all members have participated, they may break up into small groups according to their own discretion to further explore each other's values.

   e. After fifteen minutes, the group discusses the experience.

Suggestions for Facilitator Process

Concentrate on the following during processing:

   a. Was it hard to express your values? If so, why? What did you learn about yourself? About other members? How did you deal with the ambiguity of the instructions?

   b. When you broke up into small groups, how did you decide what group to join? Have your feelings changed towards any members? If so, in what way?

Variations

Variation I

   a. Repeat the basic exercise, but have members express what they want.

MEET THE PRESS

Subsidiary Goal(s)

   a. To develop rich and meaningful relationships.

   b. To explore dynamics involved in learning about other members.

   c. To encourage self–disclosure.

   d. To ascertain members' self–concept.

Group Application

Twelve members or less. To be used with encounter, personal growth, marathon and t–groups in the initial stage of development.

Application Variables

Thirty minutes. The exercise is 100% verbal. The room

must be large enough to allow members to move about unrestrained.

Administrative Procedure

a. The facilitator asks members to form dyads with members they do not know well and find a private spot in the room.
b. He informs the members that they are going to conduct interviews. The partners in the dyads are to interview each other one at a time for twenty minutes. Ten minutes are allowed for each person to be interviewed.
c. The facilitator informs the interviewer that he may ask any question he wishes but the interviewee is *not* obligated to answer any question he feels is too personal.
d. After twenty minutes the group reforms and each member introduces his partner to the group, stating anything he feels is of importance.
e. After each member has introduced his partner, the group discusses the experience.

Suggestions for Facilitator Process

Concentrate on the following during processing:

a. How much did you really learn about your partner? Did you ever feel the questions were too personal? Did you exercise your right not to answer? If not, why? Did you learn anything new about yourself?
b. What types of feelings did you have about being interviewed? Do you feel your partner accurately presented you to the group? If not, why? How much did you actually reveal about yourself to your partner? Was it difficult to disclose yourself?

Variations

None.

PLAYING HOUSE

Subsidiary Goal(s)

a. To emphasize the dynamics involved in generalization and first impressions.

b. To explore member perceptions of each other as related to past experiences.

Group Application

Twelve members or less. To be used with any group during the initial stages of development.

Application Variables

One hour. The exercise is 100% verbal. The room should be large enough to allow members to move unrestrained.

Administrative Procedure

a. The facilitator asks a volunteer to "establish a home." The member does this by giving each member including himself a role in his fantasy family (*i.e.*, brother, twin sister, cousin, dog, garbage collector, etc.) .

b. The volunteer is to physically place all members according to the roles. This can be done by placing the father in the middle of a circle, dog next to father, distant cousin furthest away, etc. Rooms may be done in the same manner; see step **d**.

c. The member is to assign roles according to his impressions of how the member chosen relates to his, the assigner's, past perceptions of family.

d. After the family roles have been assigned, the volunteer is told to assign roles according to rooms in the house (bathroom, closet, kitchen, bedroom, etc.) .

e. Each member is given an opportunity to establish his house and family.

f. The group discusses the experience.

g. After discussion, members should have an opportunity to discuss feelings which may have been aroused with individual members.

Suggestions for Facilitator Process

Concentrate on the following during processing:

a. **Did** you have trouble placing certain members? If so, why? What type of feelings and thoughts did you have when other members placed you as they did?

b. Where did you put yourself in relation to the rest of the group? Is this consistent with your self–concept? Do you feel this tells us anything about first impressions? Do you feel any of your feelings have changed toward any members? If so, in what way?

Variations

None.

PROJECTIVE INTRODUCTIONS

Subsidiary Goal(s)

a. To discover the place projection plays in meeting people.
b. To serve as a means for establishing dyadic partners.

Group Application

Twelve members or less. The smaller the number of members, the better. The exercise is very difficult to conduct with more than twelve members. Applicable to any group, but best results are obtained with encounter, personal growth, marathon and t–groups.

Application Variables

One to one and a half hours. The exercise is 100% verbal. The room should be large enough to allow the dyadic partners to interview each other without unduly distracting other dyads.

Administrative Procedure

a. The facilitator asks the group at the first session to choose a member they want to get to know.
b. After dyads have been picked, the facilitator tells them to spend twenty minutes interviewing each other. Each part-

ner will spend ten minutes interviewing the other, then
roles will be switched. The partners are instructed to
remember as much as they can, for they will introduce
their partner to the group.

c. After twenty minutes, the group gets back into a circle.
    The facilitator tells them "You are to introduce your part-
    ner to the group. Stand behind him, with your hands on
    his shoulders, and speak to us as if you were your partner.
    Use the word *I*, not *he*."

d. After all have finished, the group discusses the experience.

Suggestions for Facilitator Process

Concentrate on the following during processing:

a. What did your partner omit in his introduction of you
    that you feel we should know? Why were you pleased or
    displeased with his introduction of you?

b. What factors were responsible for what you remembered
    about your partner? What place did projection play in
    what you remembered and what you forgot?

c. What reasons did you have for picking your partner?

Variations

None.

TALKING TO A BRICK WALL

Subsidiary Goal(s)

a. To illustrate the dynamics involved in inattentive listening.
b. To help facilitate more meaningful relationships.
c. To gain further insight into members' behavior concern-
    ing physical contact.

Group Application

Twelve members or less. To be used with encounter,
personal growth, marathon and t–groups. Best results are
obtained when the exercise is utilized in the early stages
of a group's development.

Application Variables

Thirty minutes. The exercise is 90% verbal, 10% non–verbal. The room should be large enough to allow the members to move around unrestrained.

Administrative Procedure

a. The facilitator asks the group to form dyads.
b. He then gives the following instructions to the dyads: "One of you is to talk to your partner about something important to you. The person listening should not answer and is to react in an unresponsive manner (*i.e.,* looking around the room, moving slowly away)."
c. After five minutes the person doing the listening should become attentive and touch his partner as he is speaking.
d. After five minutes the roles are reversed and steps **b** and **c** are repeated.

Suggestions for Facilitator Process

Concentrate on the following during processing:

a. As you were speaking, what feelings did you have for your partner when he was unresponsive? When he became responsive? What have you learned about the dynamics involved in listening? What did you learn about your partner?
b. When you were listening, what types of feelings did you have for your partner? How did you feel about yourself when you were forced to be unresponsive? When you were asked to be responsive?
c. Did you hesitate about touching your partner? If so, why? How did you feel when being touched? Did it make a difference in what you heard or said?

Variations

None.

* THE GROUP AND I

Subsidiary Goal(s)

a. To encourage participation.

   b. To establish initial relationships.

   c. To introduce self–disclosure.

Group Application

Twelve members or less. Since dyads are used, the group number should be even. To be used with encounter, personal growth, marathon and t–groups.

Application Variables

Thirty minutes. The exercise is 100% verbal. The room must be large enough to accommodate the amount of dyads on hand.

Administrative Procedure

   a. The facilitator has the group form dyads.

   b. He then tells them: "Take turns in responding to each other. I will give you some open–ended statements. You are to communicate using *only* that sentence. The partners listening are not to respond verbally. Any questions? Communicate to your partner by completing the following open-ended statement." (We urge the facilitator to devise statements more appropriate to his group, if he so desires.) "In this group I will. . ."

   c. Have partners' rotate roles after two minutes. Stop the dyadic communication after four minutes.

   d. After four minutes the facilitator says: "Now use *only* the following in your communication: 'In this group I expect others to. . .' "

   e. After four minutes the facilitator tells the dyads to complete the following: "My reactions to what you've told me are. . ."

   f. After four minutes the facilitator says: "Now use the following: 'My feelings for you are. . .' "

   g. After four minutes the facilitator stops the dyads and tells them to take ten minutes getting to know more about each other. They may now ask questions of each other and communicate in the normal, dialogue fashion.

Suggestions for Facilitator Process

Concentrate on the following during processing:
a. Which of the four statements was hardest to respond to? Why?
b. Which was easiest and why?
c. Was it difficult to talk for two minutes using only one statement? Did you overcome these difficulties? How? If not, why not?
d. Was it difficult to listen for two minutes without interacting? Why was this so?
e. Share with us the things you revealed or found out about your partner.

Variations

None.

* UNFOLDING

Subsidiary Goal(s)

a. To provide an initiation into self-disclosure.
b. To set the communication tone at a feeling level.
c. To recognize the differences between thinking and feeling.
d. To begin developing relationships and building rapport.

Group Application

Twelve members or less. To be used at the first meeting of encounter, personal growth, marathon and t–groups.

Application Variables

One to one and a half hours. The exercise is 100% verbal. Each member will use five or six minutes. A stopwatch is needed.

Administrative Procedure

a. The facilitator presents a (brief) lecturette on the need to get to know each other. He stresses that knowing another goes beyond knowing facts about him. Self–disclosure is covered as a means to letting others get to know you.

b. He explains that the session will be spent getting to know one another through an unfolding process. Each member will have five minutes to let others know him. The first three minutes he will introduce and talk about himself. The fourth minute he is to relate what his happiest or saddest life experience has been. The fifth minute he is to share his immediate feelings with the group.

c. The facilitator keeps time. He may wish to start the exercise by introducing himself, talking of himself, sharing his happiest or saddest life experience, and revealing his feelings.

d. All members take a five–minute turn. The facilitator should make sure the fifth minute of each presentation is conducted at a feeling level, not a thinking level.

Suggestions for Facilitator Process

Concentrate on the following during processing:

a. Why did some of us have difficulty in talking about ourselves for three minutes?

b. Did you have difficulty revealing your feelings? How did you cope with them?

c. Who don't you feel you know yet? Why?

d. Who do you feel particularly close to? Why?

Variations

None.

WHAT DID YOU SAY?

Subsidiary Goal(s)

a. To gain awareness of the dynamics involved in expression.

b. To reduce the anxiety associated with meeting new people and situations.

Group Application

Twelve members or less. To be used with encounter, personal growth, marathon and t–groups in the initial stage of development.

Application Variables

Thirty minutes. The exercise is 100% verbal. The room must be large enough to allow members to move about unrestrained.

Administrative Procedure

a. The facilitator asks members to pair off in dyads and find a private spot in the room.
b. He then tells the members to engage in a conversation using only nonsense words or sounds (*i.e.*, oinking, gibberish, grunting, squeaking, etc.) .
c. After five minutes the facilitator asks the member to discuss fear. They are to continue to use nonsense words and sounds.
d. After five minutes the members are told to discuss happiness, again using nonsense words and sounds.
e. After another five minutes the members are told to discuss love, again using nonsense words.
f. The group then reforms and processes the session using nonsense words. This activity is to continue for ten minutes.

Suggestions for Facilitator Process

Concentrate on the following during processing:
a. What types of feelings did you have when using nonsense words? Did these feelings change as the exercise progressed? If so, in what way? What did you learn about your partner? About yourself?
b. Were you able to express the topics you were asked to discuss? If not, why? What does this tell us about the use of words?
c. When processed as a group, did you understand and express feelings to your satisfaction? If not, why do you think

this was so? Did you touch your partner at any time? If not, why?

Variations

None.

WHY I CAME

Subsidiary Goal(s)

a. To encourage participation.
b. To recognize similarities and differences in member expectations.

Group Application

Twelve members or less. Since dyads are used, the group number should be even. To be used with any group.

Application Variables

Thirty minutes. The exercise is 100% verbal. The room must be large enough to accommodate the number of dyads on hand.

Administrative Procedure

a. The facilitator asks each member to respond to the following: "I came to this group because. . ."
b. After each member has responded, the facilitator says: "Determine whose response was most similar to yours. Go to that member, form a dyad, and spend fifteen minutes getting to know each other."
c. After fifteen minutes, the dyads join the original circle. The facilitator tells the members to repeat their *original* answer to "I came to this group because."
d. After each member has responded, the facilitator tells the members to reform dyads based on whose response was most dissimilar from theirs. They again have fifteen minutes to get to know each other.

Suggestions for Facilitator Process

Concentrate on the following during processing:
a. Who was it easier to get to know, people whose reasons for coming were similar or dissimilar to yours? Why?
b. Share with us what you learned about your partners.
c. Who took the initiative in forming the dyads? Why? Why did the others sit and wait?

Variations

None.

XI

ICEBREAKERS

THE PRIMARY GOAL for each exercise in this chapter is development of an environment which is anxiety–reducing and which allows members to "break the ice" by having fun.

The authors have differentiated icebreakers from getting acquainted exercises, although the distinction between the two is very fine. Icebreakers are intended to be tension–reducing rather than providing encounters on a direct interaction basis. Icebreaker exercises should be used with any group that appears to be extremely anxious in the initial stage of development.

The following exercises should not be used to avoid dealing with anxiety but rather to provide a less threatening environment. Many facilitators believe that a non–threatening environment initiated at the early stage of development may make way for more meaningful interaction and relationships during the life of the group. Such facilitators are urged to use icebreakers, for they definitely reduce anxiety.

We suggest that the facilitator review both getting acquainted exercises as well as icebreakers before reaching a decision on specific exercise usage.

A FAVORITE THING

Subsidiary Goal(s)

  a. To facilitate the getting–acquainted process.
  b. To help alleviate first session anxiety.
  c. To encourage participation.

Group Application

Group size is unlimited, but should be such that dyads can be formed. The exercise loses efficiency if the size exceeds twenty members. Applicable to any group.

Application Variables

Thirty to forty-five minutes, depending on the size of the group. The exercise is 100% verbal. The room should be large enough to accommodate the dyads on hand.

Administrative Procedure

  a. The facilitator asks each member to introduce himself to the group and to then tell the group about a "favorite something" from his past (person, activity, relationship, hobby, etc.) .
  b. After each member has finished, dyads are formed. The facilitator tells the members to choose a partner whose "favorite something" you could most easily identify with. He tells them they will have ten minutes to get to know each other better.
  c. After ten minutes the group reconvenes. The facilitator asks each member to again introduce himself and repeat the same statement he originally made about his "favorite something."
  d. Dyads are again formed. The facilitator tells the members to choose a partner whose "favorite something" you find very difficult to identify with. The dyads have ten minutes to get to know each other better.

Suggestions for Facilitator Process

Concentrate on the following during processing:

a. Which dyadic encounter was easiest to enter into, the first or second? Why?
b. What types of favorite things were revealed? Why did you reveal the information you did?
c. Share with us some of the things you got to know about your partner.

Variations

None.

* BINGO

Subsidiary Goal(s)

a. To encourage participation.
b. To facilitate the getting–acquainted process.
c. To encourage self–disclosure.

Group Application

Size is unlimited. The exercise is best used with large groups of twenty or more members. It can be used with any group and is especially suitable for the classroom.

Application Variables

Time is unlimited and depends upon the size of the group. The exercise is 95% verbal, with 5% non–verbal being written. Bingo Sheets, paper, and pencils are needed. Bingo Sheets are designed according to the sample in Diagram II, with the amount of squares corresponding to the number of participants.

Administrative Procedure

a. The facilitator asks each member to write his name on a sheet of paper and then to write any piece of information about himself which he feels makes him *unique* from the other members.
b. He then collects the sheets and *randomly* inserts the names and data on *his own* Bingo Sheet (see Diagram II).

Tom Student Body President	1	Bill Athlete	4		7		10
Sue Groupie	2	Etc.	5		8		11
Ed Freshman	3	Etc.	6		9		12

Diagram II. Sample Facilitator's Bingo Sheet.

    c. He then reads the information statements to the group and they write the data in the appropriate square. *Do not read the names, only the information!*

    d. The facilitator then tells the members: "Take your sheets with you and go from member to member until you can match names with the information you have on your Bingo Sheet. You are to ask *only one* question per member. For example, you would ask me, 'Are you the athlete?' I would say: 'No.' If you receive a 'No,' go to another member. If you receive a 'Yes,' write that member's name in the appropriate square. The first person who fills his sheet brings it to me. If you are right, the exercise is ended and you win. Any questions? Go!"

    e. After someone wins, the facilitator stops the exercise and has each member tell his name and information to the group so every member will have a completed sheet.

Suggestions for Facilitator Process

Concentrate on the following during processing:

    a. Who had the least amount of squares filled? Why?

    b. *To the winner:* What strategy did you use?

    c. What reactions do you have to the exercise? Was it frustrating, fun, etc.?

---

* Dynamic, more effective exercises are marked with an asterisk.

Variations

None.

BLIND INTRODUCTIONS[1]

Subsidiary Goal(s)

a. To help eliminate visual stereotyping.
b. To enhance honest communication between members.

Group Application

Twelve members or less. Can be used with any group, but most frequently used with beginning encounter, personal growth, marathon and t–groups at the first session.

Application Variables

Thirty to forty-five minutes. The exercise is 90% verbal and 10% non–verbal. Blindfolds for every member are needed. A cassette recorder is also needed. The room must be large enough to allow the members to mill comfortably. The facilitator should have an assistant who can run the exercise.

Administrative Procedure

a. As members arrive at the session, the assistant (or the facilitator if no assistant is available) takes them aside and says: "I am going to blindfold you and take you to a seat. Do not talk to anyone until you are told to do so."
b. When all members have arrived, the assistant turns on the cassette recorder. Prerecorded on it, by someone *other* than the facilitator, is the following: "This is an exercise to help us avoid stereotyping each other. Every member, including the facilitator, is blindfolded. Now, get up from your chair and mill around. Try to meet the other members. You may do this by any means you choose, such as talking and touching. You *may not*, however, remove your

---

[1] Adapted from an exercise developed by Mike Willett, Central Michigan University.

blindfold. Try to remember voices, body sizes, hair length, etc. Form mental pictures from the feelings you get from the people you make contact with. When you have met everyone, raise your hand and the assistant (facilitator) will escort you to a seat. Make sure that you have met everyone and that you have formed a mental image of them."

c. After all members are seated, the blindfolds are removed and the group discusses the experience.

Suggestions for Facilitator Process

Concentrate on the following during processing:

a. How did your mental images of each other compare with the real, physical beings you now see? How do you explain the similarities and differences?

b. Did stereotyping play any role in your mental images? Why?

c. Which member (s) did we, as a group, have a consistent mental image for? Why? Whom did we have the least consistent image for? Why?

Variations

Variation I

a. Follow the same procedure, but instead of removing blindfolds, have the members (still blindfolded) pick someone they want to know better and form a dyad.

b. Tell the dyads they have fifteen minutes to get to know each other better.

* GROUP CAROUSEL

Subsidiary Goal(s)

a. To facilitate the getting acquainted process.

b. To recognize the place stereotyping plays in first impressions.

c. To recognize the difference between thinking and feeling.

d. To encourage participation.

Group Application

Twelve members or less. The exercise becomes unwieldly when the group size exceeds fifteen. Applicable to any group, but most frequently used at the first session of encounter, personal growth, marathon and t–groups. A fairly equal distribution by sex is recommended for eliciting data about stereotyping.

Application Variables

Time unlimited, depending on group size. With twelve members the time required would be twenty to thirty minutes. The exercise is 100% verbal.

Administrative Procedure

a. At the first session, *before* any member interaction has occurred, the facilitator tells the group: "We will engage in an icebreaker exercise. Each member will have a turn to be the center of a group carousel. The member remains stationary, facing another member. He tells the member 'I think you. . .and I feel. . .' The outer group then moves to the right until another member is opposite the center member. He repeats the statement, the group carousel will continue until the inner member has made a statement to each member. Then another member goes to the center. We will carousel until every member has been in the middle."

b. The facilitator asks for a volunteer to start the group carousel. The volunteer stands in the middle of the circle and the exercise begins.

c. The facilitator will have to be sure that each member shares a thought *and* feeling with *every* other member.

Suggestions for Facilitator Process

Concentrate on the following during processing:

a. How did you feel when you first stepped into the center? How did you feel as the carousel continued?

b. What did you learn about the effect of stereotyping on your first impressions of others? Did you experience difficulty separating thoughts from feelings? Why?

c. What did we learn about ourselves? Were we seen the same or differently by the inner members? What accounts for the differences between first impressions?

Variations

None.

PROJECTING

Subsidiary Goal(s)

a. To facilitate the getting–acquainted experience.
b. To encourage participation.
c. To initiate the self–disclosure process.

Group Application

Twelve members or less. To be used at the first meeting of encounter, personal growth, marathon and t–groups.

Application Variables

Fifteen to thirty minutes. The exercise is 100% verbal.

Administrative Procedure

a. The facilitator asks *all* members to help break the ice by taking turns in responding to some projective questions.

b. He has the group respond to any or all of the following (we encourage the facilitator to design his own questions) :

1. Who would you want to be if you couldn't be *you?*
2. What animal, food, and inanimate object would you like to be?
3. What is the worst attribute of mankind and why?
4. What is man's best attribute and why?
5. How would you change your life if you could live it over?

c. Each member responds to the questions posed by the facilitator.

Suggestions for Facilitator Process

Concentrate on the following during processing:
a. What effect did our icebreaker have on us?
b. What did you learn about each other? What would you like to know now? Ask that person your question.
c. Whose responses did you identify with most? Why?
d. Which question was the easiest to answer? Why? Which was the most difficult to answer? Why?

Variations

Variation I

a. Describe the exercise and give some examples of projective questions.
b. Then allow the members to ask their own projective questions. As before, all members are to respond, but all do not have to ask questions.
c. In processing, discover why the members asked the questions they did. You will usually find they are high in personal meaning for the asker and are, therefore, really self–disclosing and revealing of member values.

XII

LISTENING

THE PRIMARY GOAL for each exercise in this chapter is to develop and to increase awareness of listening skills.

The ability to listen (as opposed to hear) is essential for any group and its members. Without such skill a breakdown in communication is the inevitable outcome. The following exercises allow members to "check out" their listening skills. They also enhance and deepen member interaction.

It is our suggestion that the facilitator consider using listening exercises periodically throughout the group's life. Such a pattern will enhance each member's listening skills and further communication in the group. The appropriateness of each exercise is easily determined if the facilitator considers the subsidiary goals listed under each specific exercise.

The development of listening skills is a dynamic often overlooked in small groups. Because of this oversight and the fact that accurate listening is a basis for interaction, we suggest that the facilitator pay special attention to the processing stage of each exercise.

EXPERIMENT IN AWARENESS

Subsidiary Goal(s)

    a. To explore the basic concepts in communication.
    b. To allow the experiencing of member creativity.
    c. To explore word usage.

Group Application

Twelve members or less. To be used with any group. Best results are obtained if the exercise is used during the initial stage of the group's development.

Application Variables

Thirty minutes. The exercise is 100% verbal. The room must be large enough to allow dyads to work without undue distractions from other dyads.

Administrative Procedure

    a. The facilitator asks members to mill around verbally and pair off into dyads.
    b. The facilitator then makes the following statement. "Each member in the dyads is to inform his partner of his feeling for him/her. The only stipulation is that only the pronouns 'I' and 'you' may be used by either member."
    c. The facilitator may want to make suggestions as to the use of voice fluctuation, body language and other levels of communication which may be utilized.
    d. After fifteen minutes the dyads are to reform into the larger group and share what they have learned. Again, the only words that may be used are "I" and "you".
    e. After every member has had an opportunity to share his experiences, the facilitator initiates processing.

Suggestions for Facilitator Process

Concentrate on the following during processing:
    a. What did you hear your partner saying? Was it accurate?

Was what you were saying interpreted correctly? How did
you communicate? What have you learned from your
partner?

b. How did you feel when you were sharing your experiences with the rest of the group? What have you learned
about the use of words? What have you learned about
yourself?

Variations

None.

I HEARD YOU SAYING

Subsidiary Goal(s)

a. To further understand the complexity and difficulties involved in communication.
b. To gain awareness of our perceptions of other members
and their awareness of us.
c. To encourage the feedback process.

Group Application

Twelve members or less. To be used with any group. Best
results are obtained if the exercise is used early in the
group's development.

Application Variables

Thirty minutes. The exercise is 100% verbal. The room
must be large enough to allow members to move about
unrestrained.

Administrative Procedure

a. The facilitator selects a controversial issue appropriate to
stimulating interaction between group members (*i.e.,*
women's rights, abortion, drugs, premarital sex).
b. He then asks that two volunteers who have opposing opin-
ions on the issues enter the middle of the circle.

c. The facilitator informs the two volunteers that the only rule they must follow is: "Before either of you may respond to the other, the listener must state to the other's satisfaction what the speaker has just been telling him before any reply is allowed."

d. While the group is observing, the two members discuss the controversial issue.

e. The group members are to act as monitors and may intervene if they feel the rule in step c has been violated.

f. After fifteen minutes the group is to divide into two subgroups (one volunteer is in the first one, and the other volunteer in the second group). The subgroups are to give feedback appropriate to the specific volunteer in their group.

g. After fifteen minutes, the group discusses the experience.

Suggestions for Facilitator Process

Concentrate on the following during processing:

a. *To the volunteers:* What have you learned about your listening skills? What type of feedback did you receive from your subgroup? Do you feel the feedback was accurate? If not, why? How do you feel about the other volunteer?

b. *To the other group members:* Can you relate with the interaction that took place between the volunteer and yourself? Can you relate this exercise to other examples of group behavior?

Variations

None.

*LEARN TO LISTEN

Subsidiary Goal(s)

a. To get better acquainted.

b. To provide an opportunity for self–disclosure.

c. To make feelings the center of communication.

---

* Dynamic, more effective exercises are marked with an asterisk.

   d. To look at the decision–making process.

   e. To provide feedback to the group.

Group Application

Twelve members or less. Applicable to any group, but most frequently used with encounter, personal growth, marathon and t–groups. Can be very effective when used early in the life of the group in pointing out the differences between hearing and listening.

Application Variables

Time is unlimited. Each participant will use from five to ten minutes. The exercise is 100% verbal.

Administrative Procedure

   a. The facilitator asks each member to relate to the group the experience from past sessions which aroused the strongest feelings in him. Do not define "strongest feelings."

   b. After each presentation, members may ask questions for clarification purposes, but they are not to discuss the experience.

   c. After each member has responded, the facilitator asks the group to decide which experience should be investigated further.

   d. The member who is chosen is to amplify on his original statements. Members interacting with him are to first check with him that they heard him right and understood what he said. For example, the members should say, "I heard you say . . . and I think that means. . ." before *any other* interaction is allowed.

   e. The discussion continues until it is clear that everyone has heard and understood the member's experience.

   f. The exercise is continued until all members who wish the opportunity to elaborate on their experience have had a chance to do so.

Suggestions for Facilitator Process

Concentrate on the following during processing:

a. How did we decide whose experience we would listen to first? For example, by majority or minority consensus, volunteering, etc.?
b. What did you learn about your listening skills? Was it easier to listen (as opposed to hear) as the exercise progressed? If so, why?
c. *To members recounting experiences:* Did you feel any of us were consistently mishearing you? Who? How did their reaction to your experience make you feel?

Variations

Variation I
a. Conduct the exercise as above, but have members recount an experience in the group which created positive feelings.
Variation II
a. Conduct the exercise as above, but have members recount an experience in the group which created negative feelings.

WHITE LIES

Subsidiary Goal(s)

a. To gain insight into the dynamics involved in deception.
b. To explore member attitudes toward lying.
c. To help develop listening skills.

Group Application

Twelve members or less. To be used with encounter, personal growth, marathon and t–groups.

Application Variables

Forty-five minutes to one hour. The exercise is 90% verbal, with 10% non–verbal being written. Pencils and paper are needed.

Administrative Procedure

a. The facilitator asks for three to five volunteers (depending on the size of the group) to report a set of three childhood incidents.

b. The volunteers are told to relate a set of incidents in which all are true, or all are fictional, or a set in which two are fictional and one is true, or two are true and one is fictional.

c. The facilitator informs the volunteers that the incidents may be reported in whatever manner they deem most effective in misleading the group, as to which incidents are true and which are false.

d. The facilitator asks the group to listen carefully to the first volunteer's three episodes and then to write down their judgment as to which incidents actually occurred and which are false.

e. The volunteer then discloses which incidents, if any, were true. Each member should make note of the number of times he/she was misled.

f. The foregoing procedure is repeated for each volunteer.

g. The facilitator now asks each member to disclose the amount of times he/she was misled.

h. The group discusses the experience.

Suggestions for Facilitator Process

Concentrate on the following during processing:

a. *To the volunteers:* Did you feel any conflict between the truth and fantasy? How did you feel about being required to deceive the rest of the group? What type of strategy did you adopt? What assumptions about the group were your strategies based upon?

b. *To the rest of the group:* How did you feel about the situations in which you were deceived? Did some volunteers mislead you more than others? If so, why? What do you feel the choice of real or invented incidents reflected about the volunteers?

Variations

Variation I

a. The facilitator may ask all members to write out three incidents in the same manner as described in step **b** of the original exercise.

b. The recorded incidents are then read to the entire group while each member judges the authenticity of the statement.

XIII

PERCEPTION

THE PRIMARY GOAL for each exercise in this chapter is to allow members the opportunity to investigate their methods of perceiving other individuals and objects. It is hoped that members will learn to improve their mental, emotional, and physical perceptive abilities.

Most members enter a group with pre–conceived perceptions about groups, people, life, inanimate objects, and so forth. The exercises in this chapter are designed to allow members to become aware of their pre–conceived perceptions and to experience the fact and fiction of such perceptions.

One of the goals for human relations training groups is to increase the perceptive abilities of the members. The exercises in this chapter help in the attainment of this goal. Since considerable learning can be gained by engaging in these exercises, the facilitator is again urged to emphasize the processing stage so that such learning will occur.

* BECOMING CLOSE

Subsidiary Goal(s)

a. To give members insight into spatial relations.
b. To gain a sense of "group" opposed to "oneness."

Group Application

Twelve members or less. To be used with encounter, personal growth, marathon and t–groups. Is best utilized during the initial stages of a group's development.

Application Variables

Thirty minutes. The exercise is 60% verbal and 40% non–verbal. The room must be large enough to allow members adequate freedom of movement.

Administrative Procedure

a. The facilitator asks the group to form a circle by standing up and holding hands.
b. He tells the members to concentrate on their feelings about the circle.
c. He then asks the members to widen the circle. They are to stretch the perimeter *without* breaking it.
d. The group is then told to shrink the circle. They are to become as close as possible, but circular form is to be maintained.
e. The facilitator then tells the group to move the circle in any direction or shape they please, indicating why they are doing so.
f. Individuals may now leave the circle if they wish and go in the center or outside the circle, indicating why they are doing so.
g. After the group stops from its own volition, the group discusses the experience.

---

* Dynamic, more effective exercises are marked with an asterisk.

Suggestions for Facilitator Process

Concentrate on the following during processing:
a. How did you feel about the circle? Did your feelings change as the circle changed?
b. Did you lead or follow in forming the circle's perimeter? Was there stress, tension, etc.?
c. *To those who left the circle:* Why did you leave? Did you perceive the circle differently from the outside? The inside?
d. *To those who remained in the circle:* Did you resent those members who left? Did your perception of the circle change? Why did you stay?
e. After the circle broke up, how did you feel? Do you feel closer to other members and the group? If so, why? If not, why not?

Variations

Variation I
a. Conduct the exercise as above, but add the following instructions to stage f (under Administrative Procedure): "You may now leave the circle if you wish. You may go inside or outside it. You may also ask others to leave the circle."
b. During processing, concentrate on the reasons for some members asking others to leave the circle or go inside it.

* FIRST PERCEPTIONS AND EXPECTATIONS

Subsidiary Goal(s)
a. To discover and compare a member's perceptions of the group, the facilitator, and himself.
b. To help overcome false perceptions and expectations.
c. To encourage participation.
d. To facilitate the getting–acquainted process.

Group Application

Twelve members or less. Applicable to any group, but

most frequently used at the first session of beginning encounter, personal growth, marathon and t–groups.

Application Variables

Time is not limited. Each participant will use from five to ten minutes. Paper and pencils are needed.

Administrative Procedure

a. The facilitator asks each member to write a brief but inclusive reaction to *one* of the following statements:
   1. My perceptions of my role in this group are. . .and I expect to. . .
   2. My perceptions of the other members are. . .and I expect them to. . .
   3. My perceptions of the facilitator are. . .and I expect him to. . .
b. After all members have finished writing, the facilitator asks those who responded to statement one to raise their hands. Each of these members reads his paper and the members react to it, indicating where they agree or disagree with his perceptions and expectations.
c. Members who wrote a reaction to statement two read their papers. Members again react, indicating where they agree and disagree.
d. Members who wrote a reaction to statement three read their paper. Member reactions follow as before.
e. If no members wrote on a particular statement, the facilitator asks the group to write a one–sentence paragraph based on the statement in question. Reading of the sentences and reactions is then conducted.

Suggestions for Facilitator Process

Concentrate on the following during processing:
a. Why did you write on the statement you did? (We find that seldom do members write about statement two and almost never on statement three. The dynamics behind this reveal a large amount of data for discussion.)

b. Which of our perceptions and expectations were different from those of other members? Why? Whose were more "right" or accurate? Why?
c. Whose perceptions and expectations did you find it easiest to identify with? Why? Whose did you find it difficult to identify with? Why?

Variations

Variation I
a. Designate which statement you want responses to.
b. Conduct the exercise as above, but get verbal reactions to the two omitted statements.

GROUP MEMORY

Subsidiary Goal(s)
a. To explore the dynamics of first impressions.
b. To enrich and deepen interpersonal relationships.
c. To facilitate the closure process.

Group Application

Twelve members or less. To be used with any group. The exercise should be used in the next to the last or last group session.

Application Variables

One hour. The exercise is 80% verbal, with 20% non-verbal being written. Paper and pencils are needed.

Administrative Procedure

a. The facilitator passes around paper and pencils to all members.
b. He then asks each member to write his first memory of every other member of the group.
c. The members are to read, one by one, their first memories of another member to the group. Along with the first

memory, the member is to express how he now views this particular member.
d. The facilitator initiates discussion after all members have read their first memories.

Suggestions for Facilitator Process

Concentrate on the following during processing:
a. Was it difficult for any of you to recall *your* first memory of any of the members? If so, why? Why was it easy for you to recall your memories of certain members?
b. Were you surprised at some of the first memories other members shared about you? How important do you feel first memories are?

Variations

None.

HUMAN NATURE

Subsidiary Goal(s)

a. To become aware of your feelings about other members' basic beliefs.
b. To gain insight into individual values.
c. To further and deepen member interaction and understanding.

Group Application

Twelve members or less. Applicable with any group but most frequently used in the early sessions of encounter, personal growth, marathon and t–groups.

Application Variables

Forty-five minutes. The exercise is 100% verbal.

Administrative Procedure

a. The facilitator asks members in the group to discuss the

basic origin of man. Members should be encouraged to make statements rather than ask questions. The facilitator may also wish to make a general statement that there are no "right" or "wrong" beliefs.

b. After fifteen minutes the facilitator asks members to look around the group and summarize each member's position on the origin of man to the rest of the group.

c. The facilitator now asks members to state the basic origin of themselves rather than the origin of man. If members ask for clarification, the question may be rephrased to "What is the basis for your being?"

d. After twenty minutes the group rejoins for discussion.

Suggestions for Facilitator Process

Concentrate on the following during processing:

a. Have your perceptions changed toward any members? If so, which member (s) and why? Were you surprised at any of the beliefs expressed? How much did you feel you disclosed about yourself during the first part of the exercise?

b. Did you really invest yourself in sharing what you felt your basis for being was? What have you learned about other members' perceptions of themselves? Of yourself? Have any of your feelings changed toward any member (s) ?

Variations

None.

I AM A ROCK

Subsidiary Goal(s)

a. To help members relate more easily with an object or a person.

b. To gain insight into each member's thought process.

Group Application

Twelve members or less. To be used with encounter, personal growth, marathon and t–groups.

Application Variables

One hour. The exercise is 100% verbal. Various common objects are needed such as a chair, a pencil, a radio, etc.

Administrative Procedure

a. The facilitator places one object in the center of the circle.
b. He then asks the members to project themselves into the obect and, one at a time, express their feelings.
c. *No other* directions are given. Leaving the instructions somewhat ambiguous should allow for the greatest creativity and variation.
d. After each member has had an opportunity to project himself into the first object, a second object is placed into the circle and step **b** is repeated.
e. After three objects have been placed in the circle, the facilitator asks for a volunteer to become an object in the middle of the circle. The volunteer tells the group what object he is, and step **b** is repeated.
f. The exercise continues until all members who wish to volunteer have had the opportunity to do so.

Suggestions for Facilitator Process

Concentrate on the following during processing:
a. Were you able to project yourself and become the object in the center? If so, how did you accomplish this? If not, what stopped you?
b. Did you find some objects easier to relate to than others? If so, which ones and why? What did you learn about yourself from this exercise? What did you learn about the other members in the group?
c. Was relating to a person different from identifying with an object? If so, in what way? How did you deal with the ambiguity of the exercise?
d. *To volunteers:* Why did you choose to be the object you were? Did you feel we reacted to you as person or as object?

Variations

None.

SEE SAW

Subsidiary Goal(s)

a. To explore hidden agendas.
b. To gain insight into self–concept.
c. To further expand and deepen member relationships.

Group Application

Group size is unlimited, but the most successful experiences will occur with twelve members or less. Applicable with modification to any group; however, it is suggested that the exercise be used most frequently in the latter stage of encounter, personal growth, marathon and t–groups.

Application Variables

Forty minutes. The exercise is 100% verbal. The room should be large enough to allow dyads to interact undisturbed.

Administrative Procedure

a. The facilitator may wish to give a brief talk on perception and its importance to the group.
b. He then asks members to pair off into dyads, joining any member he/she has some unfinished business with.
c. The dyads are to find some private space in the room. The facilitator then gives the following instructions: "I would like you to discuss any unfinished agendas or undisclosed feelings you may have with your partner. The only restriction is that you make only statements (no questions) beginning with the words 'I see' or 'I saw.' This applies to both members, whether responding or being responded to."
d. After twenty minutes the facilitator asks members to form new dyads and step c is repeated.
e. After twenty minutes the group reforms for discussion.

Suggestions for Facilitator Process

Concentrate on the following during processing:

a. What did you learn about your partner's perceptions of you? Were you surprised at any of the statements made? Did your dyad begin most sentences with "I see" or "I saw"? If not, why did you stray from the directions?

b. What have you learned about your own perceptions? Have they changed? If so, in what way? Do you still feel you have any unfinished business with any other members? If so, with whom?

Variations

None.

SENSING STRANGERS

Subsidiary Goal(s)

a. To gain awareness into one's stereotyping behavior.
b. To examine the cues which members receive, process and formulate impressions on.
c. To explore the dynamics involved in receiving feedback.

Group Application

Twelve members or less. To be used with encounter, personal growth, marathon and t–groups. Best results are obtained if the exercise is used early in the group's development.

Application Variables

One hour. The exercise is 100% verbal. The room should be large enough to allow members to move unrestrained. Paper and pencils are needed. A guest for each member is to be brought in.

Administrative Procedure

a. Before the session, the facilitator is to arrange to bring one guest for every member (ten members—ten guests, etc.) .

b. When the session starts, the members are blind–folded (before the guests are brought in).

c. After the members are blind–folded, they are to be led to separate sections of the room.

d. The facilitator brings the guests into the room and places one guest in front of every member.

e. The members are then instructed to interview the guests without asking personal questions (*e.g.,* what is your occupation, are you married, do you like to travel?).

f. After two minutes the interviewing is to stop and the member is to describe the guest according to his feelings (*e.g.,* sensitivity, security, realness, depth).

g. The guest then rates the accuracy of the member's description on a one–to–ten scale accordingly. This is to be written down.

h. The guest now moves to another member. Steps **e** through **g** are repeated.

i. After all guests have been with all members, the group reforms and the rating sheets are distributed to the appropriate members.

j. Discussion now follows.

Suggestions for Facilitator Process

Concentrate on the following during processing:

a. *To members with high ratings:* Why do you think you were so accurate? What type of "cues" were you receiving? What do you feel this says about your perceptive ability?

b. *To members with low ratings:* If your ratings were low, what do you feel went wrong? What types of "cues" were you zeroing in on? What have you learned about yourself through this exercise?

c. *To all members:* What do you feel the exercise shows us about the way we perceive each other? The way we perceive strangers?

Variations

None.

STRIVE FOR ATTENTION

Subsidiary Goal(s)

a. To deal with feelings of success in getting attention.
b. To deal with feelings of failure in getting attention.

Group Application

Any group of any size so that quartets can be formed. Very dynamic when used with members who engage in attention–seeking behaviors.

Application Variables

Twenty minutes. The exercise is 100% verbal. The room must be large enough to seat quartets far enough away from each other so that noise from other groups does not negate the experience.

Administrative Procedure

a. The facilitator divides the members into groups of four. Drop the observer role if there is an uneven number of members.
b. Place three chairs close together with one chair outside for use by the observer.
c. The quartets are told to select one observer from their quartet and one Hot Chair occupant.
d. The facilitator tells the remaining quartet members: "Both of you are to try to get the undivided attention of the person in the Hot Chair. Ignore each other. Do not communicate in any way with each other. All your communication is to be directed at the person in the Hot Chair. You want to get him to pay attention solely to you."
e. He tells the observer to (1) enforce the rules given in the facilitator's instructions; and (2) observe the interaction which occurs. He should concentrate on what the members do in gaining attention, what verbal and non–verbal feelings they emit, how the attention seekers react to each

other and how they react to success or failure in getting
the attention of the Hot Chair occupant.

f. After four minutes, have the quartets change roles and
repeat the exercise.

g. Continue until all have had a chance to seek attention, observe, and sit in the Hot Chair.

Suggestions for Facilitator Process

Concentrate on the following during processing:

a. How did you feel during each role stage?

b. What frustrations were met? How did you cope with
these?

c. What attention seeking behaviors and maneuvers did you
try?

d. *To Hot Chair members:* What did you pay attention to
and why?

Variations

Variation I

a. Have individuals in the Hot Chair ignore both attention
seekers. *Do not* tell the attention seekers he is deliberately
ignoring them.

b. Process their feelings about failure in getting the Hot Chair
member's attention.

VIEWPOINT

Subsidiary Goal(s)

a. To explore the dynamics involved in empathy.

b. To explore new roles and members' reactions to them.

Group Application

Twelve members or less. To be used with any group. Best
results are obtained if the exercise is used in the early stage
of group development.

Application Variables

Forty-five minutes. The exercise is 100% verbal. The room

should be large enough to allow members to move unrestrained.

Administrative Procedure

a. The facilitator describes a scene that is familiar to all members in the group (student union, downtown, local park, etc.) .

b. He then asks each member to assign himself a role that can appear in this scene (*e.g.,* bird, mailman, receptionist, four-year old child) .

c. Each member is to inform the group of the role he is assuming.

d. The facilitator then asks each member to actively participate in his role. (The member should act out his chosen role according to his perception of it.)

e. After fifteen minutes the members discuss their perception of their roles and of the scene they participated in.

Suggestions for Facilitator Process

Concentrate on the following during processing:

a. Why did you choose the role you did? Did you act out your role with consistency or did you fluctuate? Did you see the activity in the scene differently than you normally would have? If so, in what way?

b. What have you learned about perception? What have you learned in the group? About yourself? Can you relate this experience to our perception in the group?

c. Did you join with others or perform by yourself? If you joined with others, why? If you performed alone, why?

Variations

None.

XIV

PROBLEM SOLVING

T HE PRIMARY GOAL for each exercise in this chapter is to create a problem solving situation, thereby allowing members insight into the behavior which occurs in such situations. They, therefore, have the opportunity to recognize how they and their fellow members react in a problem solving situation.

Although any group can benefit from exposure to a problem solving situation, such exercises are especially appropriate for use with t–groups and task oriented, problem solving groups.

A number of group dynamics are exposed and investigated through the use of such exercises (*e.g.*, feedback, assessment, awareness of member roles, etc.). Therefore, we suggest that the facilitator thoroughly familiarize himself with the processing stage for any problem solving exercise before he uses it. This suggestion is based on our belief that extensive processing is needed for accurate assimilation and learning by the members.

Since problem solving exercises are task oriented, it is essential that the proper procedures be taken in the presentation of the exercises (*i.e.*, materials needed, time required, room size, etc.).

The facilitator is urged to make alternations to these exercises in accordance with the needs of his group.

CREATE A PROBLEM

Subsidiary Goal(s)

a. To encourage participation.
b. To investigate the roles members assume in problem solving situations.
c. To recognize the dynamics operating in a competitive situation.

Group Application

Group size is unlimited, although most effectively used with groups of twenty-five or less. Applicable to any group.

Application Variables

Time is unlimited, although most exercises will run thirty to forty-five minutes. Any materials required are to be furnished by the "problem creators." The room must be large enough to allow the competing sub–groups to work without undue interference from each other.

Administrative Procedure

a. At the end of the session *prior* to the use of this exercise, the facilitator asks for three volunteers who are willing to develop a problem solving situation.
b. He tells the volunteers: "Come to the group next session with a problem solving task. That is, create a problem or task which sub–groups can *competitively* attempt to re-solve. Bring any materials that are needed. Be sure to supply a prize or reward for the winning sub–groups." (No other instructions are to be given).
c. At the beginning of the next session, the facilitator tells the volunteers: "The problem solving exercise is yours to run. Do it!"
d. After the volunteers have finished, the facilitator has the group discuss the experience.

Suggestions for Facilitator Process

Concentrate on the following during processing:

a. *To the problem creators:* What difficulties did you encounter in resolving your task? Why did you choose the problem you gave us? How did it feel to "run" the group?

b. *To other members:* Did you understand the problem? If not, why not? What feelings were present in your sub–groups as they tried to resolve the problem and win the competition? What feelings do you have for the winning sub–group members?

Variations

None.

FUMBLE TOGETHER

Subsidiary Goal(s)

a. To gain insight into dealing with ambiguity.
b. To develop problem solving skills.
c. To gain insight into member roles.

Group Application

Twelve members or less. To be used with any group. Best results are obtained if the exercise is used early in the group's development.

Application Variables

Forty-five minutes. The exercise is 80% verbal and 20% non–verbal. The room should be large enough to allow members to form separate groups of four comfortably.

Administrative Procedure

a. The facilitator asks members to mill around and non–verbally pair off into groups of four.
b. Each group is instructed to go to a separate corner of the room.
c. The facilitator tells all the quartets they will have thirty minutes to complete a task. After this time, they will be evaluated by the rest of the group.

d. He then tells the quartets that their task is to become a group. No other instructions are to be given.

e. After thirty minutes, groups one at a time present their completed task to the rest of the group for evaluation.

f. The group discusses the experience.

Suggestions for Facilitator Process

Concentrate on the following during processing:

a. How did you deal with the ambiguity of the exercise? What types of roles did members assume in the group? Did you ever feel ignored? If so, why?

b. Did the fact that the task was going to be evaluated influence your group's behavior? Do you feel you successfully completed the task? If not, why?

c. On what basis did you evaluate other groups' tasks? Did you consult with other quartets in handling your task? If not, why?

Variations

Variation I

a. Assign each quartet a different task (*e.g.,* become a group, make yourself known, become real, love each other).

b. Repeat basic exercise structure.

GATHERINGS

Subsidiary Goal(s)

a. To explore the dynamics involved in social gatherings.

b. To gain awareness of one's perceptive abilities.

Group Application

Twelve members or less. To be used with any group. Best results are obtained if the exercise is used early in the group's development.

Application Variables

One hour. The exercise is 60% verbal, with 40% non–verbal being written.

Administrative Procedure

a. The facilitator asks members to observe a social gathering before the next session. The member may observe a group of people at a bar, church gathering, football game or any other function which hosts several people. The member is to take notes on the types of behavior he sees occurring as well as the dynamics involved in specific interactions.

b. At the next session, the facilitator asks the members to report and discuss their observations.

c. Volunteers are asked to role play the most common types of observations.

d. The group discusses the experience.

Suggestions for Facilitator Process

Concentrate on the following during processing:

a. When observing the gatherings how did it feel not to be actively involved? How did the social gathering behavior you observed differ from the behavior in our group?

b. What type of behavior did you observe? Did you see yourself participating in the same way you usually would? In what ways has this group changed your perceptions, if at all? When role playing did acting come naturally or was it forced?

Variations

None.

SURVIVAL OF THE FITTEST

Subsidiary Goal(s)

a. To gain awareness of other members' self–concepts.

b. To explore members' perceptions.

c. To help members give and receive feedback.

Group Application

Twelve members or less. To be used with encounter, personal growth, marathon and t–groups.

Application Variables

Forty-five minutes. The exercise is 100% verbal. It is suggested that the facilitator be prepared to handle any intense emotional feelings which may arise from the exercise.

Administrative Procedure

a. The facilitator asks the group to fantasize that they are stranded on a desert island and in order to survive four members must be eliminated from the group.

b. He also informs the group that majority vote is allowed and failure to eliminate four members results in the destruction of all due to shortages of food and water.

c. Each member is to, one at a time, go around the group and offer a rationale for his continued existence.

d. After all members have participated, the group is given thirty minutes to make their selections.

e. The only stipulation is that no member may make a self–sacrifice under any condition.

f. After thirty minutes group re–assembles for discussion.

Suggestions for Facilitator Process

Concentrate on the following during processing:

a. *To those not surviving:* How do you feel about the decision made by the group for you not to survive? Have your feelings changed toward any members? If so, in what way? What have you learned about other members' values? About your own?

b. *To those surviving:* What are your feelings about those members who were chosen not to survive? Did you agree with all selections made? If not, why? What criterion did you use when choosing members not to survive? How do you feel at this moment?

c. *To all:* What have we learned about difficult choices? Does this exercise tell you anything about your behavior outside the group? How do you feel about the feedback you received during the course of the exercise?

Variations

None.

USE YOUR HEAD

Subsidiary Goal(s)

a. To further personal expression and creation.
b. To reveal personal agendas.
c. To encourage participation.
d. To recognize how one copes with ambiguity.

Group Application

Twelve members or less. To be used with encounter, personal growth, marathon and t–groups whose members are familiar with the structures and purposes of exercises.

Application Variables

One hour. The exercise is 60% verbal, with 40% non–verbal being written. Paper and pencils are needed.

Administrative Procedure

a. The facilitator tells each member to create an exercise which the group can utilize and which is appropriate to the group at this point in time.
b. The exercise is to be written. The facilitator is *not* to give specifics. Twenty minutes is alloted for this task.
c. After approximately twenty minutes the facilitator stops the written section of the exercise.
d. The facilitator asks that each member read his exercise.
e. After the descriptions are read, the reasons for the directions and/or goals are discussed.

Suggestions for Facilitator Process

Concentrate on the following during processing:
a. Why did you direct the goal of the exercise the way you

did? How much consideration did you give to your personal needs as opposed to the group's needs?

b. Was it hard or difficult for you to create your own exercise? Why? Why not?

c. Do we have similar or dissimilar goals? How do you explain the similarities and dissimilarities?

d. Did you look for direction in creating the exercise? How did you deal with the ambiguity?

Variations

Variation I

a. Divide the group into triads or quartets.

b. Have the sub–groups develop an exercise. Give them thirty minutes.

c. Process, concentrating on the differences between sub–group exercises, the reasons for choosing the particular exercise goals, and the consensus difficulties encountered.

Variation II

a. Have the entire group develop the exercise. They should be allowed forty-five minutes for this task.

XV

REJECTION

T HE PRIMARY GOAL for each exercise in this chapter is to expose the group and its members to the dynamics involved in rejecting and being rejected.

Rejection exercises are quite stressful. However, they are frequently used to help members deal with the concept of rejection. The appropriateness of the use of such exercises is totally contingent upon the facilitator's discretion. He should have reason for exposing the group and its members to a rejection experience.

The rejection concept is a difficult dynamic to deal with for group members. Because of this, many facilitators overlook the use of the rejection experience. Yet, rejection in life is a reality, and members should learn how to cope with it.

We believe rejection exercises can often lead to increased self–awareness, deeper interpersonal relationships, and greater insight into the coping behavior of oneself and of fellow members.

Because of the stress placed on individuals involved in a rejection exercise, the facilitator is asked to pay particular attention to the processing stage.

*BLIND ALLEY

Subsidiary Goal(s)

 a. To examine the dynamics involved in cruelty and one's re-action to it.
 b. To gain insight into one's empathic ability.

Group Application

Twelve members or less. To be used with encounter, personal growth, marathon and t–groups. Best results are obtained when the exercise is used in the earlier stage of group development.

Application Variables

Fifteen minutes. The exercise is 60% verbal and 40% non–verbal. The room should be large enough to allow members to move about unrestrained.

Administrative Procedure

 a. The facilitator asks the group to stand in a circle.
 b. He then asks for a volunteer to enter the middle of the circle.
 c. The facilitator now gives the following instructions: "The volunteer is to stand in the middle of the circle, close his eyes and fantasize that he is blind. In order to simulate the feelings of rejection, the members in the circle are to tease, taunt, insult and physically reject the blind person. The volunteer will be moving around the circle while this is being done."
 d. After five minutes the group is told: "Now try to get a feel for what the inner member is going through and feeling. Help him in any way you feel is appropriate."
 e. After five minutes, the group discusses the experience.

Suggestions for Facilitator Process

Concentrate on the following during processing:

---

* Dynamic, more effective exercises are marked with an asterisk.

a. *To the member in the center of the circle:* What type of feeling did you have toward the members in the circle? Did your feelings change as time went on? What were your feelings toward yourself? Did you convey these feelings to the group? What have you learned about rejection?

b. *To the members in the circle:* What did you learn about your reactions to giving rejection? Did your feelings change during the fifteen–minute period? If so, in what way? What did you learn about the other members of the group? What did you learn about the person in the middle? What have you learned about yourself? Were you able to empathize with the "blind" member? How did you help him?

Variations

None.

DO YOU WANT TO COME?

Subsidiary Goal(s)

a. To explore the dynamics involved in risk behavior.
b. To examine the effect stereotyping has on one's behavior.

Group Application

Twelve members or less. To be used with encounter, personal growth, marathon and t–groups in the initial stage of development. The balance between male and female members should be fairly even. Best results are obtained when the exercise is used with a group whose members are hesitant to risk or take a chance.

Application Variables

Fifteen minutes. The exercise is 50% verbal and 50% non–verbal. The room should be large enough to allow the members to move about unrestrained.

Administrative Procedure

a. The facilitator asks the female members to line up on one side of the room and the male members to line up on the other side of the room.

b. He then gives the following instructions: "The female members are to, one at a time, go across the room and non–verbally ask a male member to join them back in their line. The male member being asked to come may accept or reject the invitation, but again this must be done non-verbally. If the male member rejects the female member, she must go back to her line alone. If he accepts, both go back together. In either case, as I said before, this is done one at a time."

c. After the female members have participated, the roles are reversed and the male members now do the inviting, re-peating step **b.**

d. After the male members have finished, the group discusses the experience.

Suggestions for Facilitator Process

Concentrate on the following during processing:

a. What feeling did you have when inviting another member to join you? How did it feel when you were accepted? When you were rejected? How did you invite the other member non-verbally?

b. Were you afraid not to accept a member's invitation? If so, why? If you were not invited by anyone, how did this make you feel? In what ways did you answer your invita-tions non–verbally?

c. What have you learned about roles (women inviting men)? What have you learned about other members? About your-self?

Variations

None.

GET OUT

Subsidiary Goal(s)

a. To gain awareness of the dynamics involved in competi-tion.

b. To develop meaningful relationships through member confrontation and group consensus.

Group Application

Twelve members or less. To be used with encounter, personal growth, marathon and t–groups. Caution should be applied if exercise is used too early in the group's development. Best results are obtained if the group has held enough sessions to develop a supportive, but honest rapport.

Application Variables

Thirty minutes. The exercise is 80% verbal and 20% non–verbal. The room should contain ample floor space to allow for unrestrained movement.

Administrative Procedure

a. The facilitator asks the group to mill around non–verbally and form triads.
b. The triads are to go to separate corners and discuss meaningful feelings they have about themselves and each other.
c. After ten minutes the facilitator tells the triads they have five minutes to reach a consensus and form dyads (one member is to be eliminated).
d. The members who have been rejected may form new dyads with other rejects, or try and convince an already established dyad to reject one member so he may take his place.
e. After fifteen minutes all members must be in dyads (no triads are accepted).
f. The group discusses the experience.

Suggestions for Facilitator Process

Concentrate on the following during processing:
a. *To the members rejected:* What type of feelings did you have when you were rejected? How did you feel about the

members rejecting you? How did you form your dyad? Did you feel a great deal of competition in staying in a dyad? After you were first rejected did you try to break up any already established dyads? If so, what happened?

b. *To the members who were not rejected:* Was it difficult to reach a consensus on which member to originally reject? How did you feel when you finally did reject one of your partners? If other rejects tried to break up your dyad, how did you handle it? Did you ever feel safe from being rejected? If so, when?

Variations

None.

*GROUP REJECTION

Subsidiary Goal(s)

a. To recognize how one copes with rejection from other members.
b. To recognize the feelings created by rejection.

Group Application

Twelve members or less. To be used only with encounter, personal growth, marathon and t–groups after considerable rapport has been developed.

Application Variables

Five minutes. The exercise is 100% verbal.

Administrative Procedure

a. Prior to the group session, the facilitator tells four members about the exercise and asks that they help him (we advise choosing outgoing, dynamic, respected individuals).
b. The facilitator, after the session has started, says, "I need some volunteers to engage in an exercise today. (Here name the four "informed" students) have volunteered already. Any other volunteers?"

c. The four "informed" members now dominate the group, rejecting all other volunteers. They should be close–minded, unfair, etc. to other volunteering members.
d. After five minutes, the facilitator says, "You have just experienced a 'rigged' exercise dealing with rejection. (Name the 'informed' students) were helping me."
e. A discussion of the experience is held.

Suggestions for Facilitator Process

Concentrate on the following during processing:
a. *To rejected members:* Did you feel rejected? How did you cope with that feeling? What other feelings did you have toward me, the "informed" members, and the rest of the group?
b. *To the "informed" members:* What feelings did *you* have?
c. What have we learned about how it feels to reject and be rejected? What did we learn about how we cope with rejecting and being rejected?

Variations

None.

*LEAVE THE GROUP

Subsidiary Goal(s)

a. To explore the dynamics involved in dealing with a member who is difficult to reach.
b. To gain awareness of member perceptions.

Group Application

Twelve members or less. To be used with encounter, personal growth, marathon and t–groups which are having difficulty communicating with one specific member. This exercise should not be used until other attempts to reach a member have been fully explored.

Application Variables

Thirty minutes. The exercise is 100% verbal.

Administrative Procedure

a. The facilitator tells the group to decide which member they have the greatest difficulty communicating with.

b. After arriving at a consensus, the member is asked to leave the room for fifteen minutes. The facilitator says: "We seem to have a difficult time talking to you. Give us fifteen minutes to talk among us about you and where you are with us."

c. The group is to discuss the member while he is gone.

d. When the member returns, the group is not to talk about what they have discussed during the last fifteen minutes.

e. The group discusses the experience.

f. After discussion, the group is to form a circle with the member who was asked to leave on the inside. The group is to then move in and give him a group hug.

Suggestions for Facilitator Process

Concentrate on the following during processing:

a. *To the member who was asked to leave:* What are your feelings? Were you surprised that you were chosen to leave? What did you think about during the fifteen minutes you were gone? Have your feelings changed towards the group? Towards any specific members? What is your reaction to the group hug?

b. *To the rest of the members:* Was it hard arriving at a consensus? Have any of your feelings changed towards the member who was asked to leave? What do you feel was the purpose of the exercise? Were you afraid at any time you might be asked to leave? If so, why?

Variations

*Variation I

a. *Anytime* the facilitator becomes aware of the fact that a member is resisting communication, he may stop the group discussion and initiate the exercise as above, starting with the statement in step **b.**

* REJECTION

Subsidiary Goal(s)

a. To recognize how one copes with an authority figure.
b. To self–disclose negative self–concept perceptions.
c. To recognize how one copes with acceptance or rejection.
d. To provide feedback.

Group Application

Twelve members or less. To be used only with encounter, personal growth, marathon and t–groups.

Application Variables

Ten to fifteen minutes. The exercise is 50% verbal, with 50% non–verbal being written. Paper and pencils are needed.

Administrative Procedure

a. The facilitator says that he needs two members to help him conduct a very serious exercise in the group.
b. The facilitator surveys the group and chooses two members whose hands are *not raised*. (If all volunteer, choose two members who, you are sure, do not expect to be picked).
c. Take the two volunteers aside and conduct a brief discussion with them about why they volunteered and how they feel about being picked by you. Tell the other members, "While we are discussing the exercise, write down your predictions as to why I did not pick you to help me."
d. After seven to ten minutes, the facilitator and volunteers rejoin the group. The facilitator tells the group they have just experienced an exercise dealing with acceptance and rejection. He asks for reactions.
e. After member reactions have been dealt with, the facilitator asks each member to read his paper about why he felt he would not be chosen.
f. A discussion of the written data and the entire experience is held.

Suggestions for Facilitator Process

Concentrate on the following during processing:

   a. How did you feel about not being chosen? How do you feel now?

   b. Let's assume your written statements are indicative of some of your negative self–concept perceptions. Do any of the other members disagree with them? Which ones and why?

   c. *To the two you accepted:* Share with the group the feelings you had when I accepted you.

   d. *To others:* How did you cope with your feeling of rejection? Why did you use that particular coping mechanism? Did it work? If not, why?

Variations

None.

YES, I ACCEPT YOU

Subsidiary Goal(s)

   a. To establish more meaningful relationships.
   b. To gain insight into the dynamics involved in acceptance.
   c. To recognize how one copes with rejection.

Group Application

Twelve members or less. To be used with encounter, personal growth, marathon and t–groups that have a member or members who feel they have been rejected. Best results are obtained if the exercise is used only after direct interaction has been utilized without effect. The exercise is not to be used as a "cure" for dealing with feelings of rejection but rather as a supplement.

Application Variables

Ten minutes. The exercise is 50% verbal and 50% non–verbal.

Administrative Procedure

   a. The facilitator asks the member who feels rejected to go to each member and ask if he will accept him.

b. The members are to respond in any manner they feel appropriate. (If a member answers "yes" he should be encouraged to hug the member).
c. The member who feels rejected should now ask the group as a whole if they will accept him.
d. After the group has answered, the members discuss the experience.

Suggestions for Facilitator Process

Concentrate on the following during processing:
a. *To the member(s) who felt rejected:* Have your feelings changed? If so, in what way? Towards what members? What have you learned about acceptance? About rejection?
b. *To the rest of the members in the group:* Was it hard to accept the member(s)? If so, why? Have your feelings changed towards any members in the group? If so, in what way? What have you learned about acceptance?

Variations

None.

XVI

RESENTMENT

THE PRIMARY GOAL for each exercise in this chapter is the identification and exploration of feelings of resentment.

It is the authors' belief that, in many instances, feelings of resentment are frequently present in the group situation. Many facilitators overlook or inadequately deal with them. "Gunnysacking" resentment often leads to a breakdown in communication between individuals and among the group. The following exercises have been designed to avoid such gunnysacking situations and to provide a structure which is conducive to dealing with feelings of resentment in a positive manner.

Although feelings of resentment are often considered adversive, it is our belief that a great deal of value can be received by all members if resentments are dealt with competently.

It is recommended that the following exercises not be used in lieu of confrontations, for we believe that the best method of dealing with resentment is without structure. The structured experiences should be used *only* after it becomes evident that spontaneous confrontations are being avoided.

Because in many situations, dealing with resentment tends to intensify emotional states, it is advised that the facilitator pay very close attention to the processing stage of the specific exercise being utilized, so that members will not leave the session with negative feelings and reactions.

BEEF BOX

Subsidiary Goal(s)

a. To gain an understanding of the dynamics involved in confrontation.
b. To remove barriers which may be getting in the way of establishing deeper, more meaningful relationships.
c. To give and receive feedback.

Group Application

Twelve members or less. To be used with encounter, personal growth, marathon and t–groups in the latter stages of development.

Application Variables

One hour. The exercise is 100% verbal.

Administrative Procedure

a. The facilitator asks for a volunteer to enter the middle of the circle.
b. He then instructs the volunteer to select any group member he feels resentments toward. The member selected enters the middle of the circle.
c. The facilitator then instructs the two members in the center of the circle to take turns in verbalizing their resentments about each other. The only rule they must follow is that they cannot deal with the here and now, but only the past.
d. The rest of the group members are told to observe the interaction.
e. After the two members in the circle have expressed their feelings, the observers give them feedback about their interaction.
f. After all members wishing to participate have had the opportunity, the group discusses the experience.

Suggestions for Facilitator Process

Concentrate on the following during processing:

a. *To members who participated:* Were you hesitant about volunteering? If so, why? Was it difficult dealing only in the past? Did you listen to the other person? What did you learn about yourself? About your partner? Have your feelings changed? If so, in what way?

b. *To the group members observing:* What dynamics did you see going on in the center of the circle? Could you identify with what was being said? What type of body language was taking place? Did you see the interaction as constructive or destructive? Why do you feel it was constructive? Why do you feel it was destructive?

Variations

None.

* BLASPHEMIES

Subsidiary Goal(s)

a. To "clear the air" between members who may be harboring hidden hostilities.

b. To give members an opportunity to confront themselves and others.

Group Application

Twelve members or less. To be used with encounter, personal growth, marathon and t–groups whose members have had ample sessions to establish meaningful relationships.

Application Variables

Fifteen to thirty minutes. The exercise is 100% verbal.

---

* Dynamic, more effective exercises are marked with an asterisk.

The room must be large enough to allow members to move about unrestrained.

Administrative Procedure

    a. The facilitator asks the group to stand up in a circle.

    b. He then makes the following statement: "We are now going to try to 'clear the air' among ourselves by dealing with underlying resentments. Each member is to make blasphemous statements toward any member of the group (*i.e.*, you're a son of a bitch, I can't stand you, you make me sick, etc.). There should be no interaction except for the verbalization of your statements."

    c. Standing still, the members are to begin all at the same time. They are to maintain eye contact with the members they are addressing.

    d. The facilitator should encourage yelling, shouting, and screaming. If silence occurs he is to act as a catalyst.

    e. When it becomes obvious that all resentments have been "aired," the facilitator stops the exercise and leads a discussion of the experience.

    f. After discussion, members still feeling resentments toward one another should sub–group and attempt to deal with them.

Suggestions for Facilitator Process

Concentrate on the following during processing:

    a. Did you express your feelings? If not, why? Did the tone of your voice stay the same? If so, why? Do you feel you relieved resentments which may have been building up? If not, why not?

    b. Did you look the member you were speaking to directly in the eyes? If not, why not? What type of useful feedback did you receive? What type of feedback did you give? What type of differences did you find between making statements rather than interacting?

    c. Have your feelings changed toward any one in the group? If so, in what way?

Variations

Variation I

a. Instead of directing blasphemies toward other members, have the members direct the statements toward themselves.

* I RESENT

Subsidiary Goal(s)

a. To facilitate communication.
b. To give and receive feedback.
c. To help members stop gunnysacking.

Group Application

Twelve members or less. To be used with encounter, personal growth, marathon and t–groups whose members have developed rapport, care and warmth with each other. Since negative feedback is elicited, the facilitator should process diligently to insure that the involved members do not leave the session with negative reactions and feelings.

Application Variables

Fifteen to thirty minutes. The exercise is 100% verbal.

Administrative Procedure

a. Whenever the facilitator notices that two or more members are experiencing great difficulty in communicating with each other, he says: "I have noticed that you (name the members) are not communicating well with each other. I have a hunch that you are gunnysacking your resentments for each other. Sit in the middle of the group, facing each other, and communicate with each other. However, you may only use the statement 'I resent.' Continue until you have exhausted yourself of your resentments for the other person."
b. After the members involved have completed the exercise, they are urged to discuss their feelings and reactions to

each other. Other members should be willing to give feedback to the members concerning the accuracy of the "I resent" statements.

Suggestions for Facilitator Process

Concentrate on the following during processing:

a. *To the members involved:* How do you feel now about the member(s) you were resenting? How did you feel being in the center of the group? How have your thoughts and perceptions about yourself and the member(s) you resented changed?

b. *To observers:* How did you feel as the involved members were resenting each other? What feedback can you give them about their behavior?

Variations

*Variation I

a. When the facilitator notes that one (or more) member seems to be unwilling to communicate with the group, he says: "I notice that you (name the member) seem to be unwilling to communicate with us. I have a hunch you're gunnysacking resentments toward us. Tell them to us, using only the statement 'I resent'."

b. After the member has finished, any members who have resentments for him are urged to share them. Again, only the statement "I resent" may be used.

e. After all resentments have been expressed, the group discusses the experience. The facilitator should have them concentrate on their feelings for each other, any perceptual changes which have taken place, and what insights have been gained.

* RESENTMENT

Subsidiary Goal(s)

a. To release hidden anxieties.

b. To gain insight into individual blocking and defense mechanisms.

Group Application

Twelve members or less. To be used with encounter, personal growth, marathon and t–groups. The exercise is most effective in groups whose members have established caring, supportive environments.

Application Variables

Forty-five minutes to one hour. The exercise is 60% verbal and 40% non–verbal.

Administrative Procedure

a. The facilitator makes the following statement: "We all have resentments. Many of us have been carrying around these feelings for most of our lives. We are going to try to face these feelings and deal with them 'head on.' "
b. He then asks each member to find a private spot in the room.
c. After this is done the facilitator asks each member to close his eyes and imagine someone who he is harboring resentments for (i.e., mother, brother, other group member, friend, etc.) .
d. After giving each member ten minutes to think about his person, he instructs members to do the following: "The person you have been thinking about is now beneath your feet. Let that person know exactly how you feel (*i.e.*, kick, stomp, jump, etc.) ."
e. After fifteen minutes the facilitator asks the members to now talk to "their" person.
f. After five minutes repeat step **d**.
g. After ten minutes repeat step **e**.
h. The facilitator stops the group after five minutes have elapsed and leads a discussion of the experience.

Suggestions for Facilitator Process

Concentrate on the following during processing:

a. Who did you pick and why? Were you actually able to have a resentful fantasy about this person? If not, why?

b. What did you do to the person beneath your feet? What did you say to him afterwards? Did your feelings change about the person?

c. Did you express your resentments? What did you learn about yourself and about the person beneath your feet?

Variations

*Variation I

a. Conduct the exercise as above except during phase **c**, the facilitator says, "Close your eyes and think of someone in this group you are harboring resentments for."

* SHOVE IT

Subsidiary Goal(s)

a. To increase skills in listening when being confronted.

b. To gain insight into one's reaction to aggressive behavior.

Group Application

Twelve members or less. To be used with encounter, personal growth, marathon and t–groups. The exercise is most effective in dealing with underlying resentment when other forms of communication have failed.

Application Variables

Thirty minutes. The exercise is 100% verbal.

Administrative Procedure

a. The facilitator asks for a volunteer who feels an underlying resentment for another member in the group.

b. If the other member is willing, the two participants come to the center of the group.

c. The facilitator gives the following instructions: (1) *To the member feeling the resentment:* "You are to verbalize all your feelings about the member you chose and then assign him to complete a task you feel appropriate to his actions *i.e.,* scrubbing toilet stools, cleaning out animal cages, doing the dishes, etc.).*"* (2) *To the member receiving the resentment:* "You are not to interrupt. You must say 'thank you' after the other member assigns you your task."

d. After step c is completed, the two members reverse roles and step c is repeated.

e. The two members then rejoin the group and the facilitator asks for more volunteers to enter the circle.

f. Steps c and d are repeated.

g. After all members have had an opportunity to voice resentment the group discusses the experience.

Suggestions for Facilitator Process

Concentrate on the following during processing:

a. *To the members expressing hostility:* Have your feelings changed towards the member you were feeling your resentment towards? If so, in what way and how? How did you decide what type of task to assign the other member? When roles were reversed what did you learn about the other member's feelings about you?

b. *To the members receiving resentment:* Were you surprised that the member expressing resentment chose you? How did you feel about having to say thank you to the other member? When roles were reversed how did you decide on what task to assign? Were you harsher or more lenient in your task than your partner? Why? Did your feelings change about the member?

c. *To all other members who were observing:* What types of changes did you see going on when roles were reversed? Was body language congruent with what was being said?

Did you perceive both members listening to each other? Did you personally agree with the task assigned each member as representing their past actions? If not, why?

Variations

None.

XVII

ROLES

THE PRIMARY GOAL for each exercise in this chapter is the examination and exploration of member feelings and beliefs about roles and stereotypes.

The distinction between member role and member identity is a fine one. For some facilitators, the use of the word "role" denotes dishonesty, whereas member identity denotes honesty. The following exercises are not intended to make value judgments on member behaviors. Instead, the exercises help members explore the meaning of their role and stereotyping behavior and its relationship to the group.

Awareness of role and stereotyping is essential for most groups, for role expectations and stereotyping are frequently barriers to real, honest, genuine communication. Through the recognition of specific role behavior, members may gain greater insight into their own behavior and self-concept, and communication in the group will be facilitated.

In some of the following exercises, members are asked to exaggerate both their own role behavior and their perception of other members' roles. Therefore, the processing stage in each of the following exercises is essential to interpretation and integration of the insights developed about role and stereotyping behavior.

* BE EACH OTHER

Subsidiary Goal(s)

a. To provide feedback to a member.
b. To increase empathic understanding.

Group Application

Twelve members or less. To be used with encounter, personal growth, marathon and t–groups with adult members who have developed rapport and insight into each other.

Application Variables

Time is unlimited, although most exercises will last five to fifteen minutes. The exercise is 100% verbal.

Administrative Procedure

a. When the facilitator notes that two members are having a very difficult time communicating, understanding each other, or seeing each other's point of view, he tells them to form a dyad in the center of the circle.
b. He says: "Carry on your original conversation, but be each other. Respond as if you *are* the other person."
c. He tells the observers: "Whenever you perceive one of the dyadic members is not being the other person, but has reverted to himself, say 'Stop! You're being yourself. Be the other person.' "
d. After it appears that the dyadic partners have reached a point of agreement and have begun to understand each other's viewpoint, the facilitator stops the dyad.

Suggestions for Facilitator Process

Concentrate on the following during processing:
a. Can you now see where the other person was coming from? Why? Did you have difficulty being him? Why? Do you

---

* Dynamic, more effective exercises are marked with an asterisk.

feel the other person did a good job being you? If not, why not?

b. *To observers:* Did the dyadic partners accurately represent and play the other person? If not, where were they off? What behavior did you see them engaging in? What feedback can you give them?

Variations

Variation I

a. Have all members form into dyads and be each other.
b. During processing, concentrate on the accuracy or inaccuracy of portrayals, the feelings created by trying to be another person, the effect of the exercise on the relationship, etc.

GOING THROUGH CHANGES

Subsidiary Goal(s)

a. To develop listening skills.
b. To gain deeper insight into one's self–concept.
c. To experience a variety of roles.
d. To encourage self–disclosure.

Group Application

Twelve members or less. To be used with encounter, personal growth, marathon and t–groups. Best results are obtained if the exercise is used early in the group's development.

Application Variable

Forty-five minutes. The exercise is 100% verbal. The room should be large enough for the group to divide comfortably into separate triads.

Administrative Procedure

a. The facilitator asks members to form triads.

b. He tells the members they will be working in three different roles. Each triad is to assign roles among themselves as (1) presenter: a member who will discuss interpersonal changes he is going through; (2) consultant: a member who will discuss the topic with the presenter; and (3) observer: who will be listening to the discussion and make comments concerning the dynamics of the interaction after the discussion.

c. After ten minutes of discussion between the presenter and consultant, the observer is to make comments concerning the interaction.

d. Members are now to switch roles, again discussing interpersonal changes. Repeat step **c.**

e. Members now exchange roles for the last time, again repeating step **c.**

f. The group discusses the experience.

Suggestions for Facilitator Process

Concentrate on the following during processing:

a. *To the presenters:* Did you feel you were being listened to? If not, why? How much did you actually disclose about yourself? Were you surprised at the observer's comments? If so, why?

b. *To the consultants:* Did you feel you were acting in the constructive capacity? Did the observer confirm this? If not, why do you feel there was a discrepancy? Did you feel distant or close to the presenter?

c. *To the observers:* What type of dynamics did you observe taking place? How do you feel the interaction could be more constructive? What types of feelings did you have about your role?

Variations

None.

* HELP ME WITH MY GHOST

Subsidiary Goal(s)

a. To overcome inter–member communication problems.

b. To help a member recognize how past experiences interfere with current relationships.

c. To remove barriers between members.

Group Application

Twelve members or less. To be used only with encounter, personal growth, marathon and t–groups.

Application Variables

Time unlimited, depending upon the needs of the participants involved. The exercise is 100% verbal.

Administrative Procedure

a. The facilitator will frequently find that a member is failing to interact or has biased interactions with another member because "he reminds me of a person in my past who did such and such to me." When this is seen by the facilitator, he tells the two members, "Form a dyad in the center of the circle."

b. He tells the member who has past experiences interfering with his relationship and communication (member A) : "Tell this member everything you can about this person from your past."

c. He tells the partner (member B) : "Listen carefully. In the ensuing confrontation, try to *be* the person who is being described."

d. He then says to member A: "Confront (member B) as if he were the other person. If he is not responding as the other person would, tell him so and he will adjust his reaction. Get it all out, until you feel you've vented all your anger, frustration, pain, etc."

e. When it becomes apparent that member A has finished his confrontation with his ghost from the past, the facilitator stops the dyad and says: "Now, repeat your problem, but you, member B, react as yourself."

f. When it becomes apparent that the dyad has exhausted communication, the facilitator stops the interaction.

Suggestions for Facilitator Process

Concentrate on the following during processing:

a. *To member A:* Do you still react to member B because he reminds you of a past ghost? If no, why? If yes, why? Do you feel you've drained the past from interfering with your relationship with member B? Can you now recognize the falseness of your original interactions with him? What feelings do you now have toward member B?

b. *To member B:* What feelings do you now have for member A? Are they different than those you had about him when you entered the dyad? If yes, why? If no, why?

c. *To observers:* What feedback can you give the two participants?

Variations

None.

I WISH I WERE

Subsidiary Goal(s)

a. To explore the dynamics involved in member perceptions.
b. To become better aware of member expectations.
c. To give and receive feedback.

Group Application

Twelve members or less. To be used with encounter, personal growth, marathon and t–groups. Best results are obtained if exercise is used in the early stage of development.

Application Variables

Forty-five minutes. The exercise is 80% verbal, with 20% non–verbal being written. Paper and pencils are needed.

Administrative Procedure

a. The facilitator asks each member to write a description of the type of person they would like to become.

b. The member to the left of the facilitator is to read his description. The other members are to give feedback on the member's description according to whether or not they feel he already possesses any of his descriptive qualities.

c. Step **b** is repeated until all members have given their description and received feedback.

d. The group discusses the experience.

Suggestions for Facilitator Process

Concentrate on the following during processing:

a. Did you agree with the feedback the members gave you? If not, why? What did your description tell you about your own expectations? Do you feel they were realistic? If not, why?

b. What have you learned about other members in the group? Do you feel most feedback given was constructive or destructive? Have your feelings changed toward any members in the group? If so, in what way?

Variations

Variation I

a. Repeat steps **a** through **c** as above (under Administrative Procedure).

b. Have members break up into small groups according to the similarity of descriptions and discuss possible reasons for this.

MONKEY SEE, MONKEY DO

Subsidiary Goal(s)

a. To gain awareness into members' imitative behavior.

b. To give and receive feedback on members' physical behavior and to explore its meaning.

Group Application

Twelve members or less. To be used with any group that has had ample sessions to allow members to form cohesive impressions of each other.

Application Variables

Thirty minutes. The exercise is 60% verbal and 40% non–verbal. The room should be large enough to allow members unrestrained movement.

Administrative Procedure

a. The facilitator asks members to mill around and form dyads.
b. He then tells the dyads to find a private spot in the room.
c. The facilitator gives the following instructions: "To become aware of our physical behavior I would like you to copy your partner's behavior. Discuss anything you like. While your partner is talking I want you to copy his mannerisms, voice inflections, facial expressions, etc. After fifteen minutes I would like you to reverse roles and give the other person in your dyad an opportunity to become imitated."
d. After step c has been completed, the group discusses the experience.

Suggestions for Facilitator Process

Concentrate on the following during processing:
a. *To the members being imitated:* Did your partner accurately display your own behavior? If not, why? How did you feel when being imitated? What did you learn about your own behavior?
b. *To the members imitating:* Was it difficult for you to display your partner's behavior? If so, why? Did you feel yourself taking on the characteristics of your partner? If so, how did it feel? Do you feel you learned anything about your partner's behavior? If so, what?

Variations

Variation I

a. Have a volunteer enter the middle of the circle.

b. As he talks to the group, have all members answer while using imitative behavior.

c. Give all members an opportunity to participate.

PETER PAN

Subsidiary Goal(s)

a. To explore members' self–perceptions.

b. To gain awareness into the dynamics involved in sensing physical "cues."

Group Application

Twelve members or less. To be used with encounter, personal growth, marathon and t–groups. Best results are obtained if the exercise is used in the initial stage of group development.

Application Variables

One hour. The exercise is 60% verbal and 40% non–verbal. Members are required to create their own costume before coming to the group.

Administrative Procedure

a. The facilitator asks each member to create a costume and wear it to the next session. The costume should exaggerate what the member feels he is. For example, a member wearing a Peter Pan outfit may be representing feelings of being able to support, help and guide other members, etc.

b. At the beginning of the next session, the members are to mill around for fifteen minutes non–verbally exploring each other's new facade.

c. After this time each member is to act out his costume role and explain why he chose it.

d. Members now divide into small groups according to their perceptions of costumes that are in contrast with their own, and discuss possible reasons for this difference in contrast.

e. After thirty minutes the group discusses the experience.

Suggestions for Facilitator Process

Concentrate on the following during processing:

a. Did wearing a costume change your perceptions of yourself? If so, in what way? Did it change your perceptions of other members? If so, in what way?

b. How did you feel as you explained your costume to other members of the group? When other members explained their costumes to you, did you perceive their descriptions as being accurate? If not, why?

c. When you broke up into small groups did you learn anything new about the members whose costumes were in contrast to yours? If so, what did you learn? What have you learned about yourself?

Variations

None.

* TAKE IT OFF

Subsidiary Goal(s)

a. To gain insight into defense mechanisms.

b. To establish more open channels of communication between members.

c. To give and receive feedback.

Group Application

Twelve members or less. To be used with encounter, personal growth, marathon and t–groups which have had ample sessions to have established a supportive group environment.

Application Variables

One hour and thirty minutes. The exercise is 90% verbal,

with 10% non–verbal being written. Paper and pencils are needed.

Administrative Procedure

a. The facilitator asks each member to list one role for every group member including the member himself on a separate slip of paper. The roles assigned should be indicative of that member's behavior as the participant assigning the role perceives it (*i.e.*, Mr. Stud, Mr. Goody Two Shoes, Mr. Know It All, etc.).

b. The facilitator collects the slips of paper and gives them to the appropriate member. (If twelve members are in the group, each participant should have twelve slips of paper stating his role.)

c. The facilitator asks a volunteer to enter the middle of the circle and act out three roles from the twelve he received which he feels are most appropriate to his behavior.

d. The group is told to interact with the member in the center and explore each role and how it relates to the group.

e. During the interaction the member in the center should answer all questions according to the role assigned to him and is *not* allowed to switch roles until he has informed the group.

f. After the first member has explored three roles, another volunteer is asked for. This procedure continues until all members have had an opportunity to participate.

Suggestions for Facilitator Process

Concentrate on the following during processing:

a. Did the roles you received correspond to the roles you assigned yourself? Why or why not? Were you surprised at the roles assigned to you? If so, why?

b. How did you decide which roles to act out? What did you learn from the interaction that took place during your roles? Were you hesitant about volunteering? If so, why?

c. What did you learn about other member's roles from this exercise? Did you feel that the other members were sincere in acting out their roles? Has your perception changed about yourself or any other member in the group? If so, in what way?

Variations

*Variation I

a. Repeat steps **a** and **b**.
b. Have members choose one role they feel most appropriate and interact as a group rather than having a member enter the circle. This means that all members would be acting out their roles at the same time.
c. After thirty minutes have members act out another role as a group.
d. Process the exercise, concentrating on the change in communication resulting from role playing, the accuracy of role portrayal, the reasons members chose the role they acted out, etc.

* WOMEN'S LIB

Subsidiary Goal(s)

a. To recognize the place stereotyping plays in our interactions with members of the opposite sex.
b. To increase empathic ability.
c. To increase communication skills.

Group Application

Twenty members or less, although most effective with twelve or less. The group number should be even and have an equal amount of men and women, for man–woman dyads are used. Applicable to any group, but most frequently used with beginning encounter, personal growth, marathon and t–groups. The exercise can be especially effective when used in the classroom situation.

Application Variables

> Thirty minutes. The exercise is 100% verbal. The room should be large enough to accommodate the number of dyads on hand.

Administrative Procedure

a. The facilitator has the male members line up on one wall, the female members on the opposite wall.
b. The facilitator tells the females: "Choose a male to be your partner. Go across the room, indicate your partner, and sit together somewhere in the room."
c. When all dyads have been formed, the facilitator tells them to take ten minutes getting to know each other better. He tells them to at least explore the feelings they had about choosing and being chosen.
d. After ten minutes all the dyads reconvene. Three chairs are placed in the center of the circle. A dyad is asked to volunteer to discuss Women's Lib in the center.
e. The dyad in the center is told: "Discuss Women's Lib, but be each other. The male member is to respond as if he were the female and vice versa."
f. The facilitator tells the group: "The third chair is the 'input' chair. If you want to make input to the dyadic discussion, sit in the chair and share your input. However, you too are to be a member of your opposite sex. Male members making input are to be females and vice versa. You are to give your input and *immediately* depart. you are *not* allowed to enter into the dyadic discussion."
g. After ten minutes, the facilitator stops the dyadic encounter and has the dyad continue the discussion being themselves, not the other person. The input chair is to be used by members who are also to be themselves.

Suggestions for Facilitator Process

Concentrate on the following during processing:
a. What feelings did you have about choosing and being chosen? What were the reasons for your choices?

b. *To female members:* How did it feel to be the aggressor? Did you have difficulty being a male? Why?

c. *To male members:* How did it feel to be in a woman's place and role? Did you have difficulty being a woman? Why?

d. *To all:* Were the role reversal reactions accurate? If not, why not? What have we learned about the accuracy of our knowledge of the opposite sex? What stereotypes were evident in our role reversal interactions?

e. What differences did you perceive in the relationship and interaction when members were allowed to be themselves? How do you explain these differences?

Variations

*Variation I

a. In your initial instructions to the female members, say: "Choose a male to be your partner. Go across the room, indicate your partner, and find a seat together somewhere in the room. However, do the choosing as if you were a man picking a woman. Walk as you think a man would. Talk as he would. Pick a male partner as if *he* were the female and *you* were the male."

b. Process this phase of the exercise, concentrating on male and female reactions and feelings, the stereotyping evident in the female's actions, the feelings in the males of seeing their behavior imitated, etc.

c. Continue the rest of the exercise as above.

*Variation II

a. When used with groups whose members have developed considerable insight into each other, have the members be the other person. That is, the males are to interact as if they were their female partner *specifically* rather than interacting as if they were any female.

XVIII

SELF-CONCEPT

THE PRIMARY GOAL for each exercise in this chapter is to facilitate the exploration and identification of each member's self-concept.

Awareness of one's self–concept is essential for the individual member and disclosure of one's self-concept is essential for the group as a whole. The appropriateness of self-concept exercises is contingent upon the development of the group rather than the group type, although suggestions are made concerning the groups with which the specific exercises may be used (see the Group Application section of each exercise).

In exploring and identifying self-concept it may be assumed that members must be willing to engage in risk behavior. Since risking denotes vulnerability, it is suggested that the facilitator pay close attention to processing the heightened emotional interaction which may occur.

It is the authors' belief that by understanding one's self-concept and by becoming aware of other member's self-concepts, deeper and more meaningful relationships will be developed. The utilization of the following exercises is designed to provide a structure in which awareness and growth are cultivated through self-concept insight and disclosure.

* BRAGGING

Subsidiary Goal(s)

a. To encounter the self–disclosing process.

b. To recognize and learn how one copes with the embarrassment caused by bragging about oneself.

c. To compare one's positive self-concept with other member's positive perceptions.

d. To give and receive positive feedback.

Group Application

Twelve members or less. To be used only with encounter, personal growth, marathon and t–groups with adult members after considerable rapport and a climate of care, warmth, and concern have been established.

Application Variables

Five to ten minutes per participant. The exercise is 100% verbal.

Administrative Procedure

a. The facilitator tells the group they will have an opportunity to disclose the positive aspects of their self concept. He asks for a volunteer who is willing to reveal "good" things about himself and receive feedback from other members about the positive things they see in him.

b. The volunteer is told to spend from three to five minutes "bragging" about himself. If the member falters or attempts to stop before three minutes have elapsed, the facilitator urges him on, saying, "I don't believe you've exhausted responses. Keep going."

c. After the member has finished, the facilitator asks that other members provide the volunteer with feedback as to their positive perceptions of him. He tells the members to spend three to five minutes doing this. If they stop, he says,

---

* Dynamic, more effective exercises are marked with an asterisk.

"I don't believe we have exhausted positive responses. Keep going."
d. The exercise is repeated until all members who wish to participate have had the opportunity to do so.

Suggestions for Facilitator Process

Concentrate on the following during processing:
a. Bragging is usually a taboo behavior. What feelings did it create in you? How did you cope with them? How did it feel to be inundated with positive feedback?
b. What kind of data did you give us and why? For example, did you share positive facts, values, feelings, etc? In reverse, what was the nature of the positive feedback you got?
c. What feedback surprised you? Which do you disagree with? Why?

Variations

*Variation I

a. Whenever a member appears to be too positive or negative in his self concept, is failing to self disclose, is not receiving feedback, is non-participative, etc., he is asked by the facilitator to spend three minutes "bragging."
b. The rest of the members then spend three minutes inundating him with positive feedback.

GROUP LIFE AUTOBIOGRAPHY

Subsidiary Goal(s)

a. To give and receive feedback.
b. To encourage self–disclosure.
c. To recognize the place projection plays in one's self-description.

Group Application

Twelve members or less. To be used in one of the last two

r three sessions of encounter, personal growth, marathon
nd t–groups.

Application Variables

Forty-five minutes to one hour. The exercise is 80% verbal,
with 20% non–verbal being written. Paper and pencils
are needed.

Administrative Procedure

a. The facilitator tells the group members: "You have ten minutes to write an autobiography of your life as a group
member. The autobiography cannot exceed one page."
b. After ten minutes, the facilitator stops the written portion
of the exercise.
c. Each member reads his group autobiography to the group.
d. After *each* presentation, the group reacts, focusing on the
accuracy and inaccuracy of the autogiography read, significant facts omitted, etc. The member should attempt
to explain why certain member's names appear in his
autobiography, what place projection occupied in his autobiography, why he chose to write about the things he did,
etc.
e. The exercise continues until all autobiographies have been
read.

Suggestions for Facilitator Process

Concentrate on the following during processing:
a. Whose autobiographies did you perceive as being inaccurate representations of their life in the group? Why?
Whose were the most accurate? Why?
b. What reasons did you have for picking the events you did?
Looking back, what didn't you put in your autobiography
that you think should have been there?

Variations

Variation I

a. To add the factor of anxiety, have the members think
about the project for a few minutes.

b. Then have each member recite verbally his group life autobiography. No member should be allowed to take less than three minutes for his presentation.

c. In processing, concentrate on the place anxiety played in what was included and omitted from the member's presentation.

* HERE'S HOW I SEE MYSELF

Subsidiary Goal(s)

a. To encounter the self–disclosing process.

b. To compare one's self–concept with other member perceptions.

c. To give and receive feedback.

Group Application

Twelve members or less. To be used only with encounter, personal growth, marathon and t–groups with adult members after considerable rapport and a climate of care, warmth, and concern has been established.

Application Variables

Five to ten minutes per participant. The exercise is 100% verbal.

Administrative Procedure

a. The facilitator asks for a volunteer who is willing to reveal his self–concept and receive feedback as to how other members see him.

b. The facilitator tells the volunteer to respond for three to five minutes and to use the statement "I see myself" as many times as he can. If the member stops after a minute or so, the facilitator urges him to continue, saying "I don't believe you've exhausted responses. Keep going."

c. After the member has finished, the facilitator asks that other members provide the volunteer with feedback as to their perceptions of him. He tells them to complete the statement "I see you" to the volunteer for three to five

minutes. If they stop before three minutes, he urges them
on, saying "I don't believe we've exhausted responses.
Keep going."
d. The exercise is repeated until all members who wish to
participate as volunteers have had the opportunity to do
so.

Suggestions for Facilitator Process

Concentrate on the following during processing:
a. What kind of perceptions were shared by the volunteers?
For example, thoughts, feelings, values, facts, etc? Why did
you share the perceptions you did?
b. What kind of feedback did you receive? Did it support
your self-concept? If so, how? If not, why?
c. Why did you experience difficulty in talking about yourself for three minutes? When I pushed you on, how did
you feel?
d. What were your feelings during the two stages of the
exercise? How did you cope with them?

Variations

*Variation I

a. Whenever a member appears to be having difficulty revealing himself, exhibits a negative self concept, is failing
to receive feedback, is non-participative, etc., he is asked
by the facilitator to spend three minutes responding to
the statement "I see myself."
b. The rest of the members then spend three minutes providing feedback to him, using the phrase "I see you."

* HOW I AM – HOW I'M SEEN

Subsidiary Goal(s)

a. To compare a member's predictions of how others see
him with their actual perceptions.
b. To encourage self-disclosure.

c. To accentuate the differences between how one sees one-self and how he believes others see him.

d. To give and receive feedback.

Group Application

Twelve members or less. To be used with encounter, personal growth, marathon and t–groups whose members have developed rapport and insight into each other.

Application Variables

One to one and one–half hours. The exercise is 80% verbal, with 20% non–verbal being written. Paper and pencils are needed.

Administrative Procedure

a. The facilitator tells the group they will write two statements of no more than one page each.

b. He tells them: "The first is to describe how you see yourself in this group. You will have five minutes."

c. After five minutes he says: "Now write the second. Describe what you believe is the group's impression of you as a member. You have five minutes."

d. After five minutes the facilitator collects the self descriptions (the first paper). He says: "I will read a description. If, when I am done, you feel you know who wrote it, point to that person and say 'I feel it is ——— because. . .' If the member you name is not the member, we will continue until we have ascertained the author. When we find the author, he will read his second paper dealing with how he feels we see him. After he has finished reading we will respond to his perceptions."

e. After the member has read his second statement, the facilitator leads a discussion, concentrating on the accuracy and inaccuracy of the members' prediction, the reasons for such accuracies and inaccuracies, whether the prediction was predominantly positive or negative and why, etc.

f. The exercise is continued until each member has had his first paper read, been guessed, and read his second paper.

Suggestions for Facilitator Process

Concentrate on the following during processing:

a. Was your second paper an over or underestimation of how others saw you? Why?
b. What did you learn during the discussion about our perceptions of you that surprised you? Why?
c. What difficulties did you encounter in writing the second paper? Why? If you were now to rewrite your first or second statements, what would you leave out or put in and why?
d. In your second paper, did you concentrate on what the group thought of you or how they felt about you? Why such a concentration?
e. Who did we misguess the most and why?

Variations

*Variation I

a. Limit the papers and feedback by telling the members to write: (1) a statement about the negative perceptions you have for yourself as a member of this group; and (2) a description of what you believe is the group's negative impression of you as a member.

*Variation II

a. Limit the papers and feedback by telling the members to write: (1) a statement about the positive perceptions you have for yourself as a member of this group; and (2) a description of what you believe is the group's positive impression of you as a member.

*I

Subsidiary Goal(s)

a. To encourage self–disclosure.

b. To determine the most meaningful self–concept data for each member.
c. To encourage participation.
d. To give and receive feedback.
e. To recognize how pressure affects us and how we cope with it.

Group Application

Twelve members or less. Applicable to any group, but most frequently used with encounter, personal growth, marathon and t–groups after rapport and trust have been developed.

Application Variables

Thirty to forty–five minutes. The exercise is 95% verbal, with 5% non–verbal being written. Paper and pencils are needed.

Administrative Procedure

a. The facilitator says: "We will go through a three phase exercise designed to elicit self–concept data. *It is important* that you write your answer within thirty seconds. If you have not written a response within thirty seconds, you will be eliminated for that phase of the exercise. *Remember this!*"
b. *Phase one*–The facilitator continues: "Write an answer to the following as rapidly as possible. I am . . ." He stops the exercise after thirty seconds. Any member who has not written his reply is eliminated from participating *in any way* in that round.
c. A member volunteers to read his response. After he has done so, the facilitator says: "What other things do we think this member is?" Members then respond, indicating who or what they believe the member to be.
d. Step c is repeated until all members who are eligible have participated.
e. *Phase two*–The facilitator says: "Write an answer to the

following as rapidly as possible. My worst characteristic as a group member is . . ." Again, members who fail to finish in time are eliminated.

f. A member volunteers to read his response. After he has done so, the facilitator says: "What other negative characteristics do we perceive in this member?"

g. Step f is repeated until all members who are eligible have participated.

h. *Phase three*–The facilitator says: "Write an answer as rapidly as possible for the following: My most valuable asset as a group member is. . ." Again eliminate members who do not finish in time.

i. A member volunteers to read his response. After he has done so, the facilitator says: "What other valuable characteristics do we perceive in this member?"

j. Step i is repeated until all members who are eligible have participated.

Suggestions for Facilitator Process

Concentrate on the following during processing:

a. What feelings did the eliminated members experience? Why were you unable to cope with the time pressure?

b. To others: What did you learn about yourself during the three feedback phases? What written responses would you change if you had to do the exercise over? Why?

c. Who got the most positive feedback? Why? Who got the most negative feedback and why?

Variations

*Variation I

a. Eliminate the verbal feedback sections and replace them with the following:

1. "If you feel the member's response is significant, look at him."

2. "If you feel it was non–significant and a cop–out on his part, turn your back to him."

b. Then process the responses, concentrating on why mem-

bers voted for choice 1 or 2, how the member feels and
reacts to their votes, etc.

OBITUARY

Subsidiary Goal(s)

a. To help increase awareness of self–concept.
b. To further facilitate the concept of group concept.
c. To encourage self–disclosure.

Group Application

Twelve members or less. To be used with encounter, personal growth, marathon and t–groups with adult members
who have developed rapport and insight into each other.

Application Variables

One hour and thirty minutes. The exercise is 70% verbal,
with 30% non–verbal being written. Paper and pencils are
needed.

Administrative Procedure

a. The facilitator asks each member of the group to write a
series of obituaries one paragraph long. He is to write one
for himself, one for *every* other member of the group and
one for the group itself.
b. After this is done the facilitator asks for a volunteer to
read his personal obituary.
c. The facilitator then has the rest of the members read the
obituaries they wrote about the volunteer.
d. Steps **b** and **c** are repeated until all members who wish to
participate have had the opportunity to do so.
e. The facilitator asks that members read their obituary of
the group.
f. The group discusses the experience.

Suggestions for Facilitator Process

Concentrate on the following during processing:

a. Was your personal obituary positive or negative? How did you decide what to put in your one paragraph?
b. Did the other members' obituaries about you differ from yours? Why? Were you surprised? How did it make you feel? What did you learn about how other members see you?
c. What did the group's obituary tell us about our perceptions of the group? What differences can we see in terms of member consensus? Did you discover any hidden agendas?

Variations

Variation I
a. Repeat initial exercise.
b. Have the group as a whole write a one paragraph obituary for the group, using group consensus.

Variation II
a. Instead of obituary, use birth announcements, having members concentrate on their birth as members. They are *not* to write about their natural birth.

PICTURE ME

Subsidiary Goal(s)

a. To explore the dynamics involved in self-confrontation.
b. To enable members to self–disclose in a low–risk setting.

Group Application

Twelve members or less. To be used with encounter, personal growth, marathon and t–groups. Best results are obtained if the exercise is used in the middle stage of group development.

Application Variables

One hour. The exercise is 50% verbal, with 50% non–verbal being drawn. A large sheet of paper and a box of crayons are needed for each member. The room must be large enough to allow members to spread out comfortably within the room.

Administrative Procedure

a. The facilitator gives each member a sheet of paper and a box of crayons.
b. He then tells the members to spread out within the room in such a manner that each member may work comfortably and undisturbed.
c. The facilitator instructs the members to draw a picture of themselves. It may be realistic or abstract. They will have twenty minutes to complete the task.
d. After twenty minutes the members sit in a circle.
e. The facilitator asks the members to show their portraits to the group and give verbal descriptions of them. Members observing should be encouraged to make comments and share impressions.
f. After all members have participated, the facilitator initiates discussion.

Suggestions for Facilitator Process

Concentrate on the following during processing:
a. What have you learned from your own self-drawings? What have you learned from other member's drawings? If your drawing was abstract, what held the most meaning for you, colors, shapes, etc.?

Variations

None.

* SELF CHASTISEMENT

Subsidiary Goal(s)

a. To encounter the self–disclosing process.
b. To compare one's negative self-concept with other members' perceptions.

c. To give and receive negative feedback.

Group Application

Twelve members or less. To be used only with encounter, personal growth, marathon and t–groups with adult members after considerable rapport and a climate of care, warmth, and concern has been established.

Application Variables

Five to ten minutes per participant. The exercise is 100% verbal.

Administrative Procedure

a. The facilitator tells the group they will have an opportunity to disclose the negative aspects of their self-concept. He asks for a volunteer who is willing to reveal "bad" (negative) things about himself and receive feedback from other members about the negative things they see in him.

b. The volunteer is told to spend from three to five minutes "self chastising" himself. If he falters or attempts to stop before three minutes have elapsed, the facilitator urges him on saying "I don't believe you've exhausted responses. Keep going."

c. After the member has finished, the facilitator asks that other members provide the volunteer with feedback as to their negative perceptions of him. He tells the group to spend three to five minutes doing this. If they stop or falter, he says "I don't believe we've exhausted negative responses. Keep going."

d. The exercise is repeated until all members who wish to participate have had the opportunity to do so.

Suggestions for Facilitator Process

Concentrate on the following during processing:

a. What kind of perceptions did you share and why? For example, thoughts, values, facts, feelings, etc? Why did you share the perceptions you did?

b. How did you feel being inundated with negative feedback? How did you cope with these feelings?

c. Did other member's feedback surprise you? Why? Which did you agree with? Why?

d. To those who did not participate: Why were you unwilling to participate?

Variations

*Variation I

a. Whenever a member appears to be having difficulty self–disclosing, is too negative or positive in his self–concept, is failing to receive feedback, is non–participative, etc., he is asked by the facilitator to spend three minutes "self chastising" himself.

b. The rest of the group then spends three minutes providing negative feedback to him.

SELF IDEAL[1]

Subsidiary Goal(s)

a. To increase self-awareness.

b. To identify areas of personal dissatisfaction with self.

c. To deepen and enrich relationships.

d. To give and receive feedback.

Group Application

Twelve members or less. To be used with any group. Best results are obtained if the exercise is used in the initial stage of group development.

Application Variables

One hour and thirty minutes. The exercise is 50% verbal, with 50% non–verbal being written. Paper and pencils are needed, as well as one copy of the Self Appraisal Inven-

---

[1] Permission to reproduce this exercise was granted by the Youth Office, Lutheran Church of America.

tory for each member. The room should be large enough for members to spread out comfortably.

Administrative Procedure

a. The facilitator passes out a Self Appraisal Inventory to each member in the group.

b. He reads the directions at the top of the inventory. Members are asked to find separate spots in the room and begin filling out the forms.

c. After members have filled out the forms, the "additional directions" are read (listed at the bottom of the Self Appraisal form).

d. Members, having completed the Self Appraisal Inventory, are to compare totals for Column B, as entered in the top left-hand corner of the first page.

e. Members are now asked to share the five encircled items which they most want to change.

Suggestions for Facilitator Process

Concentrate on the following during processing:

a. *To members having high totals in Column B:* Do you feel you have over-exaggerated the need to change? Are you being overly critical of yourself? Does the feedback from other members correspond with your feeling of self?

b. *To members having low totals in Column B:* Do you feel you may be unaware of some need to change which others can see? Can you act as a resource for members who feel the need to change? What have you learned about yourself?

c. *To all members:* What have you learned from the other members in the group? Do you feel this exercise has increased your awareness? Do you feel you've been completely honest with yourself? If not, why?

Variations

None.

SELF APPRAISAL INVENTORY

DIRECTIONS: *Read each item and decide how truly it describes you. Answer by placing in the blank in Column A in front of each number:*

+2   if it is *very true* of you; *very like* you.

+1   if it is more *like* you than unlike you.

0   if you can't decide; 50–50.

−1   if it is more *unlike* you than like you.

−2   if it is *quite untrue* of you; *very unlike* you; just the opposite of what you are.

RATE HERE

Col. A (As I Now Am)	Col. B (Desire to Change)	Item No.	Descriptive Items (How true is this of you?)
_____	_____	1.	I have a horror of failure in anything I want to accomplish.
_____	_____	2.	I am contented.
_____	_____	3.	I am no one. Nothing seems to be me.
_____	_____	4.	I am relaxed and nothing really bothers me.
_____	_____	5.	I usually like people.
_____	_____	6.	I feel completely blocked emotionally.
_____	_____	7.	I am a responsible person.
_____	_____	8.	I am aware of being somewhat at cross-purpose with myself.
_____	_____	9.	I feel emotionally mature.

_____ _____ 10. I often do things when I'm in one mood, which doesn't make sense to me later.

_____ _____ 11. Sometimes I feel that the things I do are genuinely right for me; sometimes I don't.

_____ _____ 12. All you have to do is just insist with me, and I give in.

_____ _____ 13. I feel cut off from other people.

_____ _____ 14. If others don't appreciate me, I feel that they don't know a good thing when they see it.

_____ _____ 15. I have the feeling that I am just not facing things.

_____ _____ 16. I can stand up for myself.

_____ _____ 17. I feel as if I were several very different persons each struggling against the others.

_____ _____ 18. I feel helpless.

_____ _____ 19. I often kick myself for the things I do.

_____ _____ 20. I am optimistic.

_____ _____ 21. I have initiative.

_____ _____ 22. I am assertive.

_____ _____ 23. I express my emotions freely.

———————— ———————————— 24. My decisions are not my own.

———————— ———————————— 25. I often feel humiliated.

———————— ———————————— 26. It's pretty tough to be me.

———————— ———————————— 27. Sex is a problem to me.

———————— ———————————— 28. I feel worthless.

———————— ———————————— 29. I keep starting things I don't finish.

———————— ———————————— 30. I don't know how I feel about things.

———————— ———————————— 31. I can usually make up my mind and stick to it.

———————— ———————————— 32. I am at ease with the opposite sex.

———————— ———————————— 33. I am afraid of sex.

———————— ———————————— 34. I feel like a zombie, walking around in a dream or a daze.

———————— ———————————— 35. I am sexually attractive.

———————— ———————————— 36. I feel apathetic.

———————— ———————————— 37. I take a positive attitude toward myself.

———————— ———————————— 38. I doubt my sexual powers.

———————— ———————————— 39. I tend to be on my guard with people who are somewhat more friendly than I had expected.

———————— ———————————— 40. I feel anxious nearly all the time.

_____ _____ 41. I am afraid of a full-fledged disagreement with a person.

_____ _____ 42. I usually feel driven.

_____ _____ 43. I feel guilty about every little thing.

_____ _____ 44. I despise myself.

_____ _____ 45. I just can't get along with people.

_____ _____ 46. I can't seem to make up my mind one way or another.

_____ _____ 47. I understand myself.

_____ _____ 48. I have few values and standards of my own.

_____ _____ 49. I am impulsive.

_____ _____ 50. I feel hopeless.

_____ _____ 51. I enjoy sex.

_____ _____ 52. I keep worrying about my health.

_____ _____ 53. It is difficult to control my aggression.

_____ _____ 54. I dislike my own sexuality.

_____ _____ 55. I feel comfortable in most situations.

_____ _____ 56. I can usually live comfortably with the people around me.

_____ _____ 57. I seldom worry about anything once I've done it.

_____ _____ 58. I really enjoy life.

_____ _____ 59. I just can't seem to get started.

_____ _____ 60. I feel whole-hearted in my actions and at one with myself.

_____ _____ 61. I have a warm emotional relationship with others.

_____ _____ 62. I don't really respect myself.

_____ _____ 63. I feel insecure within myself.

_____ _____ 64. I seldom put on a false front.

_____ _____ 65. I am moody.

_____ _____ 66. I usually feel good about what I am doing.

_____ _____ 67. I am confident that things will get better.

_____ _____ 68. I am self–reliant.

_____ _____ 69. I often find myself doing what I don't really want to do and neglecting what I think I want to do.

_____ _____ 70. I feel adequate.

FURTHER DIRECTIONS:

1. Now read over each item again and decide whether, if you could, you would like to *change* in this particular characteristic. If you are fairly well satisfied to continue as you are, with this item as answered in Col. A, put a zero (0) in Col. B.

If you'd like to change by having the item become *more true* of you than it now is, place a plus (+) in Col. B.
If you'd like to change by having the item become *less true* of you than it is now, place a minus (−) in Col. B.

2. When you have finished, count the total number of + and − items in Col. B and enter it as "Col. B Total" at the top of the first page of the inventory.

3. Finally, pick out the five items on which you now most *strongly want to change*. On these five, encircle your Col. A and B answers.

4. Share in pairs and/or with the entire group your five items. Share how you feel about these items and have others share their impressions.

SELF PORTRAIT

Subsidiary Goal(s)

a. To explore the dynamics involved in symbols.
b. To gain awareness of selfishness and sharing.

Group Application

Twelve members or less. To be used with encounter, personal growth, marathon and t–groups. Best results are obtained if the exercise is used in the initial stage of development.

Application Variables

One hour. The exercise is 50% verbal, 50% non–verbal. A sizeable number of miscellaneous objects, such as pieces of cloth, wood, string, bottle caps, balloons, marbles, cotton, etc. are needed equalling approximately ten items for each member.

Administrative Procedure

a. The facilitator dumps the miscellaneous objects in the center of the circle.
b. He then instructs each member to construct a symbolic

self portrait utilizing the materials on the floor. Members are encouraged to use their imagination and free their inhibitions in assembling their portrait.

c. After twenty minutes the members are to stop work and reform a circle. Their newly made portrait is not to be destroyed or altered.

d. The facilitator asks the members to, one at a time, present their portrait to the group and explain its symbolic meaning. Other members should feel free to make comments and share impressions.

e. When all members have had an opportunity to participate, the facilitator initiates discussion.

Suggestions for Facilitator Process

Concentrate on the following during processing:

a. How many pieces did you take when creating your portrait? What happened if another member wanted the same piece that you wanted to use? How did you resolve any other conflicts that occurred when creating your portrait?

b. How did you decide what to create to represent yourself? Do you feel you adequately accomplished what you set out to do? Were you surprised with the final product? If so, why? How did you feel when sharing your portrait?

Variations

None.

* TALK TO YOURSELF

Subsidiary Goal(s)

a. To recognize some of the internal dialogue one carries on in a decision making process.

b. To disclose positive and negative attitudes concerning risk taking behavior.

Group Application

Twelve members or less. To be used with encounter, personal growth, marathon and t–groups whose members have learned some of the principles involved in "tuning into" oneself.

Application Variables

Thirty to forty-five minutes. The exercise is 80% verbal, with 20% non–verbal being written. A chalkboard, paper and pencils are needed.

Administrative Procedure

a. The facilitator writes the following on the chalkboard and asks for a show of hands as to which members are most hesitant to engage in such behavior. (We recommend that the facilitator design questions appropriate to his particular group.)
 1. With anger and rage confront another member.
 2. With anger and rage confront the facilitator.
 3. Be confronted by another member's anger and rage.
 4. Be confronted by the facilitator's anger and rage.
b. The facilitator then says: "Take ten minutes to write a dialogue between the part of you that is unwilling to risk the behavior you are hesitant to engage in and that part of you that is willing." (Give a three or four sentence example if necessary.)
c. After ten minutes, the facilitator has each member read his dialogue. Members should listen, but refrain from prolonged questioning, as such will add significantly to the time spent conducting the exercise.
d. When all members have finished reading their dialogue, the exercise is ended. However, members should be encouraged to question and attend to any dialogues which they perceive as particularly significant and/or self–disclosing.

Suggestions for Facilitator Process

Concentrate on the following during processing:
a. What did you learn about yourself and the inner dialogue

you inevitably conduct in situations which you are hesitant to engage in?

b. What have we learned about other members? Which of what we learned is new data, which is old data?

c. Did you experience any difficulties in "tuning into" your inner dialogue? If so, what were they and why?

Variations

*Variation I

a. When the facilitator perceives that a member is indecisive about engaging in a particular discussion or behavior, he asks the member to verbally voice his inner dialogue. The member should use two different voice levels, one to indicate the positive side of the dialogue, the other to indicate the negative side.

YOU ARE

Subsidiary Goal(s)

a. To develop and maintain greater insights into one's "self."

b. To perpetuate and enrich relationships of meaningful importance among members.

c. To encourage self–disclosure.

Group Application

Twelve members or less. To be used with encounter, personal growth, marathon and t–groups. Best results are obtained when used in a group whose members have had ample sessions to develop trust and group unity. Caution should be used when using this exercise too early in the group's development.

Application Variables

Thirty minutes. The exercise is 100% verbal. The room must be large enough to allow the members to form dyads without feeling restrained.

Administrative Procedure

a. The facilitator asks members to mill around and form dyads.
b. Each dyad is instructed to find a private spot in the room.
c. The facilitator gives the following instructions: "Your partner is to ask 'Who are you?' every fifteen seconds for the next fifteen minutes. Each time you ask your partner who he is, you are to vary inflections and tone of voice. The person answering may make any response he feels appropriate but should answer in short statements."
d. After the fifteen minutes, the partners are told to reverse roles and repeat step c.

Suggestions for Facilitator Process

Concentrate on the following during processing:

a. Did your response change significantly during the fifteen minute period? If so, in what way? Did your response vary according to the way your partner asked who you were?
b. Did silence occur during the fifteen minutes? If so, why? What have you learned about yourself? About your partner?
c. What did this exercise tell you about your own self–image? About your partner's? How did you deal with the ambiguity of instructions concerning appropriate responses?

Variations

None.

XIX

SELF-DISCLOSURE

THE PRIMARY GOAL for each exercise in this chapter is the elicitation of self–disclosing behavior or data.

Self–disclosure is an essential dynamic for any group whose purpose is to facilitate interpersonal growth. The facilitator should bear in mind that self–disclosure usually denotes risk on the individual's part. Risk implies vulnerability and, when one is vulnerable, it is often easy to be hurt. However, it is our belief that without the individual's willingness to risk, growth is extremely difficult to achieve. The following exercises are designed to elicit self–disclosure within a structure which provides a supportive environment to risk.

It is the authors' belief that self–disclosure should never be forced upon an individual. The selection of a self–disclosure exercise should be given careful consideration before its utilization. The premature use of self–disclosing exercises may be a detriment rather than an asset to the group and its members. It would be advisable to implement the following exercises only when it is apparent that group trust has had an opportunity to develop.

Because self–disclosure may often lead to intense emotional interaction, it is suggested that the facilitator pay close attention to the processing stage.

FEARS

Subsidiary Goal(s)

a. To gain insight into members' hidden agendas.
b. To further understand one's self-concept.
c. To increase listening and feedback skills.
d. To encourage self–disclosure.

Group Application

Twelve members or less. To be used with encounter, personal growth, marathon and t–groups. Caution should be used if the exercise is used before a supportive group atmosphere has been developed.

Application Variables

One hour and thirty minutes. The exercise is 100% verbal. The room should be large enough to allow members to move about unrestrained.

Administrative Procedures

a. The facilitator asks the group to divide into groups of four.
b. The small groups should go to separate corners of the room.
c. The facilitator then asks the groups to discuss their expectations of themselves and the group. The facilitator should rotate between all groups.
d. After thirty minutes he tells the members to form new groups of four and discuss their greatest worries.
e. Again after thirty minutes new groups of four are formed. They are told to discuss their fears.
f. The group discusses the experience.

Suggestions for Facilitator Process

Concentrate on the following during processing:
a. How did you originally choose your group? Have your feelings changed toward any members? If so, in what way?
b. How much did you disclose about yourself? Did it vary from group to group? If so, why?
c. Have your expectations, fears, or worries changed? If so,

in what way? What have you learned about other members in your group? What have you learned about yourself?

Variations

Variation I
a. Have members express one of the topics non–verbally.
b. Repeat basic exercise.

Variation II
a. Change topics to discussing (1) their proudest moment; (2) their greatest strength; and (3) their nicest physical quality.
b. Repeat basic exercise.

* GROUP COMMANDMENTS

Subsidiary Goal(s)

a. To recognize the extent to which a member's rules for other's are representative of his value system.
b. To encourage participation.

Group Application

Group size is unlimited, but the exercise is most effectively used with groups of twelve or less. Applicable to any group, but most frequently used early in the life of encounter, personal growth, marathon and t–groups. The use of this exercise in the classroom can be especially effective.

Application Variables

One to one and one–half hours. The exercise is 95% verbal, with 5% non–verbal being written. Paper and pencils are needed.

Administrative Procedure

a. The facilitator tells the group they will have five minutes to write five group commandments. He says: " 'You should

---

* Dynamic, more effective exercises are marked with an asterisk.

not kill' is a commandment for man. Similarly, there are such "shoulds" and "should–nots" for man in a group such as ours. Write five commandments which you feel a group member should follow."

b. After five minutes the facilitator has each member read his list of group commandments. The member should explain the reasoning behind each commandment. Other members should refrain from responding during this stage of the exercise.

c. The facilitator then has each member reread his commandments. The facilitator leads a discussion, concentrating on analyzing where the commandments come from (value investigation), extent to which the member follows his own commandments, areas of other member agreement and disagreement, the reality of the commandment, etc.

Suggestions for Facilitator Process

Concentrate on the following during processing:

a. Whose commandments were too ideal? *To those members:* Do you agree? What is your reaction to the group's naming of you as having overly ideal commandments?

b. Whose list do we feel is most realistic? Why?

c. If I said we would obey *all* of these commandments, which ones would you follow? Why? Which ones would you refuse to follow? Why?

d. If you could now rewrite your list, what would you drop from it? Why? What would you now add to it and why?

Variations

Variation I

a. To encourage a vigorous, dynamic discussion about the positive and negative aspects of each commandment, have each member tell the group which of the five commandments he has written is the *most* important.

b. The other members then write down, on their paper, the other member's name, his commandment, and the words

"I agree" or "I disagree" to indicate their feelings about the commandment in question.

c. After all members have indicated their most important rule and written voting has occurred, the facilitator asks that all the "I agree" members for (name a member's) commandment sit on one side of the circle and all the "I disagree" members sit on the other side.

d. The "opposing" corps then have ten minutes to discuss the merits, inadequacies, etc. of the commandment in question. The facilitator asks that they try to reach a decision between them as to whether this commandment should or should not be included in the "best five" list.

e. The exercise continues until all the "most important" commandments have been debated.

* HONEST-DISHONEST

Subsidiary Goal(s)

a. To enhance and magnify the value of honesty.
b. To gain greater awareness of member actions and re-actions.
c. To give and receive feedback.

Group Application

Twelve members or less. To be used with encounter, personal growth, marathon and t–groups. The group should have had ample sessions to allow the members to form group identity.

Application Variables

One hour. The exercise is 80% verbal and 20% non–verbal. Paper and pencils are needed.

Administrative Procedure

a. The facilitator writes on separate cards the following instructions: (We urge the facilitator to create card statements appropriate to the needs of his particular group.)

Card #1—Do a pantomime representing the most meaningful event in your life.

Card #2—Sing a song about a person in the group you feel the most for.

Card #3—Make up a poem which expresses your feelings about your body.

Card #4—Tell us which members the group could do without and why.

Card #5—Tell us which members are essential to the group and why.

Card #6—Tell us if you are an asset or deficit to the group and why.

Card #7—Write your own tombstone epitaph.

Card #8—Non–verbally rank members in groups of three according to any characteristic similarity, except that of physical similarity. Then explain why you lumped the members you did together.

Card #9—Take away a weakness from each person and replace it with one of your strengths.

Card #10—Pick the member you have the most negative vibrations for. Look him/her in the eyes and tell him/her why you are experiencing negative vibrations.

Card #11—Do something you have wanted to do in this group, but have not done so far.

Card #12—Rank members 1–12 according to your like or dislike for them.

b. He randomly distributes the cards, one to each member.

c. The facilitator also supplies each member with a card that says "honesty" on one side and "dishonesty" on the other.

d. One member at a time is to carry out the instructions given to him. (Do not indicate who should start. Let the group decide the method of member presentation.)

e. After each member carries out his instructions the group is to turn up the card showing the "honest" or "dishonest" side depending upon how the member observing evaluates the member's performance of his task. (Some brief discussion of the reasons for the votes given is recommended.)

f. The group should show their "honesty" or "dishonesty"

card at the same time to avoid being influenced by other members.

g. After all members have participated, the group discusses the experience.

Suggestions for Facilitator Process

Concentrate on the following during processing:

a. What feelings did you experience in carrying out your instructions? How did you cope with them? Did you like or dislike your task? Why?

b. Did you agree with the evaluation of your performance? If not, why? What criteria did you use in evaluating other member performances?

c. What did you learn about other members? What did you learn about yourself?

d. If you could have chosen one of the tasks, which one would you have picked? Why?

Variations

Variation I

a. Have members select the instructions they wish to perform.

b. Repeat basic exercise.

Variation II

a. Have members create their own instructions.

b. Repeat basic exercise.

I AM

Subsidiary Goal(s)

a. To explore one's self–concept.

b. To establish more meaningful relationships.

c. To gain increased self–awareness.

d. To explore the amount of trust which has been established.

Group Application

Twelve members or less. To be used with any group, although caution should be used if the exercise is used early in the group's development.

Application Variables

One hour and fifteen minutes. The exercise is 60% verbal, 40% non–verbal being written. Pencils and paper are needed for each member.

Administrative Procedure

a. The facilitator passes out pencils and paper to each member.

b. He then asks each member to write down ten sentences beginning with the words "I am." None of the sentences may include factual information (i.e., sex, profession, height, weight). The facilitator then asks each member to make a check by the three most meaningful attributes on the list. (The papers are to be left unsigned.)

c. After all members have completed their sentences the papers are to be placed face down in the middle of the circle. Each member is to then, one at a time, select a paper at random and read it aloud to the entire group. (No member should read his own paper.)

d. After the member has read the sentences to the group, the group is to decide who wrote the sentences and why they think so.

e. After the group has had ample opportunity to guess which member wrote the sentences, the author is to identify himself.

f. After all papers have been read and discussed the facilitator initiates processing.

Suggestions for Facilitator Process

Concentrate on the following during processing:

a. How did you decide what type of information to write about yourself? Was it difficult to come up with ten sentences beginning with "I am"? How much did you really disclose about yourself? What have you learned about your own self–concept? Why did you check the items you did on your list?

b. How accurate were you in identifying the authors of the papers? What have you learned about other members' self–concepts? Do you feel other members really disclosed much about themselves? If not, why? Have your feelings changed towards any members? If so, why?

Variations

None.

* PRESSURING FOR SELF-DISCLOSURE

Subsidiary Goal(s)

a. To recognize how one copes with anxiety.
b. To recognize the place projection plays in determining what we wish to learn about others.
c. To investigate one's decision making process.
d. To investigate one's willingness to take a chance.

Group Application

Twelve members or less, although the exercise is most easily utilizable with eight members or less. Applicable, with caution, to any group, but most frequently used with encounter, personal growth, marathon and t–groups. If used with other groups, the facilitator should prepare questions to be asked rather than allow the group members to make them up.

Application Variables

Time unlimited, with each member using approximately three to five minutes. The exercise is 100% verbal.

Administrative Procedure

a. The facilitator tells the group they will experience an exercise designed to facilitate self–disclosure.

b. He says: "Each member will answer one question posed by another group member of *his* choice. The questions *must* be designed to elicit self–disclosing data. We do not want to find out things he would tell anybody, anytime."

c. The facilitator can start by answering another member's question or (as we recommend) wait to take his turn. If he waits, he asks that a member volunteer to be the first self–discloser. He tells the volunteer "Ask who wishes information. If more than one hand is raised, choose the member whose question you want to respond to. Members *cannot* tell you their question until *after* you have picked them."

d. After the first volunteer has finished, the exercise is repeated until *every* member has self–disclosed. (We recommend using a self–initiating system. That is, each member self–discloses when *he* decides to volunteer. This system produces valuable data about member willingness to take a risk.)

Suggestions for Facilitator Process

Concentrate on the following during processing:

a. Why did you volunteer when you did? Concentrate especially on the first and second volunteers and the last two or three.

b. Which questions did you perceive as eliciting self-disclosing data? Why? Why don't you see the other questions as eliciting self–disclosing data?

c. Why did you choose the member you did when more than one wished to ask you a question? (Be sure here to have the chooser respond as specifically as possible.)

Variations

*Variation I

a. When the facilitator perceives that a member is unwilling to self–disclose, is not giving or receiving feedback, is not being asked in by other members, etc., he says "We haven't heard from you much and I'm not sure many of us know you. I'd like you to answer three self–disclosing questions,

one from me and two from any two members you choose from those with questions for you."
b. The facilitator asks the first question. After the member responds, the facilitator says, "Now ask who else has questions. If more than two raise their hands, choose the two whose questions you want to answer. The members are not to tell you their questions before you choose them."
c. Process, concentrating on why the member chose the individuals he did, what the pressure to self–disclose made him feel, how other members feel toward him now, etc.

"SHIT"

Subsidiary Goal(s)

a. To deal with tasks that are supposedly taboo.
b. To gain insights into one's defense mechanisms.

Group Application

Twelve members or less. To be used with any group. Best results are obtained if the exercise is used in the early stage of development.

Application Variables

Thirty minutes. The exercise is 60% verbal, with 40% non–verbal being written. Paper and pencils are needed.

Administrative Procedure

a. The facilitator gives the following instructions: "Write out the most important memories you have concerning feces, stools or what is commonly known as 'shit.' After you have written down memories I will read them to the group anonymously."
b. Before the group starts writing, the facilitator should stop and process the reactions to the instructed task.
c. After discussion, the facilitator asks the group to begin writing. When they are finished the facilitator collects the papers and reads them aloud.

Suggestions for Facilitator Process

Concentrate on the following during processing:

a. What were your immediate feelings toward the task? Why is this topic usually thought of as "taboo?" Do you now feel talking about feces is "taboo?"

b. Were your recollections of early childhood or later in life? In either case, why was this so? Did you conjure unpleasant or pleasant memories? What have you learned about the other members in the group?

Variations

Variation I

a. Instead of writing out memories of "shit" have members discuss them verbally.

SYMBOLIC DRAWINGS

Subsidiary Goal(s)

a. To explore the dynamics of symbols.

b. To gain insight into past hidden agendas which may still be interfering with member openness.

Group Application

Twelve members or less. To be used with encounter, personal growth, marathon and t–groups. Caution should be used if the exercise is used before a supportive group atmosphere has been developed.

Application Variables

One hour. The exercise is 50% verbal, with 50% non–verbal being written. Paper and pencils are needed. The room should be large enough to allow members to move unrestrained.

Administrative Procedure

a. The facilitator passes out paper and pencils to each member of the group.

b. He then asks members to put as many or as few dots on the piece of paper as they wish and connect them by uncrossed lines.
c. The facilitator then asks each member to share his paper with the group and discuss any symbolic meaning.
d. Step **b** is repeated with the added instructions: "Connect the dots with uncrossed lines, but try to make the drawing symbolize a meaningful relationship you have or had."
e. Members should be encouraged to give their own reactions and interpretations to the drawings.
f. The group discusses the experience.

Suggestions for Facilitator Process

Concentrate on the following during processing:
a. Were you surprised at the symbols you first drew? What does this tell you about hidden agendas you might be carrying around?
b. What have you learned about other members from their drawings? Do you feel your first and second drawing differed significantly? If so, in what way?
c. Whose drawings did you appreciate most? Why? Whose drawing turned you off? Why?

Variations

None.

THREAT

Subsidiary Goal(s)

a. To establish greater and more meaningful relationships.
b. To gain insight into one's fears and problems.
c. To encourage self–disclosure.

Group Application

Twelve members or less. To be used with encounter, personal growth, marathon and t–groups. Caution should be used if the exercise is used before the group has developed a supportive climate.

Application Variables

One hour. The exercise is 100% verbal.

Administrative Procedure

a. The facilitator asks for a member who is willing to express and reveal to the group the greatest threat in his life.
b. After the member has disclosed his threat to the group, the members may ask questions and offer suggestions.
c. After every member has had an opportunity to disclose, the group is to break up into small groups according to similarities in expressed feelings of threat.
d. After thirty minutes the group discusses the experience.

Suggestions for Facilitator Process

Concentrate on the following during processing:
a. What types of feelings did you have while expressing your greatest threat? What have you learned from this experience?
b. Did you find the questions and suggestions from the other members helpful? If so, in what way? Does your threat now seem as frightening? If not, why do you feel this is so?
c. What did you learn from the members in your small group? Have your feelings changed towards any of these members? If so, in what way?

Variations

Variation I

a. Have members express their greatest threats non–verbally.
b. Repeat basic exercises.

Variation II

a. Instead of threats have members reveal and discuss the most meaningful event in their lives.
b. Repeat basic exercise.

TIME TRAVEL

Subsidiary Goal(s)

a. To explore past experiences in an effort to better understand present feelings.
b. To become aware of the dynamics involved in self–concept.
c. To develop deeper and more meaningful relationships.

Group Application

Twelve members or less. To be used with encounter, personal growth, marathon and t–groups. Since the exercise deals with the past, caution should be used in avoiding "there and then" interaction in future sessions.

Application Variables

One hour to one and a half hours. The exercise is 100% verbal.

Administrative Procedure

a. The facilitator tells the group that there will be three stages to the exercise. In the first stage, the facilitator asks members to share with the group important past experiences from age one to six. Ample time should be allowed for a chance to share and discuss feelings in between stages.
b. He then asks members to share experiences from the age of seven to twelve.
c. The last stage consists of having members relate experiences from the age of thirteen to eighteen.
d. The group then processes the exercise.

Suggestions for Facilitator Process

Concentrate on the following during processing:
a. Which members seem to have been most affected by past experiences? How can we effectively deal with the past, if at all?

   b. Were you surprised at the memories you brought up? If
      so, in what way? How do you feel past experiences relate
      to self–concept? To what extent do you see past behaviors
      repeating themselves in the present? To what extent do
      you see past behaviors repeating themselves in the group?

Variations

   None.

XX

SMALL GROUP SERIES WORKSHOP [1]

B ECAUSE THE WORKSHOP CONSISTS of several exercises to be used in succession, the format differs slightly from previous exercises.

The basic goal of the workshop is to provide a structured environment which (1) allows members to experience communication on a variety of levels, and (2) gives members, in a large group, the opportunity to "get acquainted" with all other members in a small group setting.

As the reader will observe, the small group series workshop consists of six independent exercises (the seventh exercise is processing the first six) which are unified by the basic structure (see basic instructions). It is suggested that the small group series workshop be used primarily in large groups (twenty-five to forty members). Groups with twenty-five members or less should have ample opportunity to interact in small groups.

The variety of experiences that the workshop provides elicit a number of dynamics which can both enhance and deepen member interaction and growth.

The basic purpose of the small group series workshop is to allow members to experience and reflect on the values and hindrances of a variety of verbal and non–verbal situations as they relate to interpersonal communication and self–awareness.

The workshop can be used by any group of persons who are interested in sampling and exploring a variety of interaction modes to determine which may be most productively employed. The number of participants, sex composition, and level of member experience are not critical factors.

Three and one–half to four hours are needed to allow for com-

---

[1] Developed by Robert Shelton and Robert Brook, University of Kansas.

pletion of the entire small group series workshop. A copy of the group assignment grid as well as the laboratory outline should be given to each member at the beginning of the session.

The following series of exercises are designed to permit persons to work in a group of six members, in six different groups, for twenty minutes per group (twenty-five to forty members). Two grids are given in order to facilitate a mix depending on the amount of members in the group.

It is helpful if the leader gives a brief overview of the workshop as well as a brief talk (five to ten minutes) about "processing" one's experience. Participants can be assigned or assign themselves numbers which correspond to the subgrouping grid. (The number assigned must be kept throughout the sequence if a variety of groups is to be encountered.) The participants then follow the numbered system of the grid to the designated subgroup area. It is suggested that each subgroup meeting is preceded by one or two minutes of silence. During this time each participant can look over his new colleagues, prepare himself for the new experience, and listen to instructions.

The leader must be skillful in "easing" participants "in and out" of each twenty-minute experience. An outline of events and summary instructions are attached. Instructions are to be given at the beginning of each exercise 1 through 7.

SMALL GROUP SERIES WORKSHOP EXERCISE

Information Sheet

Outline of Activities

Small Group Experiences—Each person will be in six different small group settings. Each group differs in personnel and group task. At the conclusion, one will have experienced the "getting acquainted with others" in a variety of situations, and will be able to reflect on the varying values and hindrances of the different settings for that purpose. Through this arrangement, each person will also have the opportunity to spend twenty minutes in a group experience with all of the persons in the larger group.

1. *Verbal exchange of information.* Five minutes spent deciding what kind of information you wish to exchange. Fifteen minutes exchanging the information.

2. *Close physical contact.* Five minutes deciding, as group, what to do in close, non–verbal contact. Ten minutes doing it. Five minutes discussing the experience.

3. *Group cooperation task.* Draw a picture (on one single page of paper), each person taking no more than one-half minute, next person adding to picture. Keep picture development process going for ten minutes. Discuss for ten minutes, with emphasis on the process of what happened.

4. *Intellectual discussion.* Carry on discussion on a topic e.g., "What do you think of peer teaching—its positive and negative aspects." Stick to the subject.

5. *Pantomime.* First fifteen minutes non–verbal. Each person takes three to four minutes to tell others about self in pantomime form . . . may demonstrate personal history, how you see yourself presently, hopes, fears, etc. In closing five minutes, discuss what was done and seen, perceptions, etc.

6. *Sharing of self with group.* Use three to four minutes alone to write on paper: two qualities which are positive strengths in myself; two qualities which are limitations in

myself. Fold paper, place in middle of group. Each person takes a paper and reads the four items on it. Try to decide who it is. Identify self. Discuss.

Alone Time

LARGE GROUP: *Evaluation of small group experiences.* Discuss what was learned in each situation, which seemed to be most helpful, which least, in gaining contact with others, *i.e.,* for *you.*

GRID FOR TWENTY-FIVE MEMBERS IN SIX GROUPS

No Duplications

Exercise 1						Exercise 4				
I	1	2	3	4	5	I	1	14	22	10	18
II	6	7	8	9	10	II	8	16	4	12	25
III	11	12	13	14	15	III	15	23	6	19	2
IV	16	17	18	19	20	IV	17	5	13	21	9
V	21	22	23	24	25	V	24	7	20	3	11

Exercise 2						Exercise 5				
I	1	7	13	19	25	I	1	16	6	21	11
II	2	8	14	20	21	II	14	4	19	9	24
III	3	9	15	16	22	III	22	12	2	17	7
IV	4	10	11	17	23	IV	10	25	15	5	20
V	5	6	12	18	24	V	18	8	23	13	3

Exercise 3						Exercise 6				
I	1	8	15	17	24	I	1	9	12	20	23
II	7	14	16	23	5	II	2	10	13	16	24
III	13	20	22	4	6	III	3	6	14	17	25
IV	19	21	3	10	12	IV	4	7	15	18	21
V	25	2	9	11	18	V	5	8	11	19	22

GRID FOR FORTY MEMBERS IN SEVEN GROUPS
No Duplications

Exercise 1

I	1	2	3	4	5	6
II	7	8	9	10	11	12
III	13	14	15	16	17	18
IV	19	20	21	22	23	24
V	25	26	27	28	29	30
VI	31	32	33	34	35	36
VII	37	38	39	40	41	42

Exercise 4

I	1	16	38	12	34	21
II	37	17	32	6	28	15
III	31	11	33	7	22	2
IV	18	5	27	9	24	4
V	20	42	29	3	25	40
VI	14	36	23	39	19	41
VII	8	30	10	26	13	35

Exercise 2

I	37	2	9	16	23	30
II	31	38	3	10	17	24
III	1	8	15	22	29	36
IV	25	32	39	4	11	18
V	19	26	33	40	5	12
VI	13	20	27	34	41	6
VII	7	14	21	28	35	42

Exercise 5

I	8	16	17	11	5	42
II	36	30	38	32	33	27
III	1	37	31	18	20	14
IV	29	23	10	12	6	7
V	9	3	39	26	34	28
VI	22	24	25	19	13	21
VII	2	4	40	41	35	15

Exercise 3

I	7	8	16	24	32	40
II	1	9	17	25	33	41
III	6	14	22	30	38	4
IV	12	20	28	36	2	10
V	18	26	34	42	15	23
VI	31	39	5	13	21	29
VII	37	3	11	19	27	35

Exercise 6

I	22	21	41	18	17	30
II	1	14	5	32	10	3
III	29	7	34	19	4	37
IV	8	42	33	12	39	24
V	15	35	20	11	38	23
VI	9	28	13	40	31	16
VII	36	27	6	26	25	2

Exercise 7

I	36	5	17	29	33	38
II	9	6	10	22	34	39
III	15	13	25	14	18	37
IV	42	11	16	27	32	30
V	1	41	4	8	20	31
VI	7	12	23	28	26	3
VII	21	19	24	35	40	2

NO. 1. VERBAL EXCHANGE OF INFORMATION

Subsidiary Goal(s)

a. To help members become better acquainted.
b. To explore the dynamics involved in self–disclosure.

Group Application

Forty members or less. To be used in microlab sequence (see basic instructions).

Application Variables

Twenty minutes. The exercise is 100% verbal.

Administrative Procedure

a. The facilitator asks members to go to assigned subgroups, according to the grid.
b. The facilitator now asks members in the subgroup to spend five minutes in deciding what type of information they wish to disclose.
c. The next fifteen minutes are to be spent in exchanging the information between members.
d. The facilitator asks members to regroup (see grid) after the initial exercise.

Suggestions for Facilitator Process

Processing is delayed until entire series of exercises in the microlab is completed. See Exercise No. 7.

NO. 2. CLOSE PHYSICAL CONTACT

Subsidiary Goal(s)

    a. To explore the dynamics of non–verbal communication.
    b. To gain insight into members' physical qualities and at-
tributes.

Group Application

Forty members or less. To be used in microlab sequence
(see basic instructions).

Application Variables

Twenty minutes. The exercise is 50% verbal and 50%
non–verbal.

Administrative Procedure

    a. The facilitator asks members to decide as a group what
they will do in close, non-verbal contact.
    b. After five minutes the group is to carry out their decision.
    c. After ten minutes the facilitator asks the subgroups to stop
and discuss the experience for five minutes.
    d. The facilitator asks members to regroup (see grid).

Suggestions for Facilitator Process

Processing is delayed until the entire series of exercises in
the microlab is completed. See Exercise No. 7.

NO. 3. GROUP COOPERATION TASK

Subsidiary Goal(s)

    a. To explore the dynamics of group membership roles.
    b. To gain awareness into member's resources and creativity.

Group Application

Forty members or less. To be used in microlab sequences
(see basic instructions).

Application Variables

>   Twenty minutes. The exercise is 50% verbal and 50% non–verbal. A large sheet of construction paper and crayons are needed for each subgroup.

Administrative Procedure

>   a. The facilitator asks members to draw a picture on the construction paper. Each person takes no more than one-half minute. The next member is to add to the picture, etc. No two members are allowed to draw simultaneously.
>   b. The picture development is to proceed for ten minutes.
>   c. The facilitator now asks members to discuss the experience for ten minutes with emphasis on the process which occurred within the small group during the assignment.
>   d. The facilitator now asks members to regroup (see grid).

Suggestions for Facilitator Process

>   Processing is delayed until the entire series of the microlab is completed. See Exercise No. 7.

NO. 4. INTELLECTUAL DISCUSSION

Subsidiary Goal(s)

>   a. To gain an awareness of the dynamics involved in intellectualizing.
>   b. To explore communication levels.

Group Application

>   Forty members or less. To be used in microlab sequence (see basic instructions).

Application Variables

>   Twenty minutes. The exercise is 100% verbal.

Administrative Procedure

>   a. The facilitator asks members to discuss an intellectual

issue. (i.e. Our POW's are coming home from Southeast Asia. Some have been incarcerated for more than seven years. What adjustment problems might they face, and how might they be handled?)

b. After twenty minutes the subgroups are to regroup for the next session.

Suggestions for Facilitator Process

Processing is delayed until the entire series of the micro-lab is completed. See Exercise No. 7.

NO. 5. PANTOMIME

Subsidiary Goal(s)

a. To gain insight into members' self–concepts.
b. To explore the dynamics involved in non–verbal communication.

Group Application

Forty members or less. To be used in microlab sequence (see basic instructions).

Application Variables

Twenty minutes. The exercise is 25% verbal and 75% non–verbal.

Administrative Procedure

a. The facilitator instructs each member in the subgroup to tell the others about self in pantomime form. (Allow three to four minutes for each member.) The member may present personal history, how he sees himself presently, hopes, fears, etc.
b. In the closing five minutes the facilitator asks members to discuss what was done and seen, perceptions, etc.
c. The facilitator now asks members to regroup (see grid).

Suggestions for Facilitator Process

Processing is delayed until the entire series of the micro-lab sequence is completed. See Exercise No. 7.

NO. 6. SHARING OF SELF WITH GROUP

Subsidiary Goal(s)

a. To explore the dynamics of self–disclosure and feedback.
b. To gain insight into member perceptions.

Group Application

Forty members or less. To be used in microlab sequence (see basic instructions).

Application Variables

Twenty minutes. The exercise is 70% verbal, with 30% non–verbal being written. Paper and pencils are needed.

Administrative Procedure

a. The facilitator asks each member in the subgroup to take three or four minutes alone to write on a slip of paper two of his qualities which are positive strengths and two qualities which he feels are limitations.
b. Papers are collected and placed in the middle of the group.
c. A member is to take a paper and read the four qualities on it. The members must now decide who it is.
d. The member whose paper it is identifies himself.
e. Steps c and d are repeated until all members' papers have been read and identified.
f. The remainder of the time is spent in discussion.
g. The facilitator now asks members to regroup (see grid).

Suggestions for Facilitator Process

Processing is delayed until the entire series of the micro-lab has been completed. See Exercise No. 7.

NO. 7. EVALUATION OF SMALL GROUP EXERCISES

Subsidiary Goal(s)

a. To integrate the experiences of the microlab.
b. To explore feelings about the different levels of communication.

Group Application

Forty members or less. To be used in microlab sequence (see basic instructions).

Application Variables

One hour and thirty minutes. The exercise is 100% verbal.

Administrative Procedure

a. The facilitator asks members to take five minutes to be alone and think about the experiences.
b. The facilitator then asks the members to reform the large group.
c. Members are to discuss what was learned in each situation, which seemed the most helpful, which was least helpful, in gaining contact with others . . . for you. (Further suggestions for facilitator processing are given below.

Suggestions for Facilitator Process

The facilitator might find the following questions helpful in facilitating processing:

Exercise 1: Verbal Exchange of Information

a. How did you decide what type of information to exchange? Did the discussion material deal with thoughts or feelings? Why?
b. What did you learn from other members in your subgroup? Who did you see as being the leader? Who shared the least with the group?

Exercise 2: Close Physical Contact

a. How did you decide what to do in close physical contact? Did anyone if your group refuse to take part? If so, why?

b. What types of information did your group communicate non–verbally? Did you find it difficult communicating non–verbally? If so, why? Did you feel awkward at any time? If so, why?

EXERCISE 3: Group Cooperation Task

a. What type of picture did your group end up with? How did you feel about its development?

b. How much do you feel you contributed to the picture? What type of colors did you use? How much space did it take?

EXERCISE 4: Intellectual Discussion

a. What differences did you find between intellectualizing and interpersonalizing? Which do you feel is most beneficial to you? What did you learn from the other members in your subgroup?

b. Did you "personally invest" during the discussion? If so, in what way? Were you satisfied with the topic given? If not, why? How valuable do you feel intellectualization is in getting to know others?

EXERCISE 5: Pantomime

a. What did you tell the other members in your group about yourself? What types of feelings did you have about communicating non–verbally?

b. Did you feel the other members in your group interpreted your pantomime accurately? If not, why? What did you learn from the other members in your group? Did you feel you risked in sharing yourself with others? If so, are you glad you did?

EXERCISE 6: Sharing of Self with Group

a. How much do you feel you disclosed? Was it more difficult to list negative qualities or positive qualities? If so, why? If not, why?

b. How accurate were you in deciding whose qualities were being described? If you were constantly inaccurate, why? Did any of the descriptions surprise you? If so, in what way?

EXERCISE 7: Evaluation of Small Group Experiences

a. Which exercise was the most meaningful to you and why? How much do you feel you have revealed during the course of the evening? How much have you learned from other group members?

b. Were you most comfortable with communicating verbally or non–verbally? Why? What have you learned about yourself? Which exercise would you *not* want to participate in again? Why?

XXI

UNGROUPED EXERCISES

THE EXERCISES IN THIS CHAPTER are our version of the "grab bag." Each has a specific goal (in the upper right-hand corner). However, there is not a sufficient amount of exercises in any goal category to warrant an entire chapter.

We wish to urge the reader to be aware that these exercises are equally as beneficial to groups as are those included in the previous chapters. Do not overlook them.

POSTERS

Subsidiary Goal(s)

a. To examine the dynamics of a win or lose situation.
b. To gain insight into member roles.
c. To deepen self–awareness.

Group Application

Twelve members or less. To be used with any group.

Application Variables

Forty-five minutes. The exercise is 60% verbal, with 40% non–verbal being written. Poster board and crayons are needed. The room should be large enough to allow triads to secure separate areas in the room.

Administrative Procedure

a. The facilitator asks members to non–verbally form triads.
b. He now informs the triads that they have a task. Each group is to develop a poster which exemplifies the life of the group. The entries will be judged by the entire group and the winners will receive a reward for their efforts (i.e., body rubs by the rest of the group for twenty minutes, or any other incentive which the facilitator feels appropriate).
c. Poster board and crayons are passed out. The facilitator tells the triads they will be allowed twenty minutes to complete the task.
d. The facilitator stops work at the appropriate time.
e. Each triad presents its poster to the group. The triad is to explain how the poster represents the life of the group. Members may give impressions or offer suggestions.
f. The entire group verbally judges the posters. Members are, one at a time, to give their vote and explain their reasons for doing so.

g. Winners are announced and the group discusses the experience.

Suggestions for Facilitator Process

Concentrate on the following during processing:

a. *To the winning triad:* Were you surprised you won? How did you decide what to do? What were your members' roles (leader, followers, etc.) ? Could you give suggestions to the other groups for success?

b. *To the losing groups:* Why do you feel you lost? What roles did the members take in your group? How do you feel about losing? What would you do differently if you could repeat the exercise?

Variations

None.

Creativity

GROUP SYMPHONY

Subsidiary Goal(s)

a. To give the group an opportunity to engage in a creative endeavor.

b. To allow members to give perceptions of their own individual roles.

c. To give insights into the inner workings of other member's roles.

d. To recognize how one copes with ambiguity and anxiety.

Group Application

Twelve members or less. To be used with encounter, personal growth, marathon and t–groups whose members have had sufficient sessions to have developed member identification.

Application Variables

Fifteen minutes. The exercise is 100% verbal.

Administrative Procedure

a. The facilitator informs the group that they are going to create a symphony using the members' voices.
b. Each member is to join in whenever he feels it is appropriate.
c. The facilitator states that the member's role in the symphony is to correspond with his own perception of his role in the group.
d. The members may assume roles of instruments or may simply hum, sing, etc.
e. The facilitator then asks that each member perform a solo.
f. The group discusses the experience.

Suggestions for Facilitator Process

Concentrate on the following during processing:

a. Where did you "play" during the symphony? Why? Did another member's performance get in the way? How? Why did you choose to be the instrument you were?
b. Did the group become unified or disjointed? Were there several melodies or one? Why? Did any of you join into duets, trios, etc.? If so, why? If not, why not?
c. How did you feel when performing as a soloist compared to performing as a group? Who seemed most comfortable doing a solo? Who appeared to be most uncomfortable?
d. Did you learn about other members' perceptions of themselves and of you? Were they accurate? If you could assign instruments to various members, what instruments would we be and why?

Variations

Variation I

a. Have the group select a conductor.
b. The conductor then assigns an instrument to each member.
c. He then "conducts" the group symphony. (*Do not* tell the group how to compose the symphony.)

d. During processing concentrate on why the conductor was chosen, why he assigned members the instruments he did, the dynamics behind the composition, etc.

e. If another member wishes to "conduct" the group, repeat the exercise.

Identity

MY FAMILY

Subsidiary Goal(s)

a. To develop members' perceptive abilities.
b. To explore the effects of past family experiences.
c. To gain insight into verbal and non–verbal cues.

Group Application

Twelve members or less. To be used with encounter, personal growth, marathon and t–groups. Best results are obtained if the exercise is used later in the group's development.

Application Variables

One hour and thirty minutes. The exercise is 60% verbal and 40% nonverbal. Ten percent of the non–verbal activity is written. Paper and pencils and an opaque projector are required.

Administrative Procedure

a. The facilitator asks members to bring three to six photographs of himself as a young child in which he is photographed with other members of his family to the next session.
b. At the next session, the facilitator collects the photographs as the members come into the room. (Members should be discouraged from showing their photographs to any other members before the session.)

c. The facilitator now displays the photographs on the opaque projector without disclosing the identity of the member.

d. The group is to study the photograph and study the child's facial expression, stance, etc. Members should be encouraged to share any impressions of the child's personality.

e. This procedure is repeated until all of the photographs have been shown.

f. The group reforms and the facilitator asks that each member close his eyes and then write down any or all family expressions that he can remember (e.g., "life isn't a bowl of cherries," "money doesn't grow on trees," "the early bird gets the worm") as well as the source of the statement.

g. After members have compiled a list they are asked to share these with the group. Members are encouraged to question one another about the circumstances surrounding the saying.

h. The group discusses the experience.

Suggestions for Facilitator Process

Concentrate on the following during processing:

a. *Photograph*—What have you learned about observation? How did you form impressions based on photographs? Were you surprised when you learned the member's identity? How accurate do you feel you were in observing traits? Do you feel these traits exist in the group? Did you observe the physical closeness of people in the photographs?

b. *Expressions*—Was it difficult to remember old family sayings? If so, why? Were you able to remember the source of the saying? Did the sayings conflict? Do you feel these expressions are core values and attitudes? How has this influenced your personality?

Variations

None.

BODY MACHINE

Subsidiary Goal(s)

a. To express moods through body action.
b. To release inhibitions associated with non–verbal communication.
c. To investigate how members cope with ambiguity.

Group Application

Twelve members or less. To be used with encounter, personal growth, marathon and t–groups, preferably in the latter stages of development after member identities have been established.

Application Variables

Fifteen minutes. The exercise is 50% verbal, 50% non–verbal. The room must be large enough to allow the members to move unrestrained.

Administrative Procedure

a. The facilitator informs the group that they are going to create a "machine" using only their voices and bodies.
b. A member is asked to volunteer to "start the machine." (He may do this by slapping his thighs, swinging his arms, singing non–sense syllables, etc.)
c. The facilitator asks members to join in when and wherever they feel appropriate. (They may attach themselves as parts to the member initially starting the machine, or start a machine of their own.)
d. The facilitator should encourage members to use their imagination. Their creation may be in verbal and/or non–verbal form.
e. After fifteen minutes the group discusses the experience.

Suggestions for Facilitator Process

Concentrate on the following during processing:

a. How did you decide on what part of the "machine" you would form? Did you form a machine of your own? If so, why? What is the significance of the machine you formed?

b. Did you participate verbally, non–verbally, or both? How did you decide in what way to communicate? Did you feel more comfortable communicating verbally than non–verbally? If so, why?

c. Did you see your role in the machine analogous to your role in the group? If not, why? If so, why?

d. Were you able to communicate to other parts of the "machine"? Did you learn anything about other members of the group? If so, what?

Variations

Variation I

a. Have members create the machine using only verbal communication methods.

b. Repeat basic exercise format.

Variation II

a. Have members create the machine using only non–verbal communication.

Variation III

a. Have the members create a machine while expressing their feelings (verbally and non–verbally) about it during the actual building.

b. After fifteen minutes the group discusses the experience.

Relaxation

BREAKFAST, CARS AND MACHINES

Subsidiary Goal(s)

a. To gain awareness into the value of "playing" together.

b. To release physical and emotional energies.
c. To release inhibitions.

Group Application

Twelve members or less. To be used with encounter, personal growth, marathon and t–groups. Best results are obtained if this exercise follows an intense, draining session.

Application Variables

Thirty minutes. The exercise is 50% verbal and 50% non–verbal. The room must be large enough to allow members to have adequate freedom of movement.

Administrative Procedure

a. The facilitator asks members to physically and verbally become a breakfast (i.e., four or five members may wish to form a plate or skillet while other members jump into the middle and act out sausage, bacon, or eggs sunny–side–up or scrambled). Members should be encouraged to act spontaneously.

b. After breakfast the facilitator informs the members they will need a car to travel to the machine factory. Again members are asked to physically and verbally form a car (i.e., four members can be wheels making the appropriate sounds, while other members form the body, horn, driver, etc.).

c. When the car has arrived at the factory, the facilitator asks members to form the machine they always wished to visit, explore and understand.

d. During the entire exercise, the facilitator should encourage member interactions.

e. After completion of steps a–e the facilitator asks the members to lie on the floor for five minutes and enjoy the feelings they have.

f. The group then discusses the experience.

Suggestions for Facilitator Process

Concentrate on the following during processing:
a. Were you able to achieve complete relaxation? Were you inhibited during any phase of the exercise? If so, why? Were you surprised at the amount of energy exhibited by the group? By yourself?
b. Did you find any personal value in "playing" hard? What feelings developed toward other members during the course of the exercise?

Variations

Variation I
a. Any number of hypothetical situations may be developed. For example, the group could be visiting a zoo rather than a machine factory. The facilitator is encouraged to make his own variations which better suit his group's needs.

Relaxation

"HO, HO"

Subsidiary Goal(s)

a. To communicate with other members through laughter.
b. To gain awareness of the importance of "play."

Group Application

Twelve members or less. To be used with encounter, personal growth, marathon and t–groups. Best results are obtained if exercise is utilized after a period of hard–core encounter.

Application Variables

Ten minutes. The exercise is 50% verbal and 50% non–verbal. The room must be large enough to allow members to move about unrestrained.

Administrative Procedure

a. The facilitator asks all members to lie on the floor, face up.
b. He then instructs members to put their head on another person's belly.
c. A designated member is to begin by going "ho–ho," the person whose head is on his belly is to follow and so on, until all members are going "ho–ho."
d. After ten minutes the group discusses the experience.

Suggestions for Facilitator Process

Concentrate on the following during processing:
a. What are your feelings now? Do you feel playing is important? Have your feelings changed towards any of the members? Toward the group? If so, in what way?
b. Was it difficult to laugh? If so, why? How did putting your head on another person's belly feel?

Variations

None.

Relaxation

PULLING THE TRAIN

Subsidiary Goal(s)

a. To enhance and enrich relationships through play.
b. To emphasize the dynamics involved in physical contact.
c. To encourage the practice of new behavior.

Group Application

Twelve members or less. To be used with encounter, personal growth, marathon and t–groups.

Application Variables

Fifteen minutes. The exercise is 50% verbal and 50%

non–verbal. The room should be large enough to allow members unrestrained movement.

Administrative Procedure

a. The facilitator asks the members to line up behind one another, placing their hands on the hips of the member directly in front of them.

b. The facilitator informs the group that they are now a train and he will act as the conductor.

c. He then asks all members to close their eyes and follow the member in front of them.

d. The facilitator is to leave his eyes open and encourages members to fantasize about being a car in the train. (Each member should be encouraged to verbalize sounds he feels are appropriate in representing his "car.")

e. The facilitator moves the "train" in any direction or position he feels appropriate (i.e., crouching, running, going in circles, stopping, etc.).

f. The group then discusses the experience.

Suggestions for Facilitator Process

Concentrate on the following during processing:

a. How did you feel about being led around? Were you able to fantasize you were a railroad "car"? If not, why? What "car" were you? Why?

b. What type of sounds did you make to represent your position in the train? How does this represent your concept of your role in the group?

c. Did the physical contact change your feeling toward any members in the group? If so, in what way? Did you want to change positions? If so, where would you have placed yourself and why?

Variations

None.

AC/DC

Subsidiary Goal(s)

a. To explore differences between individual members.
b. To gain insight into one's self–concept.
c. To develop listening skills.

Group Application

Twelve members or less. To be used with encounter, personal growth, marathon and t–groups. Best results are obtained if the exercise is used early in the group's development.

Application Variables

Thirty minutes. The exercise is 100% verbal.

Administrative Procedure

a. The facilitator asks a volunteer to select a member he sees as being the most similar to himself.
b. The volunteer and his partner are to enter the middle of the circle and discuss their attributes. Other members of the group are to observe the interaction. If asked for by either member in the middle of the circle, the observers can offer suggestions to facilitate further discussion.
c. After ten minutes the observers are to review the conversation and discuss observations of dynamics they perceived.
d. The facilitator now asks another volunteer to select a member he perceives as being the most dissimilar to himself.
e. Repeat step b.
f. The group discusses the experience.

Suggestions for Facilitator Process

Concentrate on the following during processing:
a. How did the first conversation compare to the second?

Which went more easily and why? In what conversation did you feel the participants learned more about each other?

b. What have you learned about the participants? Did you find yourself empathizing with any of the members? What do you find is the value of learning about someone different from you?

Variations

None.

Trust

* VERBAL TRUST WALK

Subsidiary Goal(s)

a. To develop member perceptions and awareness.
b. To further enhance member relationships.

Group Application

Twelve members or less. To be used with encounter, personal growth, marathon and t–groups. Best results are obtained if the exercise is used after ample sessions have passed to have allowed for the development of trust between members.

Application Variables

Forty minutes. The exercise is 50% verbal and 50% non–verbal. A spacious outdoor setting is more desirable although a large room or series of rooms may be appropriate. One blindfold is needed for each dyad.

Administrative Procedure

a. The facilitator asks members to pair off into dyads. At the

---

* Dynamic, more effective exercises are marked with an asterisk.

facilitator's discretion this may be done either verbally or non–verbally.

b. Each dyad receives one blindfold and is given the following instructions: "One member in your dyad should volunteer to be blindfolded. You are about to go on a trust walk. The member who is not blindfolded will lead the other member around the area. Try to lead the person over, under, around things. Let him *explore* the area. Interaction is encouraged between you and your partner. You should feel free to ask questions or share your feelings as you go through the experience. After twenty minutes I will ask you to exchange roles."

c. After all members have had an opportunity to participate, the group reforms for discussion of the experience.

Suggestions for Facilitator Process

Concentrate on the following during processing:

a. What did you learn from the experience? How did you feel about your partner while he/she was leading you? Do you feel you were hesitant about the experience? If so, when?

b. How did you feel about leading your partner? Do you feel he/she was hesitant? Did you find being led or leading the most meaningful for you?

Variations

Variation I

a. Have all the members except for two blindfolded.

b. Instruct the two members to keep the blindfolded members in a group and lead them around. Interaction should be encouraged.

c. After ten to fifteen minutes, ask for two other volunteers. Repeat process until all members have had an opportunity to lead.

NAMES

Subsidiary Goal(s)

a. To explore the dynamics of association.
b. To gain greater insight into self-identity.

Group Application

Twelve members or less. To be used with any group. Best results are obtained if the exercise is used early in the group's development.

Application Variables

Forty–five minutes. The exercise is 80% verbal, with 20% non–verbal being written. A chalkboard and chalk are needed.

Administrative Procedure

a. The facilitator asks a volunteer to go to the chalkboard and spell his name backwards.
b. The member is now to pretend that this new word is actually a word in a foreign language. The member is now to define this word according to how it would appear in a dictionary.
c. Another member is asked to repeat step **b**, until all members have had an opportunity to participate.
d. The group discusses the experience.

Suggestions for Facilitator Process

Concentrate on the following during processing:
a. Why did you define your name the way you did? What does this imply about your self–concept?
b. What did you learn from other member's definitions about their names? Do you wish you would have used other member's definitions for your name? If so, why?

Variations

Variation I

a. Have members spell their names backward on the chalkboard.

b. The facilitator instructs the members to form a word starting with each letter (left to right) and create a sentence which describes their self-concept.

c. After every member has had an opportunity to participate, the group discusses the experience.

Variation II

a. The facilitator asks a member to enter the middle of the circle.

b. The other members in the group are to say his name using different tones of voice with different implied messages. The member is not to answer but simply listen.

c. After every member has had an opportunity to participate, the group discusses the experience.

CLOSURE

THE PRIMARY GOAL for each exercise in this chapter is the facilitation of the closure experience. We consider the closure session to be the last group meeting, at which the members will be ending (closing) the group.

There are some facilitators who believe that groups should not be formally closed. Others desire a formal closure experience, but have not as yet discovered one that satisfies their needs. We respond to the first group by saying that a group of people who have lived, loved and cared for one another, who have worked *together,* merit a peak happening at the end of the group experience. The second group of facilitators are urged to read the following paragraph.

This chapter has been placed last in the book because it seemed to the authors that our Handbook should reserve the best exercise until last. We have found the Group Closure exercise to be truly a *peak* experience for our encounter and personal growth group members. Because of our experience, we wish to end the handbook with this presentation.

We hope that other facilitators and other groups find the utilization of this Group Closure as rewarding as it has been for us and for the members of our groups whom we have loved and been loved by in return.

This particular Closure session and the Handouts accompanying it are then succeeded by two final Exercises, the purpose of which is *to facilitate the closure process,* Write My Biography and You Gave the Group and Me. . . . These will effectively re–inforce the formal closing of our group experience.

*GROUP CLOSURE

Subsidiary Goal(s)

    a.   To encourage non–verbal contact and communication.
    b.   To review the life history of the group.
    c.   To achieve a peak experience.

Group Application

    Twelve members or less. To be used with encounter, personal growth, marathon and t–groups at the last session.

Application Variables

    Thirty minutes. The exercise is 50% verbal and 50% non–verbal. A cassette recorder and Closure handouts are needed. The room must be large enough to allow the group to mill comfortably.

Administrative Procedure

    a.   Prior to the last session the facilitator has the Closure handouts prepared and records the following songs on a cassette recorder.
        (1)   Make It By Yourself. James Griffin and David Gates. Sung by: Bread on Elektra Records.
        (2)   Beautiful People. Melanie Safka. Sung by: The New Seekers on Elektra Records.
        (3)   You've Got A Friend. Carole King. Sung by: Carole King on Ode Records.
        (4)   Repeat selection 2 (optional, see Administrative Procedure, step **h**).
        (5)   Repeat selection 3 (optional, see Administrative Procedure, step **h**).
    b.   One half hour before the end of the last group the facilitator stops the group and initiates the Group Closure exercise by saying: "We have experienced each other for a long

---

* Dynamic, more effective exercises are marked with an asterisk.

time. Let's take this opportunity to remember those experiences."

c. He gives out the handouts and says: "I'm going to play a song which is relevant to one of our goals, that we are responsible for ourselves. Let's listen." (He now plays selection 1.)

d. He then says: "Mill around. I will recite a history of the group. As I do so, make physical and verbal contact with those members significant to the group history moment being recited." (The facilitator plays selection 2 and *simultaneously* recites a verbal history of the group.)

e. After the milling, he says: "Let's form a circle and read the Gestalt Prayer."

f. After the Gestalt Prayer has been recited, the facilitator says: "Stay in the circle."

g. "As I play selection 3, let's remain silent and just be with each other." He plays selection 3. (The authors have found that the group will start a slow undulating sway, that members will kiss each other, smile, and weep. It is a moving, peak experience.)

h. (*Optional*) The group may end after the previous section, or the facilitator may replay selections 2 and 3 and:

   (1) Allow the group members to mill and say good–bye to one another, *or,*

   (2) Join in a circle, with one member at a time entering the middle. The member in the middle verbally and non–verbally says good–bye to his fellow members and expresses his feelings for them. (We have found this an extremely potent aspect of the Group Closure exercise and highly recommend it.)

Suggestions for Facilitator Process

Concentrate on the following during processing:
a. No processing is conducted for this exercise.

Variations

None.

CLOSURE HANDOUT

1.

MAKE IT BY YOURSELF

By James Griffin and David Gates

You say you're down and out and need some help
To get you through each day
Well here's a thought or two I've used and
Like to pass them on your way
I found them lyin' there, the answers
That you say you're lookin' for
Make what you will of them and you can change the
Way it was before.

You got to make it by yourself
You know you got to make it by yourself
I'll be your friend and I'll lend a helping hand
But you gotta try and help yourself before I can.

I hear you talk of all the happiness and
Emptiness you've known
Well let me reassure you, never were you
Really all alone
They say in quiet desperation many people cannot see
They cannot see the simple truth that's not the
Way it has to be.

You got to find it for yourself
God helps the man who helps himself, Amen
I am your friend and I'll lend a helping hand
But you gotta try and help yourself before I can.

We got to help each other
You got to help your brother when you can.

Now don't you think that I was preachin', I'm just
Reachin' out for you
'Cause that's the only way that I know how to
Get the message through

Than you in turn have got to learn and teach
It to somebody who
Felt the happiness–the emptiness the same as you.

You got to make it by yourself
You know you got to make it by yourself
I'll be your friend and I'll lend a helping hand
But you gotta try and help yourself before I can.

2.

BEAUTIFUL PEOPLE
By Melanie Safka

Beautiful People

You live in this same world as I do
But somehow I never noticed you
Before today.
I'm ashamed to say.

Beautiful People
We share the same back door
And it isn't right we never met before
But then
We may never meet again.

If I weren't afraid you'd laugh at me
I would run take all of your hands
And I'd gather everyone together for a day
And when we're gathered I'll pass buttons out that say

Beautiful People
Then you'll never be alone because there will
Always be someone with the same button
On as you
Include him in everything you do.

Beautiful People
You ride the same subway as I do
Every morning, that's got to tell you
Something.
We have so much in common
I go the same direction that you do
So if you take care of me
Maybe I'll take care of you.

Beautiful People
You look like friends of mine
And it's about time
That someone said it here and now
I make a vow that sometime, somehow
I'll have a meeting
Invite everyone you know
I'll pass out buttons to the one's who come to show

Beautiful People
Then you'll never be alone
'Cuz there will always be someone
With the same button on as you
Include him in everything you do.

Beautiful People. Beautiful People.

CLOSURE HANDOUT

3.

THE GESTALT PRAYER [1]
By Frederick S. Perls

I do my thing, and you do your thing.
I am not in this world to live up to your expectations
And you are not in this world to live up to mine.

You are you, and I am I,
And if by chance, we find each other, it's beautiful.
If not, it can't be helped.

4.

By Carole King

YOU'VE GOT A FRIEND [2]
When you're down and troubled
And you need some loving care
And nothing, nothing, is going right
Close your eyes and think of me
And soon I will be there
To brighten up even your darkest night.

You just call out my name
And you know wherever I am
I'll come running to see you again
Winter, spring, summer or fall
All you have to do is call
And I'll be there
You've got a friend

If the sky above you
Grows dark and full of clouds
And that old north wind begins to blow
Keep your head together
And call my name out loud
Soon you'll hear me knocking at your door

You just call out my name
And you know wherever I am
I'll come running to see you
Winter, spring, summer or fall
All you have to do is call
And I'll be there yes I will

---

[1] From *Gestalt Therapy Verbatim* by Frederick S. Perls. © 1969 Real People Press.

Now ain't it good to know that
You've got a friend
When people can be so cold
They'll hurt you, yes and desert you
And take your soul if you let them
Oh, but don't you let them

You just call out my name
And you know wherever I am
I'll come running to see you again
Winter, spring, summer or fall
All you have to do is call
And I'll be there
You've got a friend.

WRITE MY BIOGRAPHY

Subsidiary Goal(s)

a. To give and receive feedback.
b. To reveal to others and have revealed to you an estimation of the member's place in the life of the group.
c. To facilitate the closure process.

Group Application

Twelve members or less. To be used with encounter, personal growth, marathon and t–groups.

Application Variables

Time unlimited, with most exercises running one to one and a half hours. The exercise is 80% verbal, with 20% non–verbal being written. Paper and pencils are needed, but the written portion of the exercise is to be done *before* the group meets.

Administrative Procedure

a. At the next to the last meeting, the facilitator breaks the group into sections (*e.g.,* six in section A, six in section B) and tells them they are to perform a written task between this session and the last.

b. He says: "You are to write biographies for *every* member in your particular subgroup. In other words, you will have to write a biography about all other member's lives as members in this group, one biography for each member." (He illustrates saying "You, Tom will write five biographies, one for each member in your subgroup.") "No biography is to exceed one page in length. You will also write an autobiography of your life as a member in this group. The autobiography is not to exceed one page." (He illustrates saying "You, Tom, would write five biographies and one autobiography.") "Are there any questions about the between session task?"

c. The facilitator adds that the members are *not* to reveal, relate, compare, etc. biographies prior to the next session.

d. At the start of the next session, the facilitator says, "Will a member volunteer to read his autobiography?"

e. The volunteer reads his autobiography. Then each member in his subgroup reads his biography of the volunteer.

f. Members who did not write biographies for the volunteer are urged to express their feelings and thoughts about the volunteer's life as a group member.

g. After *each* presentation, the group discusses the material read. The facilitator should have them concentrate on differences between autobiographies and biographies, the reasons for such differences, significant omissions, etc.

h. The exercise continues as above until each member has read his autobiography, heard the biographies read, and a discussion of each volunteer has occurred.

Suggestions for Facilitator Process

Concentrate on the following during processing:

a. Whose biography did you appreciate the most? Why? Whose did you find displeasing? Why?
b. If you wrote your autobiography again, how would you change it and why?
c. What did you learn about yourself from other member's biographies? What did we learn about other members from their autobiographies?

Variations

None.

* YOU GAVE THE GROUP AND ME . . .

Subsidiary Goal(s)

a. To give and receive feedback.
b. To end the group on a positive note.
c. To establish feelings of worth in members.
d. To achieve a peak experience.

Group Application

Twelve members or less. To be used with encounter, personal growth, marathon and t–groups at the last session.

Application Variables

Thirty minutes. The exercise is 100% verbal.

Administrative Procedure

a. The facilitator stops the group about forty minutes before ending time and tells them they will engage in a closure exercise in which they will have the opportunity to thank each other for contributions made to the group and to each other.
b. The members stand in a circle, with arms around each other's waists. One member steps into the center, facing any individual he desires. He receives feedback from that member, then turns and faces another member and re-

ceives feedback. This process continues until he has faced and received feedback from every member.

c. The members in the circle, when faced by the member inside, are to say "You gave the group . . . and you gave me. . . ." The member may reply in whatever fashion he deems appropriate.

d. Each member takes his turn in the center until every member has received feedback from every other member.

e. If no processing is to occur, tell the group to mill and express their feelings for each other in whatever fashion they so desire.

Suggestions for Facilitator Process

Concentrate on the following during processing:

a. What did you learn about your contributions to the group and its members that you did not previously know?

b. How did you feel as you were receiving feedback? How did you feel giving it?

c. If there is anyone you wish to give further feedback to, do it now. If there is anyone you wish to receive further feedback from, ask for it now.

d. If you have processed, implement step e now.

Variations

Each of the following phases may be substituted for the original, thereby creating a new closure variation:

*Variation I

a. In step c substitute: "If I could take a personal quality of yours, and make it mine, I'd take . . ."

*Variation II

a. In step c substitute: "I love you because . . ."

*Variation III

a. In step c substitute: "When I first met you I thought . . . , and now I know . . ."

INDEX

343

DATE DUE

7.24 '80	
1 01 '81	
11 10 '83	
5.24 '84	
JUN 1 5 1985	
ret 6/26/85	
1.22 '86	
6 4 '86	
11 19 '88	
11.23 '88	
11.23 '88	
AUG 09 '89	
NOV 22 '89	
NOV 14 '90	
JUL 1 5 2004	

BRODART, INC.   Cat. No. 23-221